# SEEING
# the
# insane

# seeing the insane

## A Visual and Cultural History of Our Attitudes Toward the Mentally Ill

### Sander L. Gilman

ECHO POINT BOOKS & MEDIA, LLC

Published by Echo Point Books & Media
Brattleboro, Vermont
www.EchoPointBooks.com

Copyright © 1982, 2014 Sander L. Gilman

ISBN: 978-1-62654-876-3

Cover Image: *Portrait of a Woman Suffering from Obsessive Envy*
by Jean Louis Théodore Géricault

Cover Design by Adrienne Núñez,
Echo Point Books & Media

Editorial and proofreading assistance by Christine Schultz,
Echo Point Books & Media

To

DANIEL HANS-HAIM

# introduction

What a fascinating interdisciplinary book this is! Its profuse illustrations reveal a range of human distress from the passions of everyday life to those of psychiatric illness. From these, we learn much about how emotional suffering has been viewed over the centuries. As the earliest illustrations were nonmedical in origin, we enter into the area of art quite naturally, noting its aesthetics and the changes in approach to depicting the human form and face. This tradition gradually becomes influenced by the emerging debate between religion and the growing field of science. The focus of the controversy is man. What is his ultimate reality? Is he closer to the angels, or can we visualize him in a naturalistic or structural fashion which includes the dangerous implications of materialism?

A Professor of German Literature at Cornell University might not at first glance seem to be a prime candidate to take on the Herculean task of penetrating such a complex set of intellectual boundaries. Academic professors, however, bring a variety of essential attributes to these endeavors: intelligence and curiosity; a willingness to explore far and wide, to ask questions that are narrow but can also become broad enough to encompass the intermingled streams of nature and culture; the ability to transcend the restricted confines of a given discipline, and to infuse their topics with life through their enthusiasm and their skill with words.

Sander Gilman has all these attributes along with the drive to implement them. His training as an intellectual historian and its application to his literary field led him to an early concentration on the history of stereotypes: the Eastern Jew, Blacks, women, and, eventually, the insane. Pursuing these interests, he spent his sabbatical year (1977-78) in the Department of Psychiatry at the New York Hospital-Cornell Medical Center. (His contributions to the Section on the History of Psychiatry and to the Department led to his

receiving an appointment as Professor of History in Psychiatry.) In doing the research for this book, he became the first person to survey all the psychiatric volumes in the Oskar Diethelm Historical Library. He also avidly explored the resources of other libraries, museums, and private collections in the U.S. and abroad for applicable information on how the insane were viewed in the past.

The insane were the subjects of artists long before they were the objects of psychiatric study, and the development of their portrayal is a concomitant of the history of portraiture in general. The first rendering of a human being is lost somewhere in prehistoric times. Preliterate peoples created images of specific persons although their representations often were so stylized that they would be unrecognizable to us as individuals. Out of these early beginnings, three main styles of portraiture gradually evolved: the allegorical, the idealistic, and the realistic.

The allegorical portrait is especially familiar to those who have viewed paintings which were inspired by the Christian church and which presented Christ and His family as well as sundry saints in roles that served to illustrate the teachings of the church. Idealized but representational images appeared early in Egyptian and Greek art. Secular figures important to the Catholic Church were painted later, but most of the figures represented throughout history were of the powerful, the rich, and the famous. The glorified portraits of Napoleon, for example, typify this style.

Realistic portrayals also have had a long history, but their ascendancy is a Renaissance phenomenon which reached its peak in the naturalism of the nineteenth century. While Dr. Gilman devotes most of his book to this theme and period, he presents as background the earlier cultural conventions in the representation of the melancholic. Other symbolic themes can be found in his discussions of the wild man, the danger of demons, and the tradition of the ship of fools. The eighteenth century is particularly pertinent, for it was then that realism became popular and even artisans started to hang portraits of themselves in their homes. An increasing emphasis on the individual and an equally secular and eventually scientific concern for "human nature" also contributed to the growth of depicting the insane in art. This trend can be found in literature as well, with increasing attention paid to individual human detail in biographies and the emergence of the autobiography as a literary form.

Dr. Gilman guides us through some of the complexities of the onset of the nineteenth century: the extensive popularity of the physiognomical system of Lavater, the phrenology of Gall and Spurzheim, and the naturalistic art of Goya and Hogarth. Concurrently he analyzes the development of psychiatry during the late eighteenth century when a number of specialized hospitals for the mentally ill were founded under the stimulus of the concern and optimism of the Enlightenment (and, others would argue, from society's need to suppress the insane). The physicians in charge of these hospitals began to study their patients scientifically, report their findings in print, and form associations with their colleagues. Out of this trend came the first specifically medical portraiture of the insane by well-known artists and engravers under the sponsorship of doctors like Pinel, Georget, and Esquirol in France, and Morison in England.

In the visualization of the insane, a major revolution occurred during the 1840s after the introduction of photography. Sander Gilman has already written about the early use of this technique for the study of the insane in *The Face of Madness* (1976). Here was a procedure that gave great promise of precision; the insane could be caught at their most expressive moment, realistically, and less subject to the taste and inclination of the portrait artist. As photographers improved in skill and speed, a split was created in the tradition of portrayal. Portrait painters moved from realism to the freer expression of the personal reactions to a subject. This can be seen vividly in the works of Van Gogh and even more strikingly and with a greater sense of uncomfortable disorientation for the viewer in the Cubist movement early in the twentieth century. Photography, on the other hand, supposedly provided reality. Sequential photography, introduced in 1877 by Eadweard Muybridge, helped clarify the dynamic pattern of movement whether in gross motor locomotion or in the finer muscles of expression. Through the work of Thomas Edison and others, motion pictures with synchronized sound made it possible to follow in detail not only fleeting feelings and expressions but the speech and ideas that accompanied them. Eventually, tape recording and the growth of color television would lead to the current easy availability of color videotaping.

This modern period of "seeing the insane" becomes a dynamic one which still awaits its historian. The early highlights of silent movie film use must include the child development studies of Arnold Gesell, the invasion of the newborn nursery by Margaret Fries with her own movie camera around 1935, and the study of tics in children by Margaret Mahler in the mid-1940s. When sight and sound finally came together, a human being could be recorded visually and acoustically in an ongoing lifelike fashion. The focus of studies had shifted from a static snapshot frozen in time to a dynamic process that eventually spread to involve the observer interacting with his insane subject. The scientific focus was changed by this procedure and produced an emphasis ranging from the very disturbed to the near normal. Researchers are now studying the correlation of the emotions not only with expression and movement, but with the shape and context of speech. Cadences and inflections are being analyzed in detail, and this leads to deeper questions of linguistics and thought. No longer is "seeing" largely a surface phenomenon; the inner recesses of human nature and maladaptation are being explored in depth. Science in its own fashion has finally reached the point where artists who painted portraits had long since been, but with the hopeful prospects of a vast expansion of knowledge.

Sander Gilman, in surveying how the mentally ill have been represented from the middle ages to the dawn of the twentieth century, provides us with an informative, stimulating, and visually exciting book which will be the standard historical study of this complex association between psychiatry and portraiture.

ERIC T. CARLSON, M.D.
Clinical Professor of Psychiatry
Director, Section on the History of Psychiatry
New York Hospital-Cornell Medical Center

# contents

The only thing that is different from one time to another is what is seen and what is seen depends upon how everybody is doing everything.

Gertrude Stein, *Composition as Explanation*, 1926

# preface TOWARD A THEORY OF PSYCHIATRIC ILLUSTRATION

How do we learn to see?

Oscar Wilde suggested that we learn to see the world through the prism of art. "External nature," he argued, "imitates Art. The only effects that she can show us are effects that we have already seen through poetry, or in paintings."[1] We learn to perceive the world through those cultural artifacts which preserve a society's stereotypes of its environment. We do not see the world, rather we are taught by representations of the world about us to conceive of it in a culturally acceptable manner. It is not merely flora and fauna, sunset and seascape which are seen through the prism of culture. We also see man in his infinite variety through the filters of stereotypical perspective.[2]

Throughout the history of any given culture the structure most often applied to categories of man is that of the polar opposite. Each category is perceived as either the embodiment or the antithesis of the group which has provided the category. Thus in Western culture a polar antiworld of human types has been developed, populated by the Black, the Jew, the Gypsy, the madman, among others.[3] The "otherness" of the representatives of these categories is defined in many different ways, not the least of which is the strict delineation of what the culture designates their appearance to be.

The statement that someone "looks Jewish" or "looks crazy" reflects the visual stereotype which a culture creates for the "other" out of an arbitrary complex of features.[4] Examination of non-Western images of the madman, for example, reveals clearly that the perception of the appearance of the madman is determined by a sense of historical and cultural continuity, rather than any quality of the process of insanity or of the actual individual observed.[5]

Such visual stereotypes are the product of the application of existing paradigms to those aspects of the universe which a culture has defined as inherently inexplicable. When this sense of in-

explicability is externalized it takes the human form of the "other," whether as madman, Black, Jew, or Gypsy. Its concreteness is superficial as it is an extension of the perceiver and only in the most limited ways rooted in reality. Its source lies in the sense of distance between the perceiver and the perceived implicit in the polar model, a distance imposed by the perceiver based on the anxiety generated by his perception.

Thus the "other" is one of the myths resulting from the existence of polarities. It is comprehended and articulated in terms of the numerous historically determined forms applied to it from other spheres, which Stephen Pepper has called "root-metaphors." These are conceptual structures applied to those aspects of the world not readily understandable:

> A man desiring to understand the world looks about for a clue to its comprehension. He pitches upon some area of commonsense fact and tries to see if he cannot understand other areas in terms of this one. This original area becomes then his basic analogy or root-metaphor. He describes as best he can the characteristics of this area, or, if you will, discriminates its structure. A list of its structural characteristics becomes his basic concept of explanation and description. We call them a set of categories. In terms of these categories he proceeds to study all other areas of fact whether uncriticized or previously criticized. He undertakes to interpret all facts in terms of these categories. As a result of the impact of these other facts upon his categories, he may qualify and readjust the categories, so that a set of categories commonly changes and develops.[6]

The type of labeling described by Pepper also has a historical dimension. Michel Foucault has outlined a similar process in tracing the concept of the "clinical gaze" in medical diagnosis. He attributes its origin to the borrowing of what he calls "epistemological myths" by diagnosticians who converted their seeing (*voir*) into clinical knowledge (*savoir*).[7] Thus metaphors, such as those taken from chemistry, became the vocabulary of French medical diagnosis in the eighteenth century. This borrowing of metaphors from one sphere to explicate another is preserved in the multiplicity of visual representations of the insane. The act of portraying the insane interprets the reality of insanity through the use of a complicated and varied visual vocabulary based on a complex series of applied root-metaphors.

The problem of examining the appearance of reality (its noema) is parallel to that of the blind fakirs "seeing" the elephant. Each perceives his segment as unique. That the animal exists in the world is never in doubt. But how and why does each of the fakirs choose his metaphor for that tiny bit of the elephant which his hands perceive? This is the key question. Similarly, we can try to analyze the means (and perhaps the motivation) by which mental illness is envisaged. As Nelson Goodman has noted:

> We cannot find out much about the way the world is by asking about the best or most faithful or most realistic way of seeing or picturing it. For the ways of seeing and picturing are many and various; some are strong, effective, useful, intriguing, or sensitive; others are weak, foolish, dull, banal, or blurred. But even if all the latter are excluded, still none of the rest can lay any good claim to be the way of seeing or picturing the world the way it is.[8]

What we can do is study the means by which the world of the insane and the insane in the world are described.

The visual root-metaphors applied to madness coexist in uncounted numbers. They seem never to die, only to recede from the center of perception. At any given moment seemingly contradictory models may operate simultaneously. Each root-metaphor is used in the context of a specific "mental universe," following William James's term, to provide an explanation for the perception in that sphere. Most historians of psychiatry have seen the evolution of this medical specialty in relation to the patient as a lineal (whether progressive or retrogressive) process.[9] Either psychiatry has become more subtle and more accurate or it has become ever more shackled with misconceptions. Social psychiatrists, on the other hand, abandoning the lineal model, find complex and contradictory distinctions among professional as well as lay populations in regard to their understanding of the insane.[10] Both medical histor-

ian and sociologist may be measuring, at least in one respect, the same feature—the simultaneous existence of a multitude of root-metaphors that articulate a myriad of different perceptions of the basic dichotomy of insanity perceived through an infinite number of discrete mental universes.

Such a complexity could not be the subject of analysis if one did not limit the object reference. By concentrating on the metamorphosis of perceived realities into visual structures through the application of certain root-metaphors, we can acquire a sense of the complexity as well as the flux of the history of psychiatric illustration. Susan Sontag has accomplished such an analysis of the literary root-metaphors applied to tuberculosis and cancer, understanding them as "the punitive or sentimental fantasies concocted about that situation [illness] : not real geography, but stereotypes of natural character."[11] In dealing with insanity, this need to understand the relevant vocabulary is vital. To analyze a subset of this language, the iconographic language of the visual presentation of insanity, we must understand the language of the visual realization of literary metaphors in the history of art as well as the symbolic language generated by changing technology. The interpretation of a portrait of a madman is a process of disentangling some of the root-metaphors applied not only to madness but to the idea of portrayal in general.

Discussions of the realities perceived in describing the insane have usually been limited to four major categories: facial (and cranial) appearance; expression; body build; and gesture (including gait and posture). These are the classic, but arbitrary, divisions of the visual aspect of man, and it is an unusual discussion of the appearance of insanity which is able to concentrate on one aspect to the exclusion of the others. But these specific features exist in an actual or implied context. The visual environment in which the madman is portrayed is in itself the expression of an attempt to understand the insane. The resulting image of the madman is therefore the sum of the root-metaphors applied to him and his world.

Since the purpose of such a study is to understand the multiplicity of visual motifs which make up the image of the insane, no line can be drawn between the portrait of the madman in the fine arts and that in medical illustration. Painting, sculpture, and photography have been concerned with the madman in their expression of his being in the world. These aesthetic structures and their intellectual background have heavily influenced the medical illustration of psychiatric texts. Thus, to paraphrase Wilde, it is not art which imitates insanity, but the perception of insanity which imitates art. There is a constant give and take between the vocabulary of structures used in the fine arts and that employed in medical illustration.

The relationship between the realities that are being described and the mode of description extends into any historical definition of insanity. The madman is that individual seen as "other" by a culture. Thus the image of reality shifts, depending on the time and orientation. Madness includes at one time or another all of the traditional tripartite classifications of amentia, dementia, and melancholia. No distinction can be made between somatic and emotional illness if both are understood as subcategories of insanity. This introduces certain complications into any discussion of psychiatric illustration, for some illnesses now categorized as primarily nonpsychiatric, such as cretinism, have a long history of inclusion as psychopathologies. It is impossible to exclude these illnesses retrospectively, for the visual aspect of some of them served not only medically as a diagnostic sign but also historically as an "icon" of insanity. For example, the bulging eyes and goiter in hyperthyroidism led to a visual structure of cretinism which is inherent in the reality of the illness itself.[12] The understanding and implication of such an illness was rooted, however, not in the specificity of an endocrinological defect but in the subjectively

sane observer's self-definition as not belonging to the category of the cretin. Thus the myth of the appearance of cretins will long outlive their redefinition as nonpsychiatric patients.

The present study relates three closely bound areas of investigation: the image of the insane in the fine arts, in medical illustration, and in theories of physiognomy and expression. The interaction among these three areas provides a background against which to understand the visual stereotypes of the insane. There has been no attempt at exhaustiveness. Rather, examples have been selected which best demonstrate patterns in the representation and perception of the insane. The period under investigation ranges from the Middle Ages to the close of the nineteenth century; the cultural area is limited to the West. Even with these restrictions, however, the evolution of the image of the insane can be extrapolated from the material.

Today the appearance of the madman has supposedly receded in importance in art as well as medicine. The emphasis on abstraction in both modern art and psychoanalysis leaves little room for the consideration of the seemingly concrete aspects of the bizarre in appearance. Yet underlying our understanding of the mentally ill is the continued presence in society of older images of the insane, images that overtly or covertly color our concept and serve to categorize them upon first glance.

# acknowledgments

I am indebted to a number of friends and colleagues who have helped this work come into being—at Cornell Medical College, Professors Eric T. Carlson, Jacques Quen, and Robert Michels; at the University of Cologne, Professor U. H. Peters; at the Salpêtrière, Professor P. Castaigne; at Columbia, Professors Meyer Schapiro and Ludwig Kahn. Segments of this study have been presented in lectures at Mainz, McMasters, Baden-Baden, Yale, and the Cornell Medical College in New York. I am grateful for all comments made at those times.

Research materials have been placed at my disposal by a number of institutions. In particular, those that provided the reproductions for the illustrations are individually credited in the list of sources on page 241. I thank all of them, but especially the staff of the Payne-Whitney Clinical Library and the Historical Library, Yale Medical College, for their help.

Finally, I thank Ella Mazel, who helped form this book as its editor, designer, and compositor.

*Ithaca, New York*

# icons
of
madness

# the appearance of madness

In *Madness and Civilization*, Michel Foucault says that "the face of madness has haunted the imagination of Western man" from the fifteenth century.[1] The Renaissance concept of the unique appearance of the mentally ill rests on older and well-established traditions of perceiving and portraying the otherness of the insane. In these traditions the diverse representations of the madman's appearance are interrelated. The insane are branded as outsiders through their visibility.

The madman was already visible in the Middle Ages, through a vocabulary of images which blended schematic representations of various symptoms and symbolic references to madness into an integrated portrait of the insane. This iconography was extended to all the figures associated with any divergence from the society's accepted norms for sanity, whether the maniac, the idiot, the melancholic, the wild man, or the possessed. As the images of the madman evolved, aspects of the imagery of each group permeated the others, generating an interchangeable set of icons by which the insane were either observed or identified.

Such an icon of insanity can be found within the medieval romance.[2] In the Ywain legend, part of the myth associated with Brittany, a pivotal incident is Ywain's betrayal of his promise to return to his wife, Alundyne, after a year as a wandering knight. After the year has passed Ywain is confronted by his wife's handmaiden, who seizes the ring given him by Alundyne. This drives him into madness. In Hartmann von Aue's German version of the legend, written about 1200, Ywain roams through the forest, creating fear wherever he is seen.[3] In his appearance he becomes more and more the image of the madman as wild man, echoing the biblical description of the madness of Nebuchadnezzar, who, in Daniel 4:33, "was driven from men and did eat grass as oxen, and his body was wet with the dew of heaven, till his hairs were grown like eagles' feathers, and his

nails like birds' claws." Hartmann's description adds one further aspect to the appearance of the madman, not present in the biblical text. For his Ywain is black!

Ywain is not the only madman depicted as black. In Wirnt von Grafensberg's *Wiglois*, written about a decade after Hartmann's poem, the hero is confronted with a monster:

> Soon the Knight of the Wheel saw floating on the water a small raft which was tied to a post by the bank at a large willow twig. He squeezed through the dense underbrush, took the raft, and pulled it back to where he had left his horse. In a nearby rock was a cave from which he saw running toward him a woman who was all black and shaggy as a bear. She had neither great beauty nor good manners; indeed she was a monster.[4]

Here the madness of the wild woman is characterized by her description as being both hairy and black. This tradition appears again in the anonymous *Wolfdietrich* of the mid-thirteenth century:

> A monstrous woman, born from the wild, came toward him through the trees. There was never any bigger woman. The noble knight thought to himself: "O dear Christ, protect me!" Two monstrous breasts were hung from her body. "Whoever gets you," the wise knight spoke: "Gets the devil's mother, I do believe." Her body was created blacker than coal. Her nose hangs over her chin; stringy, black is her hair.[5]

The association of madness and blackness seems a commonplace, at least in the medieval German romance [Plate 1]. Richard Bernheimer, in his study of the wild man in art and literature, observes: "It must be added in parenthesis, that the writers of the romances do not regard hairiness as a necessary symptom of wildness induced by insanity; they are satisfied with describing the victim's total disarray, or with letting him turn all black as a sign of his demonic state."[6] However, just as the madness of Nebuchadnezzar is associated with hairiness, so too there is a clear biblical allusion to the association of blackness with madness.

When the biblical discussions of blackness and their exegesis in the Middle Ages are examined, one text assumes a central position. It is the passage from the beginning of the Song of Songs (1:5), "I am black, but comely." This passage provided medieval commentators with a text upon which to base a discussion of the nature (and implications) of blackness. St. Hippolytus (c. 170-c. 236), one of the early theologians of the Roman Church, in a fragment of his commentary on the Song of Songs, equates the blackness of the speaker, the Shulamite, with man's fall from grace.[7] Hippolytus, like all of the early commentators, both Jewish and Christian, reads this first dialogue of the Song of Songs as an allegorical portrayal of the relationship of God with the individual soul. The figure of the black woman becomes an allegory for the soul fallen from grace. The soul, however, still contains the potential for salvation.

Such a simplistic interpretation provided the allegorical groundwork for a more complicated presentation of the means by which the soul is blackened in the fall. St. Ambrose (c. 339-397),

in his commentary on this text in his discourse *On Isaac, or the Soul*, also refers to the concept of madness as a means of perceiving the state of the soul after the fall:

> And yet the selfsame soul, knowing that she has been darkened by her union with the body, says to the other souls or to those powers of heaven that have charge of the holy ministry, "Look not on me, because I am of a dark complexion, because the sun has not looked upon me. The sons of my mother have fought against me"; that is, the passions of the body have attacked me and the allurements of the flesh have given me my color; therefore the sun of justice has not shown on me.[8]

St. Ambrose sees the figure of the black woman in the Song of Songs as an indicator of the dominance of the physical (the body) over the spiritual (the soul and the mind). He articulates this within the Greek medical model, speaking of the passions, and their sources, the humors, as the determinants of mental states. After the fall the soul is trapped in a body racked by the conflicts of the humors which control the body.

The humors literally color the soul by their presence, and the visible sign of the effect of the humors on the soul is the change in skin color. This manner of perceiving the outward manifestation of the humors is exemplified in the most

PLATE 1. Image of a madwoman confronting Attila, from Valentier Alberti, *Dissertatio academica, De sagis, sive foeminis, commercium cum malo spiritu habentibus* (Leipzig: Christoph Fleischer, 1690)

famous reading of the Song of Songs, that of St. Bernard of Clairvaux (1090-1153):

> Or, blinded by the unparalleled splendours of the Divine Majesty, they may be overcast with a cloud of denser darkness than belonged to their former state. O whosoever thou be that art such a soul, do not, I implore thee, do not regard as mean or contemptible that place where the holy Penitent laid aside her sins and clothed herself in the garment of sanctity! There the Ethiopian woman changed her colour, being restored to the whiteness of her long-lost innocence. Then indeed, she was able to answer those who addressed her in words of reproach, "I am black but beautiful, O daughters of Jerusalem." Do you wonder, my brethren, by what art she effected such a change, or by what merits she obtained it? I will tell you in a few words. She "wept bitterly," she heaved deep sighs from her inmost heart, she was agitated interiorly with salutary sobbings, and thus she spat out the venomous humor. The heavenly Physician came speedily to her aid, because His "word runneth quickly." Is not the word of God a spiritual medicine? Yea, truly, and a medicine that is "strong and active, searching the heart and the veins."[9]

PLATE 2. Portrait of a melancholic with heavy cross-hatching representing the darkness of the skin. The plate, taken from *Das gross planeten buoch sampt der Geomanci, Physiognomi und Chiromanci* (Strassburg: Jostam Richel, 1558), was originally used to illustrate Bartolommeo Cocles, *Physiognomiae et Chiromantiae Compendium* (1551). The reuse of the illustrations representing human physiognomy is a tradition throughout the Middle Ages and Renaissance.

St. Bernard sees the affliction caused by the fall mirrored in the blackness of the humor. Moreover he sees associated with the dispelling of the humoral blackness a set of symptoms—the Shulamite's despair, her bitter weeping, her sighs, her sobbing—which could be categorized as an emotional or mental illness. Christ is cast in his traditional role as the heavenly physician to cure her.

Here one can return to the Ywain legend. Penelope Doob, in her study of madness in medieval English literature, explains the madness of Ywain as the direct result of his grief at having violated his word to his wife: " 'For wa he wex al wilde and wode'. . . Considered medically, this passion produces excess melancholy and deprives Ywain of his reason, after which—like other melancholy madmen—he wishes to shun men's sight by flight into the forest."[10] Grief, despair, madness and blackness are inexorably linked in the Middle Ages [Plate 2]. What Shakespeare calls "sable melancholy" in *Love's Labour Lost* (I, v) becomes a link between the classical medical theory and the visual understanding of madness.

In Galen's various works on insanity, texts that canonize numerous classical Greek medical theories, the four humors are the predominant manner of perceiving all psychopathological states. Those suffering from an excess of black bile, the melancholics, are described as bloated and swarthy.[11] The association is also present in the classic work of Greek physiognomy long ascribed to Aristotle:

> Why is it that some people are amiable and laugh and jest, others are peevish, sullen and depressed, some again are irritable, violent and given to rages, while others are indolent, irresolute and timid? The cause lies in the four humours. For those governed by the purest blood are agreeable, laugh, joke and have rosy, well-coloured bodies; those governed by yellow bile are irritable, violent, bold, and have fair, yellowish bodies; those governed by black bile are indolent, timid, ailing and, with regard to body, swarthy and black-haired; but those governed by phlegm are sad, forgetful, and with regard to the body, very pale.[12]

Among the illnesses ascribed to a dominance of black bile are a variety of psychopathologies, including melancholia, hypochondriasis, epilepsy, and hysteria.[13] Indeed mania may also be caused by the overheating of the yellow bile which in turn creates black bile. All of these illnesses have specific physical signs related to the presence of black bile, such as the blackness of the patient's skin. This symbolic perception of the uniqueness

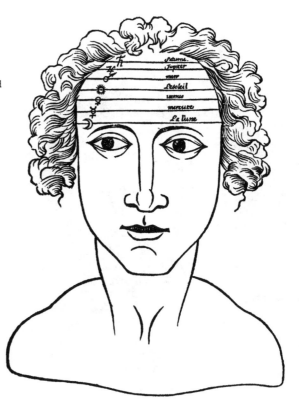

PLATE 3. Girolamo Cardano's image of the standard lines of the forehead taken from his *Metoposcopia libris tredecium* (Paris: Thomas Iolly, 1658)

of the mentally ill is rooted in the significance of the dominance of black bile as the etiology of their illness. Since black bile itself is a physiological fiction—unlike the yellow bile (gall), blood, and phlegm—it is a symbol which easily generates other symbols. The humors become a manner of structuring the universe, based on the model of man, for not only does black bile generate specific diseases, it is also the equivalent of a season (autumn), a physical quality (cold and dry), a segment of the four-fold world (earth), a zodiacal sign (Saturn), and much more.

The category of the insane changes from one such as Ywain, who is dominated by a single humor because of a specific set of circumstances, to individuals whose entire constitution predisposes them to madness. Thus the humors have evolved into the temperaments. Where Ywain's blackness is a variable sign, vanishing as his madness leaves him, in the evolution of the theories of the temperaments fixed aspects of human appearance are seen as being representative of the permanent dominance of the humors. No complete restoration to a socially approved state is possible. This, of course, broadly extends the concept of mental illness. All individuals under the dominance of Saturnian melancholy do not manifest gross psychopathologies. All, however, do possess the qualities attributable to the presence of black bile and can be seen as potentially deviant.[14]

The evolution of the theory of the temperaments from Galen's view of the humors perpetuated many of Galen's diagnostic considerations, for Galen was interested in the total individual, in his facial appearance as well as his bodily structures.[15] As the symbolic representation of the appearance of the insane evolved, all aspects of human expression, gesture, and constitution were examined for signs of the dominance of black bile. Thus in Girolamo Cardano's Renaissance study of the diagnostic and prognosticative function of the lines of the forehead, a madman is seen as one whose forehead mirrors the dominance of Saturn[16] [Plates 3 and 4]. Strik-

PLATE 4. Cardano's image of the "demented individual" with the prominent lines of the forehead

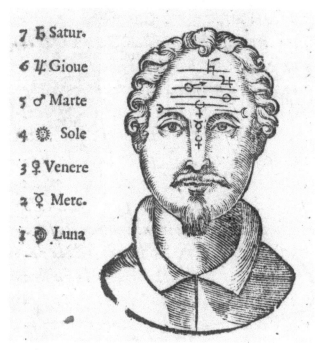

7 ♄ Satur.

6 ♃ Gioue

5 ♂ Marte

4 ☀ Sole

3 ♀ Venere

2 ☿ Merc.

1 ☽ Luna

PLATE 5. Ciro Spontone's indication of the forces represented by the lines of the forehead, from *Le Metoposcopia* (Venice: Ghirardo Imberti, 1637)

PLATE 6. A "weak minded individual," from Spontone

ing similarities can be observed in the lines of the forehead of an imbecile in Spontone's somewhat later work on the same subject **[Plates 5 and 6]**. Likewise, a sixteenth-century German manual of palmistry documents, as do many similar works, the dominance of the line of Saturn in the hand of an idiot **[Plate 7]**. Both head and hand betray the congenital weakness of the mind, or dominance of the emotions, both associated with the dominance of black bile.

Psychopathologies are seen as the result of the close relationship between the mind and the body, for as the author of a pseudo-Aristotelian physiognomy observes: "It seems to me that soul and body react on each other; when the character of the soul changes, it changes also the form of the body, and conversely, when the form of the body changes, it changes the character of the soul."[17] This is the key to the understanding of all early theories of the appearance of the mentally ill. By the Renaissance these theories have given way to a radical monistic view of the body dominating and forming the mind and soul. In terms of the appearance of the mentally ill this movement occurs on a symbolic plane. The appearance of the individual is seen as a classifiable, interpretable reference to his mental state. The loss of the significance of individual variations, of the sense of human diversity, begins with the etiology of mental illness in the humors and is easily transformed into icons of insanity, representing madness.

PLATE 7. The lines of the palm representing "weakness of the brain," from *Das gross planeten buoch. . .* (1558)

# the staff of madness

The concretion of all forms of insanity into a visual continuum of otherness can be observed in the symbolic function of one of the trappings of the madman in medieval and Renaissance representations, sometimes the only clue as to his deviation. Whatever the guise of the madman, whether as the maniac, the fool, the wild man, the idiot, or the possessed, a single image which often accompanies him is the staff of madness.[18] From the ubiquity of the staff in early portrayals of these figures it is evident that the categories were quite interchangeable. The idiot could (and did) serve as the fool; the maniac, as the wild man.

Within the initial "D" of the Latin versions of the fourteenth and fifty-third psalms in many medieval manuscripts lurks the fool. He may bear various disguises, one of them being the fool as madman. In two fourteenth-century manuscripts he carries a club (or stick) in one hand and a large white disc in the other [Plates 8 and 9]. Often the club is divided or decorated with a bladder or a small fool's head. The naked disarray of the fool as madman is a further sign of his insanity.

PLATE 8. The fool as madman, from a fourteenth-century manuscript

PLATE 9. The fool as madman from a manuscript, second half of the fourteenth century

7

The white disc may be a visual reference to Psalm 14:4: "Have the workers of iniquity no knowledge? who eat up my people as they eat bread and call not upon the Lord." The fool as madman is thus not merely ill, he is ill as the Shulamite was ill before her cure by Christ, he is ill through denying God. His madness is thus a sign of this denial.

The club also embellishes the portrait of the madman as wild man in a fourteenth-century Book of Hours [Plate 10]. His traditional coat of leaves, his flowing beard and hair are all set off by the branched club he brandishes.[19] The wild man is the madman in nature, often placed there, like Ywain, for denying God's order on earth.

In Hans Holbein the Younger's sixteenth-century illustrations for the psalms, those who deny Christ are depicted as "foolish." The illustration for the fifty-second psalm is a conflation of the visual associations with madness and folly as seen through the Middle Ages [Plate 11]. The madman, half-naked, his clothes in disarray, one shoe missing, is mocked by the children. In one hand he has the wild man's cudgel, in the other a giraculum, a child's pinwheel with its bifurcated top. The pinwheel, according to the sixteenth-century Alsatian writer Johannes Fischart,[20] is the sign of the "vain, Saturnian pinwheeler," or fool. His hair is covered with a band from which flow feathers. This feather cap, related to the wild man's leaves, is also a sign of wildness (a feature which reappears in the figure of the wild man as bird man in Mozart's *The Magic Flute*[21]).

It is not merely the maniac who is seen as bearing a divided stick. In Lucas Cranach the Elder's 1532 portrait of melancholy, Melancholy sits in the corner carving a stick into a bifurcated staff [Plate 12]. In the upper left of the painting the figures flying through the air on their zodiacal beasts represent the various humors. The dog, often associated with Saturn and melancholy—for the sensitive dog too can fall victim to madness—carries the antithetical figures of youth and old age. The standard borne by old age and that borne by the figure seated upon the boar are both variants of the staff of madness, with the latter being in turn related to the wild man's leafy cudgel.

PLATE 10. The madman as wild man, from the *Bedford Book of Hours*, a fourteenth-century French manuscript

PLATE **11**. From Hans Holbein the Younger's *Icones historiarum veteris testamenti* (Lugduni: Joannen Frellonium, 1547)

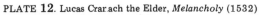

PLATE **12**. Lucas Cranach the Elder, *Melancholy* (1532)

PLATE 13. "Madness" [*Pazzia*] from Cesare Ripa's *Iconologia* (Venetia: C. Tomasini, 1645)

By the time the image of the madman is incorporated into the catalogues of iconography during the seventeenth century, his staff has become a regular part of his appearance. In what is considered the standard iconography, the collection compiled by Cesare Ripa in 1611, madness is portrayed in a manner not very different from that found in Holbein's drawing a century earlier [Plate 13]. The pinwheel, the cudgel (which the madman mounts like a hobby-horse), and the disordered clothing all reappear to provide an image of the madman readily identifiable in the seventeenth century.[22] Giuseppe Mitelli, in his collection of illustrated proverbs, uses the madman to represent the saying: "Those who believe themselves wiser than all are more foolish than everyone" [Plate 14]. Here the madman is the fool. The pinwheels are present, and tied to them are fools' bladders. His clothing is mixed up, one side not matching the other, and he is accompanied by the Saturnian dog.

The icon of the stick or cudgel of madness is associated not only with various psychopathologies such as melancholia and mania, but also with possession.[23] In the first illustration of flying witches ever published, which appeared in 1489, these demons are perched upon a bifurcated stick [Plate 15]. By the beginning of the eighteenth century the fabled broomstick is only just replacing the staff, which is still present in the form of the pitchfork [Plate 16]. Witches and demons were believed to be possessed by the devil just as they possessed others. The demonic, as will be discussed later, was perceived as a black force governing mind and body. It was a medieval concretion of black bile to explain yet another form of deviancy.

The origin of the staff of madness is not clear. It may be a version of the crutch or scythe of Saturn as Father Time.[24] It may be rooted in the royal flail portrayed with the Egyptian Seth-Typon, the trickster-god.[25] The bifurcated staff

CHI SI CREDE ESSER PIV SAVIO DE GLI ALTRI, QVELLO
E PIV PAZZO DI TVTTI.

Perche il *saggio* de'*saggi* esser presumi,
Il più folle *sei* tu di tutti i folli,
Se non empion tua mente altro, che fumi.

PLATE 14. From Giuseppe Maria Mitelli, *Proverbi Figurati* ([Bologna]: n. p. 1678)

may be the medieval animal trap which Sebastian Brant depicts the devil as using to capture men's souls.[26] Indeed, the bifurcated image of the wild man's branch may point to the implications of the icon of division symbolized by the letter "Y" in the Middle Ages.[27] This icon represented the divided path leading to the choices of life. All of these sources bear implications that are incorporated into the general image of madness through the use of the madman's staff. Like the leper's clapper, the staff comes to represent the inner nature of the one bearing an outer sign.

PLATE 15. The first published illustration of flying witches, from Ulrich Molitor, *De lamiis et phitonicis mulieribus* (Strassburg: Johann Prüss, 1489)

PLATE 16. Flying witches on broom sticks from Christian Thomasius, *Kurze Lehr-sätze von dem Laster der Zauberey* (1712)

# the position of madness

If appearance, complexion, and accessories create the aura of madness, so also do the posture, gestures and movements of the entire figure.[28] When the medieval German poet Walther von der Vogelweide places himself in the philosopher's pose, he provides yet another icon for madness:

> I sat down on a stone,
> and crossed my legs
> and set my elbows on them;
> I rested my chin and cheek
> in my hand.
> Then I pondered very earnestly
> how one ought to live one's life on earth.
> I could not find the solution.[29]

The physical position of the pensive philosopher is one of grief.[30] Here the association of the icons of melancholy with icons of grief becomes apparent. Similarly, the classical image of the melancholy Hercules, his head resting on one hand, is paralleled in religious art of the late Middle Ages by figures mourning the death of Christ.

The position of the figure of melancholy becomes one of the key images in characterizing mental illness. The seated figure, its eyes cast down, its hand grasped to its face, seems to be closed within itself. It is oblivious to the world, cut off from it. Thus the figure representing melancholy in Ripa's seventeenth-century *Iconologia* [Plate 17] is seated in such a position. Her clothing is disheveled, her face darkened, the bifurcated staff growing as a tree from the rock on which she sits.

Another grief-related image which is transfered to melancholy is that of the clenching or hiding of the hands. One of the great works of art in which this feature comes to categorize the symbolic nature of the portrait of melancholy is Albrecht Dürer's *Melencolia I* [Plate 18]. The figure representing melancholy is seated in the

pensive position, her darkened face partially obscured by her clenched fist.[31] The bifurcated staff of earlier tradition has been transformed into a pair of calipers, symbolizing her relationship to the scholarship of the liberal arts. But her tools are untouched, her clenched and hidden hands undertake no meaningful task. She thus incorporates as well the visual symbol of the medieval sin of acedia, sloth. The sleeping dog also epitomizes this aspect of melancholy, the inability to act. The medieval commentator Evagrius saw "the demon of acedia . . . tearing the soul asunder as a dog the fawn."[32] The dog, the most sensitive of the creatures in the medieval bestiary, is as passive and melancholic as the seated figure.

PLATE 17. *Melancholia,* from *Ripa's Iconologia* (1645)

PLATE **18**. Albrecht Dürer's *Melencolia* I (1514)

In Abraham Janssens van Nuyssen's *Joy and Melancholia* of 1623, the antitheses of youth and age, joy and sadness found in the peripheral figures of Cranach's painting (see Plate 12) reappear [Plate 19]. Not only does the old woman assume the half-crouching posture of the melancholic, but she also hides her hands. Again, the hidden or obscured hands symbolize the melancholic's ineffectuality. The slothful individual is likened to one suffering from paralysis which "unloosens the whole man and renders him use-

less for any good work."[33] Here too the Bible provides a text, in Proverbs 19:24: "A slothful man hideth his hand in his bosom, / And will not so much as bring it to his mouth again." The broad image of madness in all its guises also encompasses this concept, as in a fifteenth-century Flemish portrait of a fool whose hands are hidden [Plate 20]. The hidden-hand motif appears in a variety of related images of minimal men, including figures representing poverty and idleness.

PLATE **19**. Abraham Janssens van Nuyssen, *Joy and Melancholia* (early seventeenth century)

PLATE **20**. *Portrait of a Fool*, Flemish (fifteenth century)

15

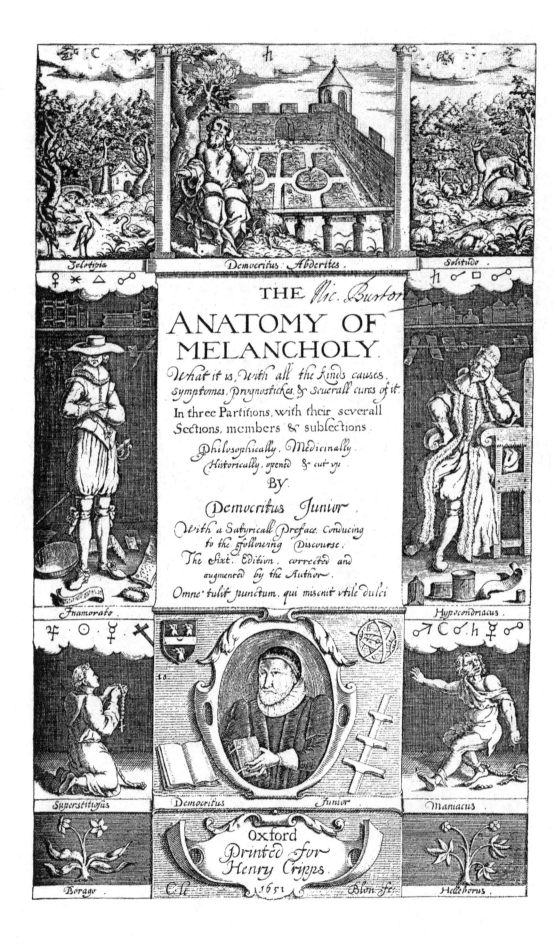

The awareness of the role of body position and gesture in characterizing the mentally ill can be judged by the frontispiece to Robert Burton's widely-read seventeenth-century psychiatric and literary classic, *The Anatomy of Melancholy*. Beginning with the third edition in 1628, the reader was supplied with a commented visual catalogue of psychopathological images[34] **[Plate 21]**. Uppermost on the page is the figure of the Greek philosopher Democritus, born, like Burton, under the sign of Saturn, in the position in which Hippocratus found him

> in his garden in *Abdera*, in the suburbs, under a shady bower, with a book on his knees, busy at his study. . . . The subject of his book was melancholy and madness; about him lay the carcasses of many several beasts newly by him cut up and anatomized . . . to find the seat of this *atra bilis*, or melancholy, whence it proceeds, and how it was engendered in men's bodies, to the intent he might better cure it in himself, [and] by his writings & observations teach others how to prevent and avoid it.[35]

The philosopher is seen in the meditative pose, which in his case is also a melancholic one. On either side are two of the causes or symptoms of melancholy, jealousy and solitude. Each relates in turn to the figure immediately below. On the left, under jealousy, is the figure representing the melancholy of love. He stands under the sign of Venus, hands hidden, face obscured, "with your hat penthouse-like o'e the shop of your eyes, with your arms crossed on your thin belly doublet, like a rabbit on a spit," as Shakespeare describes the melancholy lover.[36] Opposite him, under the sign of Saturn, sits hypochondriacal melancholy, the most severe form of the disease. Religious melancholy, signified by the kneeling monk, is seen as a form of love melancholy. For Burton, "folly, melancholy, madness are but one disease," thus the maniac with his body in an extravagant pose, which will be discussed later, stands below Saturnian melancholy.[37] At the bottom, the side panels illustrate two modes of treatment, the purgatives borage and hellebore. The author himself, with his coat of arms, is portrayed holding a copy of his book. He is also accompanied by two symbols usually associated with exploration, the armillary sphere and the cross staff. These are the scholarly versions of the fool's staff and bladder, representing here the voyage of discovery into the unknown surrounding melancholia.

Burton's frontispiece serves as a seventeenth-century summary of visual icons of mental illness, especially in regard to the body position. The fine line that divides art from the reality of mental illness was breeched in 1680 by Cajus Gabriel Cibber in the two statues he carved for the portal of Bethlem Asylum, the proverbial Bedlam **[Plates 22-24]**.

PLATE 22. Cibber's sculptures depicted *in situ* at Bedlam before they were recut in the nineteenth century. This plate formed the frontispiece to Thomas Bowen's *An Historical Account of the Origin, Progress, and Present State of Bethlem Hospital* (London: n.p., 1783)

PLATE 21. Title page of the 1651 edition of Robert Burton's *The Anatomy of Melancholy*

PLATE 23. Cibber's image of "Melancholy" (1680)

Where proud Augusta, blest with long
   Repose,
Her ancient Wall and ruin'd Bulwark shews;
Close by a verdant plain with graceful Height,
A stately Fabric rises to the Sight:
Yet tho' it's Parts all elegantly shine,
And sweet Proportion crowns the whole
   Design;
Tho' Art, in strong expressive Sculpture
   shewn,
Consummate Art informs the breathing
   Stone:
Far other Views than these within appear,
And Woe and Horror dwell for ever here.[38]

Here art is seen as providing a decorous presentation of madness in the form of Cibber's statues.
The reclining figure of melancholy, his hands
hidden from sight, contrasts with raving mania
in chains. With Burton's presentation in mind
one can see the use of relaxation and tension as
images for melancholia and mania. Despite the
constraints of the portal upon which the figures
were placed, the sculptor's subtle use of iconographic references makes clear the counterpoint
inherent in these manifestations of insanity. As
the anonymous poet observes, the statues provide a fixed, aesthetic representation of madness.
It is the polarity implicit in the balance of the
two figures, in the seeming antithesis of the two
types of insanity, which creates the "sweet Proportion."

In their representation of mental illness as a
duality, Cibber's figures are a major innovation
in the iconography of the posture of the insane.
By the seventeenth century the concept of melancholy and the reflexive position of the melancholic had become so fashionable that the immediate reference to a form of psychopathology
was substantially diluted.[39] But the figure of
mania had not been as compromised. It is little
wonder that in a contemporary sculpture [Plates
25 and 26], which stood in the courtyard of the
asylum at Amsterdam,[40] the figure representing
madness is that of the maniac, the reverse of the
classic figure of melancholy. Where melancholy
is characteristically seated, with sunken head, le-
thargic, withdrawn, self-enclosed, the maniac is
typically contorted, head and limbs thrown out,
hyperactive, and exposed. These seemingly in-
compatible images share a common source for
their iconography. Indeed, Seneca mixed the
two in his description of "a madman": "a bold
and threatening mien, a gloomy brow, a fierce
expression, a hurried step, restless hands, an altered colour, a quick and more violent breathing."[41] The gloominess, the clenching of the
hands, and the color change belong to the classic
image of melancholy, the other attributes, to the
maniac.

As the clenched fist of melancholy is taken

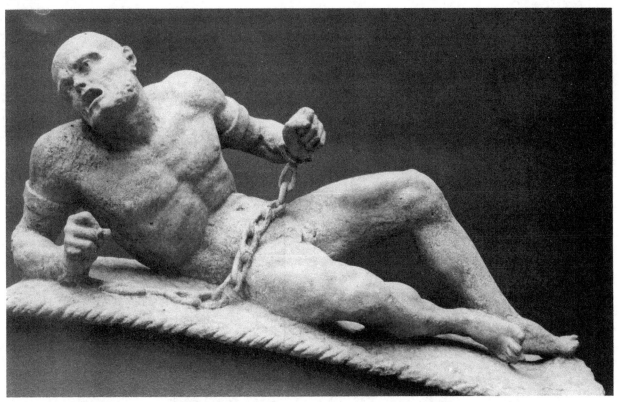

PLATE 24. Cibber's image of "Raving Madness"

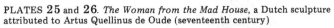

PLATES 25 and 26. *The Woman from the Mad House*, a Dutch sculpture attributed to Artus Quellinus de Oude (seventeenth century)

PLATE 27. Pieter Xavery's *Two Madmen* (1673)

from traditional images of grieving, so too is the tearing of the hair. In Pieter Xavery's terra-cotta group **[Plate 27]**, the two madmen interconnect images of melancholy and mania. The seated figure in chains tears at his clothing with the tightened hands of the melancholic; the reclining figure, in the classic *arc de cercle* position of the corybantic ecstatic, which will be discussed below, completes the visual image with his hands hidden from view. These figures emphasize the tension of mania rather than the passivity of melancholia.

By the close of the seventeenth century the iconography of insanity was well established in the West. Yet the basic structures found in the visual arts from the Middle Ages through Rococo are in no way isolated from the mainstream of medical thought. Indeed the iconography of insanity is as much the iconography of medicine as it is that of art, and not merely through the medical theories upon which the visual images are based.[42] The visual representations of the insane in medical texts are identical with those in the fine and popular arts. Nowhere is this more clearly to be observed than in a page that can serve as a Rosetta stone for medieval images of the insane [Plate 28]. Cauterization diagrams are given for the treatment of four psychopathologies: mania, epilepsy, melancholy, and frenzy. The maniac is shown half-clothed, his naked-

ness and disheveled clothing a sign of his illness. He clutches in one hand the madman's staff, here with a curved end reminiscent of the fool's sceptre. The epileptic suffers, as does the maniac, from an excess of black bile. He is portrayed in the *arc de cercle* position of the ecstatic, his arms and legs flailing. The melancholic, with clenched fist, head resting on his arm, is seen as passive rather than active. The frenetic, according to Galen, is in a state of delirium brought about by a fever and is seen seated, ready to be purged. Among these four figures are the various physical gestures, positions, and accessories associated with the image of the madman through the Middle Ages and the Renaissance. The page provided a diagnostic chart for identifying or symbolizing the appearance of the insane, as well as a set of procedures for treatment.

PLATE 28. A cauterization diagram from a thirteenth-century medical manuscript. The figures represent the maniac, the epileptic, the melancholic, and the frenetic

# the treatment of madness

If madness is the result of the imbalance of the humors, then it should be treatable. As with the cauterization diagram above, the image of the madman is found as frequently in scenes describing treatment as in all other contexts. The concept of treatment is a broad one. Within the application of the humorial theory during the Middle Ages and the Renaissance, certain basic reinterpretations of the nature of the humors occurred. Indeed, the humors themselves metamorphosed into forms not immediately identifiable as humorial. As in St. Bernard's discussion of the illness of the Shulamite, the humors can be seen as the infiltration of the evils of the world and the flesh into the purity of the soul. This contamination is perceived as the possession of the individual by actual demons, and thus exorcism becomes the appropriate means of treatment.

The basic image of curing the possessed derives from the New Testament. According to the accounts in Mark (5:1-20) and Luke (8:26-29), the madman "was kept bound with chains and in fetters; and he brake the bands, and was driven of the devil into the wilderness." Also he "ware no clothes." Here the basis for the figure of the maniac is already present.

In the earliest visualizations, the possessed is portrayed with arms askew, head tilted back, the demon fleeing from his opened mouth [Plates 29 and 30]. This position is adapted from the classical image of the ecstatic as seen in Greco-Roman presentations of Bacchic ritual.[43] The demon in its blackness is the materialization of the blackness associated with black bile, indeed a blackness associated universally in the West with evil and corruption.[44]

PLATE 29. A tenth-century ivory relief of Christ healing the man of Gerasa possessed by the devil

PLATE **30**. Remy Vuibert's image of the healing of the possessed (1639)

PLATE 31. Christ healing the demoniacs, from a fourteenth-century Byzantian manuscript

In a medieval illustration based on Matthew's version of this miracle, in which Christ heals two men rather than one (8:28-34), the two figures show the possessed before and after treatment [Plate 31]. The upright one, with the demons flying from his mouth obliterated in the manuscript, stands before Christ cured; the second lies at Christ's feet. His tousled hair as well as his position mark him as still possessed.

In all the representations of the exorcism of demons the focus is on the relationship between the victim and the figure treating him. Christ as the divine physician is as often as not replaced by a galaxy of saints, yet the concentration on healer vis-à-vis patient is perpetuated [Plate 32]. The domination of the healer over his patient, his distance from him, point toward the domination of divine power over demonic presence. Healing is thus the overcoming of the earthly, the corrupt, by the divine. It is the conquest of Saturn by Christ.

The evolution of the image of the possessed through the seventeenth century is striking. By the time of Raphael's *Transfiguration* [Plate 33] it has become so stylized as to permit the omission of literal demons.[45] The *arc de cercle* position—eyes rolled back, mouth open, appendages askew—in itself signifies the possession. As in

PLATE 32. Girolamo Di Benvenuto, *St. Catherine Exorcising a Possessed Woman* (fifteenth century)

PLATE 33. Raphael's *Transfiguration* (1519-1520) places the figure of the demoniac
in the immediate right foreground

Raphael's work, there is in Benedetto Luti's portrait of St. Romuald curing a possessed woman [Plate 34] a noticeable absence of the demonic except as indicated by the face and posture of the possessed. Yet Peter Paul Rubens, in his portrait of St. Ignatius Loyola miraculously curing the insane [Plate 35], with its clear reference to Raphael, again introduces the visible demons, but as a subtext.[46] Here the figures of the possessed, especially the one in the foreground who, like the biblical character, has broken his bonds, interact with the raised figure of Loyola in a manner paralleled above them by the demons fleeing from the angels. This materialization of the demonic has only stylized reference to the concept of possession, with the fight between demons and angels used to symbolize the struggle in the souls of the possessed.

PLATE 34. Benedetto Luti's *St. Romuald Curing a Woman Possessed* (late seventeenth century)

PLATE 35. Peter Paul Rubens, *The Miracle of St. Ignatius Loyola* (early eighteenth century)

As with the staff of madness, the image of the possessed recurs in other contexts, such as in those relating to the victims of witches. Themselves possessed by the devil, the witches can in turn possess others. The signs of possession are very specific. Francesco Guazzo, in his *Compendium Maleficarum* (1608), describes them in detail:

> The following is the customary practice to determine whether a sick man is possessed [*energumenus*] by a demon. [Priests] secretly apply to the sick man a writing with the sacred words of God, or relics of the saints, or a blessed waxen Agnus Dei, or some other holy thing. A priest places his hand and his stole upon the head of the possessed and pronounces sacred words. Thereupon the sick man begins to shake and shudder with fright, and on account of his pain makes many confused movements, and says and does many strange things. If the demon lodges in his head, he feels the most piercing pains in his head, or else his head and his face are suffused with a hot red flush like fire. If the demon is in his eyes, he makes them roll wildly. If in the back, he brings on convulsions in his limbs, in front and behind, and sometimes makes the whole body so rigid and inflexible that no amount of force can bend it.
>
> Sometimes the [possessed persons] fall down as if dead, as if they were suffering from tertiary epilepsy and a vapor rushing into their head; but at the priest's command they arise, and the vapor goes back where it came from. If the demon is in their throats, they are so constricted that they appear to be strangled. If the devil is in the nobler parts of the body, as about the heart or lungs, he causes panting, palpitations and syncope. If he tends more to the stomach, he provokes hiccoughs and vomiting, so that sometimes they cannot take food, or else cannot retain it. And he causes them to pass something like a little ball by the anus, with roarings and other discordant cries; and afflicts them with wind and gripings in the abdomen. They are also sometimes known by certain fumes of sulphur or some other strong-smelling stuff.[47]

The frontispiece for Georg Mercklin's early eighteenth-century tractate on enchantments illustrates this use of the manic figure in images of witchcraft [**Plate 36**]. At the right of the picture stands a witch, herself under the spell of the Devil. In the background is a witches' dance, dominated by another satanic being. Other witches fill the air on flying broomsticks and pitchforks. On the left is a sickroom filled with sufferers of witchcraft. Included among them is the maniac, in his classical pose, being held by two warders.

This figure of the maniac is found throughout representations of demonic possession. In Abraham Palingh's description of a mass possession in early eighteenth-century Holland it takes a pure *arc de cercle* form [**Plate 37**]. In Andreas de Conti's volume of exorcisms from the same period, the demonic presence is indicated by the Edenic serpent escaping from the mouth of the maniac [**Plate 38**]. The demonics are seen as specifically originating from the malevolent forces of evil. The portrayal of their victims incorporates the image of the madman as maniac from medieval art.

PLATE **36**. The frontispiece from Georg Abraham Mercklin, *Tractus physico-medicus de incantamentis* (Nurenberg: Joh. Friedrich Rudiger, 1715)

PLATE 37. Demonic possession, from
Abraham Palingh, *t'Aufgerukt Mom-Aansight
der Tooverye* (Amsterdam: Andries van
Damme, 1725)

PLATE 38. Portrait of Andreas de Conti,
the Franciscan beatified in 1724 by Innocent
XIII. He was supposed to have the ability to
drive out demons. From Vincent von Berg,
comp., *Enchiridium quadripartitum*
(Cologne: J. C. Gussen, 1743)

29

PLATE 39. Saul comforted by David. The position of Saul is typical of that of the melancholic. Present also are the demons of possession. Illustration from *Queen Mary's Psalter* (English, fourteenth century)

If the visual representation of the patient from whom the demon is to be exorcised by religious means is that of the maniac, the opposite figure, that of the melancholic, has his demons disposed of in quite a different manner. The concretion of black bile into black demons is no-where better illustrated than in the archetypical image of melancholy in the Old Testament, the tale of Saul and David (I Samuel 14-23). Saul is described as being troubled by "an evil spirit" from the Lord:

> And Saul's servants said unto him, Behold now, an evil spirit from God troubleth thee.
> Let our lord now command thy servants, which are before thee, to seek out a man, who is a cunning player on an harp; and it shall come to pass, when the evil spirit from God is upon thee, that he shall play with his hand, and thou shalt be well.

The image of Saul [Plate 39] is that of the melancholic, who is to be cured by music.

This method of cure is illustrated again in a thirteenth-century manuscript of Aristotle's *On Dreams* [Plate 40]. His eyes closed, the recumbent half-nude figure listens to the sounds of the stringed instrument. It is the action of the music that restores the balance of the humors.

The belief that music and dance could cure insanity permeates all Western cultures. Plato, in the *Laws*, describes how mothers, when they wish "to put fractious babies to sleep," employ not stillness, but its very opposite, movement, "as well as melody of some kind."

> . . . in fact, so to say, put a spell on their babies just as the priestess does on the distracted in the Dionysiac treatment, by this combination of the movements of dance and song.
> Clinias: And pray, sir, what explanation are we to give these facts?

PLATE 40. The melancholic cured by music. From a thirteenth-century manuscript of Aristotle's *On Dreams*

30

Athenian: Why, the explanation is not far to seek.

Clinias: But what is it?

Athenian: Both disturbances are forms of fright, and fright is due to some morbid condition of the soul. Hence, when such disorders are treated by rocking movement the external motion thus exhibited dominates the internal, which is the source of the fright or frenzy. By its domination it produces a mental sense of calm and relief from the preceding distressing agitation of the heart, and thus effects a welcome result in both cases, the induction of sleep in the one, in the other —that of patients who are made to dance to the flute in the ritual of the deities to whom sacrifice is done on these occasions—the substitution of sanity for their temporary state of distraction.[48]

Music cures the dominance of black bile; it also cures the frenzied madman through dance. Aristotle had observed that the mindless passion of the Dionysiac ritual was a direct result of the "Phrygian [mode] which inspires enthusiasm."[49] The sound of the flute playing in this mode possessed the listener and forced him to dance. His dance was the result of the total suppression of his logical faculties and his surrender to the power of music.

Of all the images of the dancing madman none is more striking than the sixteenth-century drawing by Pieter Breughel the Elder of the pilgrimage of the madmen to Molenbeek [Plate 41].

PLATE 41. Pieter Breughel the Elder's mid-sixteenth-century drawing of the procession to the shrine at Molenbeek

# VERTOONINGE

## Hoe de Pelgerimmen, op S. Ians-dagh, buyten Bruſſel, tot
Meulebeeck danſſen moeten; ende als ſy over deſe Brugh gedanſt hebben, ofte
gedwongen werden op deſe volgende maniere, dan ſchijnen ſy, voor
een Iaer, van de vallende Sieckte, geneſen te zijn.

Voor aen gaen deſe Speel-lieden ofte Moeſelaers, ſpeelende op Sack-pijpen; daer nae
volgen de Pelgrims, die met ſtercke Huyslieden gevat worden, ſeer ongaerne tegen haren wil [gelijck
in de tweede ende derde volghende Figuere vertoont wert] ſom krijtende en roepende; maer
komende ontrent de Brugge, ſoo keerenſe haer om, ende gebruycken groot tegenweer;
maer gevat zijnde, werden over de Brugge geheſt ende gedragen; over zijnde
ſitten neder als vermoeyt weſende: ende dan komen de Huyslieden
van dier plaets, haer lavende, ende wat warms in-gevende:
ende is ſoo dit werck vol-eyndt.

*dere aerdigh uyt-gebeeldt door den uytnemenden konſtigen Schilder* Pieter Breugel. *Geſneden ende gedruckt*
*ten Huyſe van* Henricus Hondius, *in 'sGraven-Hage,* 1642.

P. Breugel inv.                                                                 Hh. fec. Cum priv. 1642.

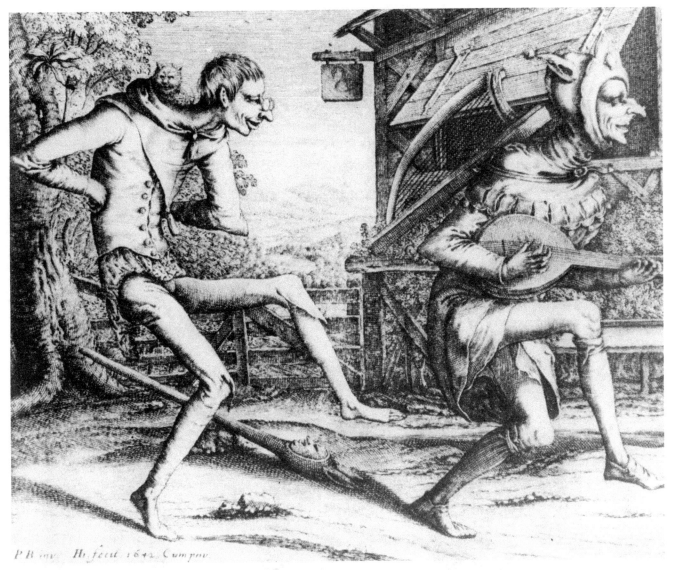

PLATE 43. One of the Hondius engravings showing the expansion of the Breughel plate to include fools

PLATE 42. Title page of the book of engravings by Henricus Hondius (1642) based on Breughel's drawing of the pilgrimage to Molenbeek

In a series of engravings based on this drawing, Henricus Hondius first depicts the antics of fools [Plates 42 and 43], thus presenting a continuum through the power of music from the fool to the possessed. The fools scamper while the possessed, in classic positions, heads thrown back, arms and legs no longer under control, are helped by warders [Plates 44 and 45]. The Breughel drawing does not provide this continuum, for the fools are not present. However, the idea of the dance of the fools was so basic as to demand their inclusion in the more detailed volume documenting the pilgrimage.

PLATE 44. A Hondius engraving based on the figures at the left of Breughel's drawing

PLATE 45. Another of the Hondius engravings, showing the right-hand figures

A contemporaneous engraving by Daniel Hopfer [Plate 46] provides portraits of two of the classic fool figures of the sixteenth century, Markolf and his consort Bolikana. The source of the madness is evident here in the iconographic depiction of the goiter, but the goiter serves as only one image for this grotesque dancing pair.[50] The leaves and bird's nest indicate the wild man, the bells signify the fool. The idea of the dancing madman, either as the fool or the possessed, with the potential for cure through music, adds one more level of interpretation to the image of flailing limbs as an icon of madness.

The modes of treatment discussed so far can be understood both as pragmatic approaches to specific typologies of mental illness and as symbolic ways of dealing with the iconographic perception of these illnesses. This complexity is also found in the images of curing insanity through the removal of the stone of madness.[51] The reality behind this method lies in treatments such as cauterization for various psychopathologies, as mentioned earlier, as well as trepanation or trephination to release the demons or pressures causing mental aberrations. In the sixteenth century, Paracelsus, in his tractate *Diseases That Deprive Men of Their Reason*, describes the opening of the skull as well as the "place from which the mania rises," which is usually the liver or the spleen.[52] The image of removing an irritant or permitting one to escape through the opening of the skull is attached in religious art to portraits of St. Luke as a healer. In the popular art of the fifteenth and sixteenth centuries this becomes one of the ways of presenting the concretion of the mode of possession.

The madman becomes but one of the actors in a world of fools. By the time Hieronymous Bosch painted the *Cure of Folly* in the 1480s [Plate 47], the image of the patient being cut for stones had assumed a proverbial quality. The proverb literally surrounds the scene: "Master cut the stone out, my name is Lubbert Das."[53] Lubbert Das, the Dutch fool figure, is portrayed as having the flower of folly removed from his head. With the doctor stand the Church and Philosophy. The position of the fool is analogous to that of the maniac, eyes rolled back, mouth open, bent backwards in his chair in an approximation of the *arc de cercle*. He is paralleled by a female figure who has assumed the position of meditative grief, her head resting on her clenched hand. The volume on her head is symbolic of false learning, and is analogous to Dürer's use of the liberal arts in his *Melencolia I* (see Plate 18). Although she is only an observer, she serves to balance the portrait in presenting the other typology of madness, that of the melancholic.

PLATE 46. Daniel Hopfer's early sixteenth-century engraving of the wild man and woman as dancing fools

PLATE 47. Hieronymous Bosch's depiction of the removal of the stone of folly from
the head of Lubbert Das (c. 1480)

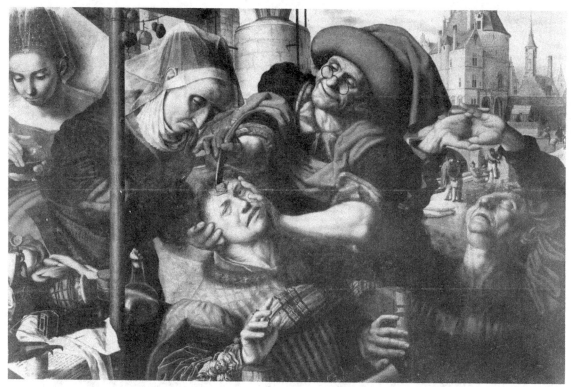

PLATE 48. Jan Sanders van Hemessen's painting of the cutting of the stone of folly (c. 1530)

PLATE 49. Theodor de Bry's engraving of the cutting of the fool's stone, with its reference to the classical concept of foolishness

Such a sense of parallelism can also be seen in Jan van Hemessen's somewhat later presentation of the same scene [Plate 48]. Here the stone of folly is removed from the bound patient who is portrayed as one possessed. In addition to the doctor and his staff (one holding the patient, the other examining his urine), a parallel figure is presented in the right foreground. Her clenched hands and head thrown back create the image of the madwoman who waits for treatment, but since Hemessen applies to her the iconography of grief this figure would be ambiguous if it were not seen in a broader context.

A sixteenth-century engraving by Theodor de Bry gives a very clear example of the parallelism among the various types of madness. Here the raving and melancholic figures wait to have their stones removed, while the doctor operates on another patient [Plate 49]. The even more chaotic scene in Breughel the Elder's *Witch of Mallegem* depicts all manner of madmen, each

waiting to have the stone of madness removed [Plate 50]. Almost framing the presentation are the figures of the raving madman with his two attendants on the left and the hooded figure of the melancholic, with the staff of madness, on the right.

The symbolic reference in Bosch's painting (see Plate 47) becomes explicit. The entire world is populated by fools. The idea of the world as madhouse is found in Carolin Allardt's drawing of stone cutting and other modes of treatment, purgation and fumigation [Plate 51]. In all these images, from Bosch on, the figure of the doctor, the quack, is part of the image of the world inhabited by fools. This usage is quite a change from the idea of the Holy Physician found in the images of exorcism, or earlier in the representation of Luke as a physician, for the image of the madman has become one with that of the fool inhabiting the world of fools. The stone, unlike the goiter or the staff, is omnipresent, signifying

PLATE 50. Pieter Breughel the Elder's mid-sixteenth-century engraving of the *Witch of Mallegem*

PLATE 51. Carolin Allardt's representation of the wide range of fools and their treatment

madness of the entire world. Each of the figures in Breughel's illustration (see Plate 50) has his hidden stone. Here the idea of the universality of the potential for madness in the presence of black bile within everyone has evolved into the universal potential for each man to have his foolishness revealed.

With Allardt's illustration of the range of mock treatments paralleling the cutting of stones, the idea of the treatment of madness is expanded. Paracelsus saw the source of madness in the abdominal region. In a seventeenth-century German broadside, the quack doctor treats his patient, placed in the traditional position of the melancholic, for "hare fever" [Plate 52]. Here the proverbial, as in the cutting of stone, is made literal. The German proverb reads: "One is covered with a hare and fed by a fool." "Hare fever" is madness, but the doctor's treatments, including feeding the patient with "the smell of a roast capon," are also mad. Hans Sachs, in his 1557 drama, "Cutting the Fool," has the doctor prescribe equally foolish treatments to drive the fools out of the patient's belly.[54] They tumble out, forming a microcosm repeating (while quoting) the image of Sebastian Brant's *Ship of Fools* (see Plates 55 and 56).

A similar mode of purgation is accompanied in Theodor de Bry's illustration [Plate 53] by a demonstration of distillation. On the left we see the opening of the gut and the release of the fool (with his ass-ears and his donkey). At the right the patient's fantasies are expelled through the top of the apparatus while the proverbial "rats

40

Ein bewehrtes Recept,

Für das vmblauffende Rädlin in den haspelhafften, ver wickleten, ver zwickleten, vnd ver wirrten köpffen, vnder den hasen haren

PLATE 52. The fool suffering from "hare fever" in a seventeenth-century German broadside attributed to Matthaus Rembold

PLATE 53. Lunacy cured by distillation in a sixteenth-century engraving by Theodor de Bry

41

of the brain," the cause of madness, are ejected from the bottom.[55] The black rats, like the demons and the stones, are the concrete representations of the humors which, when distilled out, release the fantasies of the madman. The presence of a miniscule fool in the urine glass being inspected by the doctor points to a physical cause of madness.

The distillation of madness is also found in a sixteenth-century broadside by Matthias Greuter depicting Doctor Wurmbrandt (= worm distilled) and his cure for insanity [Plate 54]. While one patient defecates demons, another has his demons literally burnt out of him. (In a later version of this broadside from 1648, the still as well as figures with the fool's staff are added to the image.[56]) The legend below the illustration points again to a physical source of madness in the "rats of madness":

You sick men and women: If you wish to entrust yourselves to a doctor, then entrust yourselves to me. I am the best healer of the human race. Just show me your urine and I shall soon see what has happened to your body and brains to make you act so foolishly and to associate with fools. I am a master of these things; can make the giddy and mad intelligent; can recognize immediately from the face what disjoints a person mentally and can conjecture easily from one's manners what else might be wrong. If you have no rest because of worms, then hurry to me, Dr. Wurmbrandt: I shall cut away skillfully the worm from your worm-eaten brains. If you struggle and pick a quarrel with a mouse (in your imagination?), which no one can very well endure, then for a little money I will catch them for you; I have cats up my sleeve which are so full of cunning that no rat is safe. If you have too many rafters in your head (i.e., if you are crazy) then you are a very great fool; if there is a spar missing in your head then you are very close to being an arrant fool and children might laugh at you. If you lose your senses, then fantastic notions, doves and other nonsense continually fly in and out of your head. Your mind then becomes its own house. See! I can name all that as vertigo and wild imaginings as when one is in-

flamed by wine or just as a coal fire burns, and as when you, having become quite drunk, do not know the east, south, west, or north. Yes. When you are conscious of nothing—whether you are man or woman—then trust me to bring you back to your right mind. If you do not get the mastery of just one of your evil troubles (so that my medicine must depart without any healing power and without proper working); if you do not wish to understand and do not wish to recognize who you are and what foolishness is in you; and if you display yourself pompously and believe that more wit is in your nose than in twelve wise minds—Oh woe!—then all medicine is useless. If my medicine is to refresh you then you must have faith in it. Faith establishes all things. Without it all craft and relief is trifling. But come! We will test it in my alchemical laboratory. There I have set up my *Brennhelm* (a dome used for distilling). Come. Present your head and do not be afraid. We will in a short while see the mist go up in full current with the thousand-fold contents of a fool's mind—contents which I noticed so well in you. Oho! They already come up. What distilling! What things fly out! What trash was stuck in your head! You confused simpleton! you have me producing more rubbish from your head than there is in almost a whole forest of monkeys. If I make you free of this illness then proclaim that I am a master.[57]

Whether as black bile, black demons, black stones, black rats (or indeed grey hares) or any other concrete form, the images of madness indicate the search for a substantial physical source for the etiology of insanity; and whether these sources have any existence in reality, such as the goiter, or exist merely in the imagination, such as the stone, they are reflected in the representation of the insane. The physical position, gesture, and trappings of the insane serve to present a concrete manner of comprehending madness. As madness is never a clearly defined and limited concept, the icons for treatment and representation tend to evolve and interrelate, reappearing more and more as the image of an undifferentiated sense of deviancy.

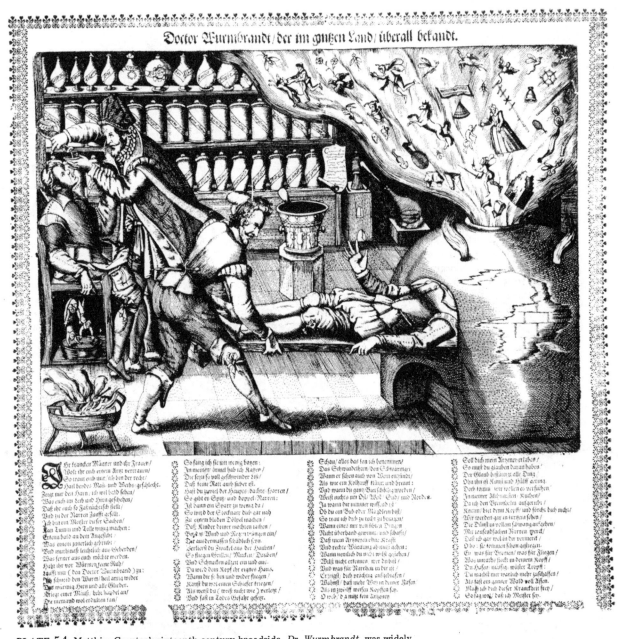

PLATE 54. Matthias Greuter's sixteenth-century broadside, *Dr. Wurmbrandt*, was widely circulated and exists also in French and Dutch versions

# the confinement
# of madness

The final context in which images of the insane are found in the late Middle Ages is that of containment. The idea of the asylum is but an extension of the early modern view that the insane should be contained, if not for treatment, then to isolate them from sane society.[58] One of the standard expressions of the concept of containment is the ship, especially the ship of fools. As early as Seneca, the view existed that the conflict of emotional states "shattered and storm-tossed" man's soul, but it was not until the late Middle Ages that the idea of the ship became so closely associated with the image of madness.[59] Perhaps its sources lie in the ship that is the icon of St. Dimphna, the patroness of the insane, or in the mock ship of the carnival procession, with its crew of fools and misfits.

The image of the ship as a closed world populated by fools was widely disseminated for the first time, however, in Sebastian Brant's *Ship of Fools* [Plates 55 and 56]. These illustrations, attributed in part to the young Dürer, became visual commonplaces of madness throughout the sixteenth century.[60]

PLATE 55. Wood engraving of a ship of fools from a 1498 Latin translation of Sebastian Brant's work

Ad narragoniã

Gaudeamus oẽs

PLATE 56. Another illustration from the Brant work

PLATE 57. Hieronymous Bosch's late-fifteenth-century *Ship of Fools*

The floating world of the fool is a microcosm in which all of the foibles, sins, and misdeeds of man are made manifest, and in such portrayals as that by Hieronymous Bosch [Plate 57] they often have sexual references. Incorporated into Bosch's painting are icons of immorality, such as the eating of cherries and the hazel branch tied to the mast. These exist parallel to icons of insanity, of which the most evident is the fool seated in the position of the melancholic, his fool's stick clutched in his hand. The stick is topped with a fool's head. But the fool with his staff is himself perched on a desiccated, divided branch which serves as the icon of madness for the entire ship, an icon made even more evident by the fool's presence. The figures in the central group, dominated by the representatives of the Church, are gathered about a circular object suspended from a line leading to the mast—the loaf of bread referred to in Psalm 14:4 and seen in earlier images of the fool as club-bearing mad-

man. Here the iconography of the insane points to the moral failings of society, a society seemingly adrift in its madness. The importance of the idea of the ship of fools lies, however, in its containment of the fools rather than in any other single aspect. What matters is not whether the ship is moored or adrift, but the sense of enclosure and the literal separation of the madman from the observer. The madman's place is clearly defined, and the satiric observer of his foibles knows that his own place is distanced from that where madness is to be found.

At least one visualization of the ship of fools expands upon the concept of the containment of the madman. In Pieter Breughel the Elder's *Dulle Grete*, Mad Meg [Plate 58], a seemingly inexplicable painting,[61] the apocalyptic vision of Breughel places the ship of fools almost at the center of the work. It is borne by a figure ladling money from his backside, a symbol of profligacy but also reminiscent of the purging of demons as

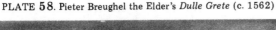
PLATE 58. Pieter Breughel the Elder's *Dulle Grete* (c. 1562)

discussed earlier. In the ship are a roast capon, which had made its appearance tied to the mast of Bosch's ship of fools as the ship's standard (a reference to the sin of gluttony), and a minute figure carrying a huge, stylized disc of bread. In the foreground, the title figure marches across the face of the earth towards the mouth (literally) of hell. Her tattered clothes, disheveled hair (under a helmet), her splayed gait, all categorize her as an icon of the madman. Moving through a world characterized by anarchy and war, she has collected the garb of the warrior—helmet, breastplate, and sword (her fool's staff). Here the ship of fools is much too small to contain the madness of the world. The entire cosmology is dominated by madmen. There seems to be no place where sanity prevails, except the implied locus of the artist.

While Breughel contains his fools in the vastness of a mad universe, Erhard Schön's woodcut of 1530, the "Fools' Cage" [Plate 59], returns them to a more clearly defined space.[62] Here the fools are confined to the burning cage of lust. That they are fools is clear from their garb, but Schön also provides a figure of melancholy and

one of raving madness, without fool's garb, at the cage gate. The males are being ordered to sing the women's song of lust, which will permit them to be released. Here, as in Bosch's work (see Plate 57), the symbolic image has definite sexual overtones. Unlike the ship of fools, however, to which the madmen are magically drawn because of their intrinsic similarity, Schön's cage provides a definite image of captivity. As in the world of Mad Meg (see Plate 58), standing outside the confined space is but an illusion, for as the female fools in the background and the divided bush at the left of the picture testify, this world is dominated by the fool.

Perhaps the oldest extant image of confinement relating to the actual world of the asylum is found in the bas-relief on the cornerstone of the asylum at 's-Hertogenbosch, founded by Jan van Arckel in the fifteenth century [Plate 60]. The cornerstone itself dates to the year 1686, and is thus contemporary with the figures that were sculpted by Cibber for the portal at Bedlam (see Plates 22-24). The central figures represent raving mania and melancholia, and are identifiable through their positions as well as their

PLATE 59. Erhard Schön's woodcut of the cage of fools (1530)

48

PLATE 60. The cornerstone of the asylum at 's-Hertogenbosch (1686)

actions. The maniac bites his own arm, while the other arm is thrown back, the legs are splayed, the hair is disheveled. This figure also exhibits the tension associated with representations of mania. Next to him hang the chains which, like those of his biblical analogue, cannot confine him. The melancholic, in a relaxed position contrasting with the opposite figure, eats the bread of the "workers of iniquity." The faces of other inmates peeping through the cell windows and from behind the melancholic exemplify active and passive states of insanity.

The concept of confinement still contains within it the idea of the closed, self-contained world of the madman. Like the world of *Dulle Grete* (see Plate 58) it is a world recognizable as such because of the images used to characterize it. Confinement means isolation. The madman, beginning in the fifteenth century, appears more and more frequently in confined situations. Here the nature of the madness is of importance, for the use of the image of the fool implies a moral aspect of the etiology of madness, associated as it often is with the seven deadly sins.

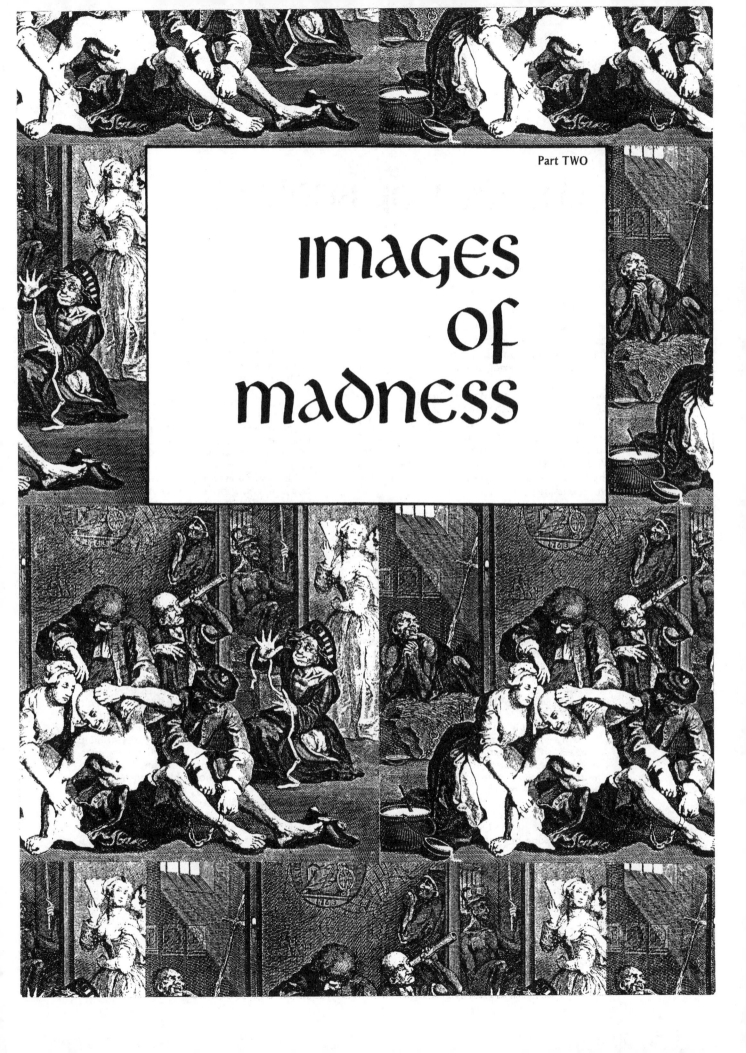

# images of madness

# the idea of Bedlam

Cibber's statues above the portal at Bethlem (see Plate 22) introduced a visual reference for madness which transcended the bounds of the asylum. These "brazen, brainless brothers"[1] are echoed in a rendition of Bedlam as the sum of the world[2] by the anonymous illustrator of the fifth edition of Jonathan Swift's *A Tale of a Tub* (1710). The engraving of visitors gawking at the inmates through the windows of one of Bedlam's open wards accompanies Swift's "Digression on Madness" [Plate 61]. Swift bitingly catalogues the inmates and their relationship to the greater world outside the asylum:

Is any Student tearing his Straw in piece-meal, Swearing and Blaspheming, biting his Grate, foaming at the Mouth, and emptying his Pispot in the Spectator's Faces? Let the Right Worshipful, the *Commissioners of Inspection*, give him a Regiment of Dragoons, and send him into *Flanders* among the *Rest*. Is another eternally talking, sputtering, gaping, bawling, in a Sound without Period or Article? What wonderful Talents are here mislaid! Let him be furnished immediately with a green Bag and Papers, and *three Pence* in his Pocket, and away with Him to *Westminster-Hall*. You will find a Third, gravely taking the dimensions of his Kennel; A Person of Foresight and Insight, tho' kept quite in the Dark; for why, like *Moses, Ecce cornuta erat ejus facies.* He walks duly in one Place, intreats your Penny with due Gravity and Ceremony; talks much of hard Times, and Taxes, and the *Whore of Babylon*; Bars up the wooden Window of his Cell constantly at eight a Clock: Dreams of *Fire*, and *Shoplifters*, and *Court-Customers*, and *Priviledg'd Places*. Now, what a Figure would all these Acquirements amount to, if the Owner were sent into the *City* among his Brethren! Behold a Fourth, in much and deep Conversation with himself, biting his Thumbs at proper Junctures; His Countenance Chequered with Business and Design; sometimes walking very fast, with

his Eyes nailed to a Paper that he holds in his Hands: A great Saver of Time, somewhat thick of Hearing, very short of Sight, but more of Memory. A Man ever in Haste, a great Hatcher and Breeder of Business, and Excellent at the Famous Art of *whispering Nothing*. A huge Idolater of Monosyllables and Procrastination; so ready to *Give* his Word to every Body, that he never *keeps* it. One that has forgot the common *Meaning* of Words, but an admirable Retainer of the *Sound*. Extreamly subject to the *Loosness*, for his *Occasions* are perpetually *calling him away*. If you approach his Grate in his familiar Intervals; *Sir*, says he, *Give me a Penny, and I'll sing you a Song: But give me the Penny first*. (Hence comes the common Saying, and commoner Practice of parting with Money for a *Song*.) What a compleat System of *Court-Skill* is here described in every Branch of it, and all utterly lost with wrong Application? Accost the Hole of another Kennel, first stopping your Nose, you will behold a surley, gloomy, nasty, slovenly Mortal, rakin his own Dung, and dabling in his Urine. The best Part of his Diet, is the Reversion of his own Ordure, which exspiring into Steams, whirls perpetually about, and at last reinfunds. His Complexion is of a dirty Yellow, with a thin scattered Beard, exactly agreeable to that of his Dyet upon its first Declination; like other Insects, who having their Birth and Education in an Excrement, from thence borrow their Colour and their Smell. The student of this Apartment is very sparing in his Words, but somewhat over-liberal of his Breath; He holds his Hand out ready to receive your Penny, and immediately upon Receipt, withdraws to his former Occupations. Now, is it not amazing to think, the Society of *Warwick-Lane*, should have no more Concern, for the Recovery of so useful a Member, who, if one may judge from these Appearances, would become the greatest Ornament to that Illustrious Body? Another Student struts up fiercely to your Teeth,

PLATE 61. Bedlam, from an engraving by
Bernard Lens and John Sturt for the fifth
edition of Jonathan Swift's *A Tale of a Tub*
(1710)

puffing with his Lips, half squeezing out his
Eyes, and very graciously holds you out his
Hand to kiss. The *Keeper* desires you not to
be afraid of this Professor, for he will do you
no Hurt: To him alone is allowed the Liberty of the Anti-Chamber, and the *Orator* of
the Place gives you to understand, that this
solemn Person is a *Taylor* run mad with Pride.
This considerable Student is adorned with
many other Qualities, upon which, at present,
I shall not farther enlarge.[3]

This catalogue is not very different in its particu-
lars from that compiled by the early seventeenth-
century clergyman Thomas Adams in his *Mysti-
cal Bedlam, or The World of Madness*.[4] These are
categorizations of representative characters rather
than a comment on the structured world of the
inmates, even though Swift knew this world as a
governor of the asylum.

Swift's delineation of the insane as captured
by his illustrator influenced in turn the most wide-

ly known portrait of confinement created in the eighteenth century [Plate 62], the eighth and final plate for William Hogarth's *A Rake's Progress* (1735/1763). The degradation of Rakewell is followed through debauchery and debtor's prison to what the German philosopher Georg Christoph Lichtenberg, Hogarth's contemporary, calls the final "burial among the civic dead."[5] Hogarth sees the influence of the passions, the humors in their seventeenth- and eighteenth-century transformation, as central to madness. Decadence is, for Hogarth, society's corruption of the passions, as he states in the caption to the plate:

> Madness, Thou Chaos of ye Brain,
> What art? That Pleasure giv'st, and Pain?
> Tyranny of Fancy's Reign!
> Mechanic Fancy; that can build
> Vast Labarynths, & Mazes wild,
> With Rule disjointed, Shapeless Measure,
> Fill'd with Horror, fill'd with Pleasure!
> Shapes of Horror, that wou'd even
> Cast Doubt of Mercy upon Heaven.
> Shapes of Pleasure, that but Seen
> Wou'd split the Shaking Sides of Spleen.
>    O Vanity of Age! here See
> The Stamp of Heaven effac'd by Thee—
> The headstrong Course of Youth thus run,
> What Comfort from this darling Son!
> His rattling Chains with Terror hear,
> Behold Death grappling with Despair;
> See Him by Thee to Ruin Sold,
> And curse thy self, & curse thy Gold.[6]

Hogarth's images of the madmen who inhabit Bedlam support the continuity of Rakewell's world, prior to his arrival in the asylum and within the world of the asylum. Lichtenberg observes that "in the microcosmos where he lives now, affairs are ordered very much as in their extended Macro-Bedlam, the world itself; not all the madmen are chained, and even the chains have their degrees."[7] These levels of sanity are represented by Hogarth's characters in a manner that differs significantly from the late seventeenth- and early eighteenth-century image of the asylum found in *A Tale of a Tub*.

Central to the image of Bedlam is the figure of Rakewell. His hand clenched to his head, in the position of Cibber's statue of raving madness, he is partly unclothed. While this aspect was present in the icons of mania as well as the related icons of grief from the Middle Ages, by the seventeenth century the idea of nakedness had become a symbolic reference for the nature of madness. Thomas Tryon wrote in the 1680s:

> For when men are so divested of their *Rational Faculties*, then they appear naked, having no *Covering*, *Vail* or *Figgleaves* before them, to hide themselves in, and therefore they no longer remain under a Mask or Disguise, but appear even as they are, which is very rare to be known in any that retain their *Senses* and *Reason*; for those two serve to cover and hide the Conceptions, Thoughts and Imaginations.[8]

The continuity of Rakewell's life is symbolized by his present state. He is a raving maniac, but thus he was in his entire life of debauchery, even though masked by the conventions of the Macro-Bedlam, of polite society.

Here he is seen being put in chains. Hogarth places Rakewell not only stage-center, but also moving from one level of Bedlam to another, as Lichtenberg observes:

> Through the long corridor, the catacomb, which we see here, the more harmless are free to walk about, at least as far as the big grating, behind which lives another class, or sect as it is called in ordinary life, having other principles, not in agreement with those on this side of the iron bars; only those of a still lower class and more dangerous degree are buried in the numbered cells.[9]

Rakewell's physical attitude is counterbalanced by the figure of religious melancholy who is seen through the door of cell 54 at the left in the position of the other statue atop Bedlam's portal. Through the next open door, that of cell 55, can be seen a man gone mad with pride, wearing a straw crown and holding a broken stick as a scepter. He is observed urinating by two visitors, one of whom shields her eyes from the spectacle with her fan. Between the two cells another madman draws a version of William Whiston's plan for travelers to determine longitude by the use of rockets. On the same wall the figure of Brittania is seen with hair flowing, an image of the Macro-Bedlam that is England. At the right are four madmen, the proverbially mad tailor, the mad musician, the melancholic—in the traditional position of melancholy, accompanied by the Saturnian dog—and a figure, with hidden hands and loosened hair, which Lichtenberg interprets as representing "faith." The triple cross of this figure and the tracings on the back wall form a composite reference to the image of madness as the exploration of the unknown in Robert Burton's cross staff and armillary sphere (see Plate 21). These images are themselves a continuation of the tradition of the fool's staff and bladder.

While Hogarth employs the standard cast of characters found in earlier renditions of Bedlam,

PLATE 62. Hogarth's Bedlam, the eighth plate from *A Rake's Progress* (1735/1763)

such as those accompanying Swift's essay, he alters the interpretation from a static to an active one. Adapting Burton's travel metaphor, Hogarth carries Rakewell step by step to Bedlam, where in the final plate Rakewell and his life stand at the center of our vision of the madhouse.

Hogarth, who knew the asylum through his charitable work, supplied a complex context for seeing the insane, a context which altered the earlier one-dimensional view of the madhouse as the gathering place of selected representatives of the world. Though Hogarth's madhouse also has this supporting cast, his view is focused on the life and world of a single individual, a change of perspective that gives added depth and meaning to this world.

BEDLAM of the WORLD.

PLATE 63. Peter Dutsman's 1781 political cartoon

In the second half of the eighteenth century the image of confinement was determined by the popularity of Hogarth's view of Bedlam.[10] The idea of the world as Bedlam is captured in Peter Dutsman's political cartoon of 1781 satirizing the war between England and Holland [Plate 63]. The "mad king" George III is portrayed in the pose of the melancholic,[11] while his ministers are exemplars of raving madness. This manner of seeing the world as Bedlam, with its claustrophobic closeness, reflects Hogarth's vision in the way it sets the figures in a total context, rather than providing merely a detailed catalogue of the inmates of this political madhouse.

A different perspective is found in Richard Newton's Bedlam, with its focus on the visitors [Plate 64]. Here one of the inmates of Hogarth's asylum, the man gone mad with pride wearing his straw crown, holds up two fingers in an obscene gesture observed through the bars of the cell. The figure accused by the madman of being a cuckold is portrayed with his mouth open, his walking stick falling to the ground. Although his

PLATE 64. Richard Newton depicts *A Visit to Bedlam* (1794)

attitude, like those of the other visitors, may be interpreted as an image of surprise, the visitors' faces can also be perceived as the pop-eyed, open-mouthed visages of madmen, for in Newton's Bedlam the visitors as well as the inmates share the madness of the world. Indeed, if it were not for the quaint headdress of the latter, it would be difficult to say on which side of the bars one found oneself. These satiric illustrations of the Macro-Bedlam stand in the eighteenth-century tradition of the image of the asylum as a reflection of the world and its passions.[12]

57

# the physiognomy of madness

The tradition of classical physiognomy based on humorial theory continued uninterrupted into the Middle Ages and the Renaissance. In 1586 the Neopolitan Giovanni della Porta published a manual of human physiognomy which provided ample visual material for the pseudo-Aristotelian correlation of human and animal characteristics in terms of the quadruple humors[13] **[Plates 65 and 66]**. Della Porta's lack of interest in psychopathologies (he discussed only one case, with no illustrative material and little detail) affected later physiognomies. From the little-known works on this subject such as that of Vaenius (1662) through the influential and oft-reprinted work of Charles Le Brun (1698), seventeenth- and early eighteenth-century physiognomies relied on the dual axis of humorial theory and animal analogies as the basis of both normal and pathological states.[14] Like della Porta they ignored psychopathological states except in passing. They placed their emphasis on fixed facial structures, seeing in the permanent lines of the forehead and face the reflection of mental or intellectual states.

While popular physiognomy remained limited by the constraints of humorial theory and its relationship to the static aspects of appearance, the rise of anatomical studies led to the first detailed analysis of the mechanics of expression. Works such as Petrus Camper's on the anatomy of expression (as well as his other studies, such as those on the structure of the skull) were originally intended to aid artists in their portrayal of human expression based on the scientific observation of muscular and structural elements.[15]

In 1747, James Parsons published his lectures on the muscular structure of human expression, focusing on the facial manifestation of the passions.[16] The passions, beginning with Juan Luis Vives in the sixteenth century, were conceived as able to be influenced by external forces and were, in turn, reflected in expression. Using Descartes' classification of the passions (1650), Parsons documented the detailed muscular structure of the expression of emotions. In the general category of "Fear and Terror," Parsons provided a context for the image of the maniac, without, however, directly referring to psychopathology:

1. Here the *Occipito-Frontalis* drags up the Eyebrows, and wrinkles the Forehead transversly.
2. The *Aperiens Palpebram* on each Side pulls open the Lids with Violence a great way above the Pupils, which are as it were suspended below the Equator, by the Remission of the *Elevators*.
3. The *Digastricus* and *Latissimus Colli* pull down the lower Jaw.

The Reason why the Eyes and Mouth are suddenly open'd in Frights, seems to be, that the Object of Danger may be better perceived and avoided; as if Nature intended to lay open all the Inlets to the Senses for the Safety of the Animal; the Eyes, that they may see their Danger; and the Mouth, which is in this case an Assistant to the Ears, that they may hear it. This may perhaps surprise some, that the Mouth should be necessary to hear by; but it is a common thing, to see Men, whose Hearing is not very good, open their Mouths with Attention when they listen, and it is some Help to them: The Reason is, that there is a Passage from the *Meatus auditorius*, which opens into the Mouth. Thus we see how ready Nature is, upon any Emergency, to lay hold of every Occasion for Self-preservation.

But when a Person is frighted, so as not to be under an instantaneous Apprehension of Danger, by being pursued, or the like; then the upper Part of the Face will be as in this Figure, and the lower somewhat different from what it appears here; that is, the Mouth will open moderately, by the Remission of the Actions of the *Temporal* and *Masseter* Muscles, having the Corners, or *Rictus Oris*, inclin'd a little downwards.

PLATE 65. The intelligent man compared to the ass, from Giovanni della Porta's *De Humana Physiognomia* of 1586

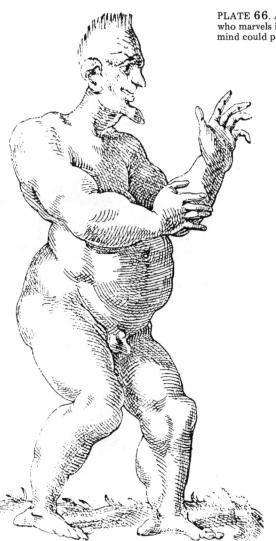

PLATE 66. A case of akromegalia from della Porta, who marvels in his commentary that an intelligent mind could possibly by found in such a body

It has been imagin'd, that the Eye-brows might be moved in Parts; that is, that one Part of a Brow may be pull'd up, while the other is pull'd down: But this cannot be, for the *Occipito-Frontalis*, which pulls up the Brow, acts all at once on either Side; so that the intire Brow must be pull'd up at once, or, by its Remission, let down at once. I never yet saw any one, who was able to give them this partial Motion, and there are but few who can raise either without the other at the same time; so that this Opinion amounts to something Nature never intended, and is an Exaggeration which renders any Figures preposterous.

*Fear, Horror,* and *Terror*, are but Terms which signify the same Passion, only in different Degrees; and are all expressed by this Figure, only rendering the Change of Features, by the Motion of the Muscles, greater or less; which, if accompanied with certain Actions of the Body, would express them more absolutely. As for Example; if on the Ground, under an Enemy resolved on the Destruction of the frighted Person, with Hands lifted up, and Fingers stretch'd far asunder, dreading the fatal Blow; or, if flying from Danger, with the Hands push'd forward, and looking back at the Object that affrights; which kind of Fear may be excited by Imagination, as well as by real Objects.[17]

PLATE 67. "Fear and terror" from James Parsons, *Human Physiognomy explain'd* (London: The Royal Society, 1747)

PLATE 68. "Melancholy" from Parsons

Parsons focused on the expression of the emotions as well as on their external cause.[18] He saw, in the expression of fear and terror [Plate 67], the external signs of a greater scale of reactions which stretched from the normal to the abnormal:

To this Class may be added *Despair*, and the same Countenance will serve to express it, with very little Alteration: For, as the first Advance to that Passion is the Fear, Terror, or Dread of any Danger, and is thus expressed, so the Deprivation of any Hope for Relief, and the perpetual Dread of meeting the fatal Shock, is *Despair*; and therefore by adding Paleness, and a livid Aspect, to this Countenance, it will be well represented; because, when all Hopes are given over, the Blood grows languid in every Part, notwithstanding the same Fear and Terror remains, from the Person's ceasing to make any Defense; and at length degenerates into a melancholy Madness: So that Flying, or Sitting, or Lying prostrate on the Ground, may be suitable Attitudes to this Passion; and then the Countenance will be chang'd, as in the Passion of Grief.

PLATE 69. A spectrum of emotions from the 1763 *Encyclopédie*: (1) simple admiration; (2) admiration with astonishment; (3) veneration; (4) ecstasy

I cannot but think it a wrong Application of the Passion of *Despair*, to represent it with flaring Hair, corrugated Face, the Brows drawn down even with the Eyes, and the Mouth open, with a weeping Aspect; for, instead of such violent Contractions, which are Signs rather of bodily Pain and Torment, there is in deep *Despair* a Cessation from those muscular Actions in the Face; and the first Actions of Fright are rather remitted, as it were, into a Relaxation of those Muscles, and a Falling of the Countenance; because all Exertion towards a Defense, as I have just said, is given up, and a Desponding and Fainting are often the Consequences.[19]

In his closing paragraph Parsons rejects the classical image of madness and stresses relaxation from tension as the underlying characteristic of melancholy, a feature common to the multitude of representations of that state [Plate 68]. Within the boundaries of the general aesthetic category of "Fear and Terror," he classifies mania—characterized by the height of tension—and melancholia—the pathological expression of relaxation—as the extremes of the passions.

The concept of a limited spectrum of Cartesian categories for the passions is reflected in the plates accompanying the Diderot and d'Alembert *Encyclopedia*, published between 1751 and 1772. In the text as well as in the plates, the Encyclopedists followed, according to d'Alembert in his "Preliminary Discourse," the Cartesian view that "there are few fields where propositions and rules cannot be reduced to simple notions and then arranged in such close order that the chain of connection is never broken."[20] It is this view that permits the schematization of the appearance of the emotions. As in the case of the early physiognomists and anatomists, the illustrations concentrate on the stylized facial expression of the passions [Plates 69-71]. The purpose, as with Camper's study, was to provide for artists a standard scale for the expression of the emotions. The result was a stereotyped set of heads with exaggerated, frozen grimaces.

In the unsigned essay on the passions in the body of the *Encyclopedia*, the author, possibly Diderot himself, divided the passions into three distinct categories: the literary, the medical, and the artistic. The literary or poetic passions are

PLATE **70**. Emotions from the *Encyclopédie*: (1) laughter; (2) tears; (3) compassion; (4) sadness

PLATE **71**. Emotions from the *Encyclopédie*: (1) envy or jealousy; (2) anger; (3) desire; (4) acute pain

those attributed by an author to his characters; the medical, the actual attractions or aversions of individuals; the artistic, the mechanical reproduction of the impressions made by the face when attracted or repelled. The Encyclopedists did differentiate between the representation of states of emotion through aesthetic means and the fluidity of the states themselves, and it was their intention to convey not the passions per se but their reflection in art. Thus some distinction was made in the eighteenth century between the manner in which the emotions, including psychopathological ones, were portrayed and the manner in which they were perceived.[21]

In the 1770s a radical rediscovery of the tradition of classical physiognomy occurred in the light of the scientific and aesthetic discussions of visual representations of the emotions. The work of the Zurich pastor Johann Caspar Lavater burst upon the European scene with an intensity that was to color the perception of psychopathological states for generations.[22] His studies, rooted in established physiognomies yet influenced by the scholarly discussion of expression, had an unprecedented popularity.

Lavater initially published his views on physiognomy in a series of essays in the *Hanoverian Magazine* in 1772. His theory amalgamated the moral implications of the temperaments held by the mystic Jacob Boehme with the "monad theory" of Leibniz. Boehme saw the soul held within a body, as in a prison, dominated by the temperaments. Leibniz saw human individuality reflected in the uniqueness of each person's physical characteristics. In these early essays Lavater wrote:

> Does not reason tell us that everything in the world has an internal as well as an external aspect, which stand in direct relationship to each other? For everything, because it is itself and not something else, has something in it, with which it can be distinguished from everything else? Does this not tell us that an exact relationship exists between the soul and the body, between the internal and the external of man, that the infinite variety of the souls or the internal nature of man creates an infinite variety in his body or externality. . . . If such differences exist then they must be recognizable; they must also be the basis for an exact science.[23]

This "not fantastic but real science"[24] was presented in Lavater's first book-length analysis of human physiognomy, published in 1772. Here he again summarized his views, but his theoretical position was cast in specifics:

Human reason revolts against one who could claim that Leibniz or Newton could have existed in the body of an idiot; that an inhabitant of a madhouse could be a great metaphysician or mathematician.[25]

Madness and genius were not only antithetical, they were also impressed on the external aspect of mankind.

Lavater devotes a segment of his early work to an outline of "mental abilities and states"[26] in which he simply lists a wide range of degrees of intelligence from "Understanding, healthy" to "Nonsense and Childishness." He does not categorize them any further. Likewise, his scale of "emotional states" lists the passions, for example "wild, horrible," in a seemingly random order. These two outlines provide a relative position for psychopathological states on one end of a scale of normal intelligence or passion. While Lavater provided neither illustrations of these states nor any detail of their appearance, his lists do reflect the scientific opinion of the day.

Lavater's major source seems to have been Albrecht von Haller's physiognomy of 1763.[27] Haller, in his chapter on "Fatuitas," weakened mental states, had summarized the literature on the appearance of the insane. He limited his discussion, however, to those cases in which clear, structural alterations could be observed, for example the cretin or the hydrocephalous idiot. Lavater used the scholarly literature of his time as proof of the difference of appearance of the insane, but underlying his discussion is Boehme's view that the madman is the most attractive prey of the devil because of his melancholic propensity. This moral underpinning of Lavater's exposition provided a double-edged way of seeing the insane.

Lavater's influence was established with the publication of his four-volume, richly illustrated study of human physiognomy which appeared between 1774 and 1778. In these volumes Lavater provides at least a dozen examples of psychopathologies, without any systematic attempt to discuss what he designated in his earlier study as "the semiotics of illness."[28] In the first and most detailed case study of insanity [Plate 72] he presents:

> A madman, who in his youth was an intelligent, first-rate, goodly individual. He was so mishandled by his wild father because of a presumed love affair that he lost his reason. When the mouth, the primary seat of madness, is once closed in death, I will wager that the prior expression of understanding will for the most part reappear. This previ-

PLATE **72**. Johann Gaspar Lavater's image of a madman from his *Physiognomische Fragmente* (Leipzig and Winterthur: Weidmann, 1774-1778)

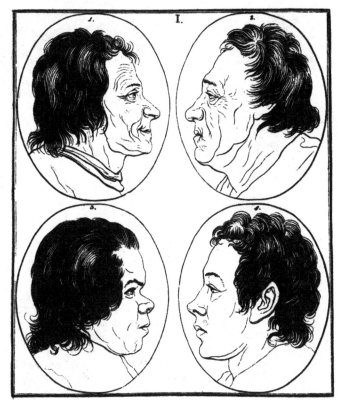

PLATE **73**. Four male idiots from Lavater's *Fragmente*

PLATE **74**. Six idiot women from Lavater's *Fragmente*

ous comprehension is still noticeable in the forehead and the profile, but not in the gaze of the eyes.[29]

This is the only time Lavater provides the etiology for a psychopathological state, also centering his discussion on the movable aspect of the individual's face. The influence of Camper and Parsons can be seen here, though Lavater stresses the open mouth and bulging eyes of the insane, features discounted by Parsons.

Lavater's most extensive discussion of psychopathologies occurs in the sixteenth fragment of the second volume of his study. This segment is headed "Weak, mad individuals," and he starts his analysis with a catalogue of the qualities of the appearance of the idiotic: "Indolent distortion, animalistic obtuseness, convulsive attitude, crooked smiles, inconstancy, indifferentiatedness, vacancy, looseness—the usual, most common, most evident signs of inherent and natural stupidity."[30] In the various "classes" of madness (which he does not categorize) he includes a discussion of four male idiots **[Plate 73]**, with the scale of idiocy running from the most apparent (numbers 1 and 3) to the least obvious (4). Without any further discussion of what he is observing as signs of pathology, he uses the illustrations alone to document his scale of abnormalities.

Lavater had a far-reaching concept of "idiocy." For a plate drawn by the famed illustrator Daniel Chodowiecki, he provided more detailed information, revealing how eclectic his concept of the insane really was.[31] The portraits **[Plate 74]** reflect senility (number 2), mental deficiency (1 and 4), stroke (5 and 6), and melancholia (3). The inclusion of the melancholic returns

PLATE 75. Two cretins from Lavater's *Fragmente*

PLATE 76. Two melancholics from Lavater's *Fragmente*

the basis of the analysis to the fixed structure of the face. Just as Lavater's portrait of two cretins [Plate 75] captures the idiocy of the subjects in their "sloping foreheads," his melancholic [Plate 76] is characterized by the (Saturnian) "unequal forehead," depressions in the temples, and sunken eyes. These permanent qualities of the melancholic are also accompanied, in the illustration, by the blackness of aspect and disheveled hair which complete the classic image.

The parallel existence of fixed structure and movable aspect theories in Lavater's work is evident in his dealing with the insane. His indebtedness to the older images of psychopathology can be seen in one of Chodowiecki's most striking illustrations [Plate 77], representing a wide spec-

PLATE 77. The physiognomy of illness and deformity, a plate by Daniel Chodowiecki from Lavater's *Fragmente*

PLATES **78-80**. Three portraits of idiots from Thomas Holcroft's *Essays on Physiognomy* (London: Whittingham, 1804)

trum of illness and deformity ranging from the dwarf to the giant, from the hunchback to the syphilitic. Present too are the cretin with his goiter (at the far right) and the madman with torn clothes, disheveled hair, arms and legs askew, flailing about with his fool's staff. Chodowiecki's theme is the contrast and the continuity of the normal and abnormal. Lavater had juxtaposed images of Plato and a cretin in the second volume, much as he had confronted the concept of Leibniz existing in a madhouse. In this plate the artist provides a "normal" couple, walking, like the visitors in Hogarth's Bedlam (see Plate 62), through the world of the deformed and the ill. Lavater stresses the continuity in his comment that "who ever scorns these individuals . . . also scorns their maker." They stand within the continuum of God's creation, yet are identifiable as unique within the pattern of creation through their appearance.

In later versions of his work, Lavater came to be seen as placing almost exclusive emphasis on the fixed aspect of facial appearance. Thomas Holcroft, in his early nineteenth-century English edition, presents a series of heads of madmen and idiots [**Plates 78-80**]. Holcroft sees the per-

ception of the appearance of the insane as immediate and universal **[Plate 81]**:

> That physiognomical sensation, which, like sight and hearing, is born with all, will not permit us to expect much from the upper profile; although, to the inexperienced in physiognomy, the proper marks of folly are not very apparent. It would excite universal surprise, should any one, possessing such a countenance, pronounce accurate decisions, or produce a work of genius. The lower is still less to be mistaken, and I would ask the most obstinate opponent of physiognomical sensation, whether he would personally declare, or give it under his hand, that the man who expects wisdom from this countenance is himself wise.[32]

Holcroft is able to reduce his perception of the psychopathologies to the most simplistic outlines of profiles **[Plate 82]**:

> Twelve outlines of idiots given promiscuously, without eyes, or additional lineaments. Who would seek, who could find, wisdom in any such countenances? Were they all animated, of which would any man ask advice? Would not the world pronounce that painter ridiculous who should give such a profile to a Solon, or a Solomon? Would not each accurate observer of the human countenance distinguish these natural idiots from such as might have become idiotical, in consequence of sickness, or accident? 1 might have been wise, perhaps, but could 3, 4, 7, 8, 9, 10, ever have been so? And would it not be affectation in any philosopher to answer,—"I do not know: wretched mortal, how knowest thou? Might not God have pleased to have permitted any one of these profiles to have written the theory of light?"[33]

Here the duality of Lavater's vision of the insane is lost. Holcroft believes himself able to see clear signs of psychopathologies in the most skeletal images, without the need to characterize what in the profile qualifies them as such. Rather, it is the immediate, unreflective reaction of the observer which is taken as the indication of the accuracy of the observation.

The impressionistic aspect of the physiognomist's mode of interpretation caused problems even for those who supported this method of analysis. One of Lavater's collaborators on the first volume, the twenty-six-year-old Johann Wolfgang von Goethe, wrote him how difficult it was to interpret the drawings, especially those representing the insane.[34] Immanuel Kant, in the section of his *Anthropology* (1800) concerned with the "manner by which one can identify the interior

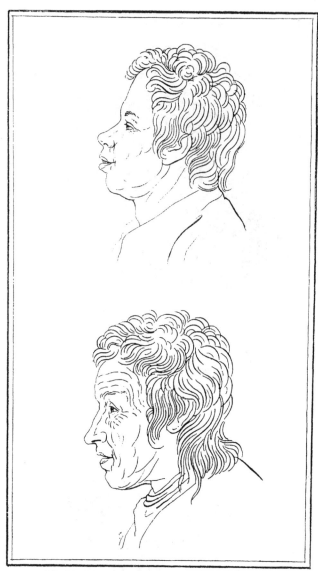

PLATE 81. Two idiots from Holcroft's *Essays*

nature through an examination of the external nature," rejected the immediate and total identification of physical characteristics with psychopathological states.[35]

In 1785 the German popular philosopher Johann Jakob Engel published his *Ideas toward a Mimetic Theory* in part as an answer to Lavater. Engel focused on the role of movement and gesture as a reflection of the intrinsic relationship between soul and body. He classified these as intentional, analogous, and physiological, with the

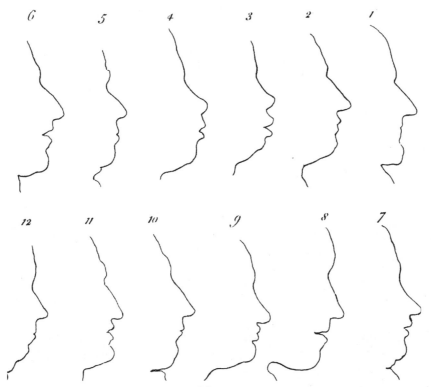

PLATE 82. Profiles of twelve idiots from Holcroft's *Essays*

PLATE 83. Depiction of an idiot from Johann Jakob Engel, *Ideen zu einer Mimik* (Berlin: Mylius, 1785)

latter being determined by the passions. Thus in his portrait of an idiot **[Plate 83]** he emphasizes the posture: the dropped head, the unclosed lips, the hanging chin, the half-open eyes, the hands in the pockets. Engel comments:

> Who does not recognize at first glance the weak, inactive mind, incapable of attention or interest; a mind, which never can bring even the limited energy to create a tension in his muscles so that the body carries itself correctly, that the limbs are held correctly. Only the most stupid and lazy can assume such a meaningless, mindless position.[36]

Thus Engel provides a further aesthetic context, that of posture, for the image of the psychopathologies. His emphasis is on the totality of the appearance of the insane, on their expression, gesture, and posture, rather than on their facial structure. However, he incorporates into his description not only older icons of insanity, such as the hidden hands, but sees these icons in their historical context as linking madness and indolence, as did the Church Fathers in their discussion of *acedia*.

PLATES 84 and 85. Sketches made at the Zurich
Asylum by Johann Konrad Fäsi-Gessner (c. 1840)

In the early nineteenth century the influence of the theories of physiognomy on the perception of the insane is evident in the images of the asylum drawn by the Swiss artist and medical administrator Johann Konrad Fäsi-Gessner,[37] director of the Zurich asylum from 1835 to 1853. In the 1830s he kept a sketchbook in which he captured the various physiognomies of his patients [Plates 84-86]. His work stands as an important, if little known, continuation of the physiognomic studies of Lavater, whose granddaughter he married and whose works he knew well. But in light of the newer emphasis on the individual, Fäsi-Gessner attempted to capture the typical expressions of specific patients rather than to portray stereotypes.

Louis Léopold Boilly's general plate of medical physiognomy [Plate 87] represents a similar effort grafted onto the image of the scale of the passions. Adolf Menzel's 1844 etching [Plate 88] presents even more individual heads interpretable in the light of physiognomic analysis.[38]

All these works stress facial expression rather than fixed structure as typical of psychopathological states. But frequently, the advocates of a more conservative approach to the physiognomy of the insane were little heard in the rush to judgment of madness by the physiognomists and their later followers.

PLATE 86. From the sketchbook of Fäsi-Gessner

PLATE 87. Louis Léopold Boilly, *Thirty-five Heads of Ill Persons,*
a colored lithograph from the first half of the nineteenth century

PLATE 88. Adolf Menzel's etching, *Studies from an Insane Asylum* (1844)

# the medical illustration of madness

By the end of the eighteenth century the association of madness with a specific physiognomy of insanity had become a commonplace in European thought. But in medical studies per se, the paucity of illustrations of psychopathological states is striking. Except in images of treatment, where the focus is on the patient as the object of treatment, medical illustrations of insanity are all but nonexistent in the eighteenth century. This lack is especially conspicuous in light of the numerous images of the insane in other contexts during that period.

It is of interest, therefore, that when Phillipe Pinel published *A Treatise on Insanity* in 1801 he included two plates, the first comparing the skulls of normal and idiotic subjects, the second illustrating the appearance of psychopathologies in two patients, an idiot and a maniac **[Plate 89]**. Thus by the first year of the nineteenth century, illustrations of the insane had been introduced into medical works on mental illness through the amalgamation of late eighteenth-century views of physiognomy with an altered philosophy of scientific description.

Phillipe Pinel's role in the introduction of humane treatment and the reform of the French asylum (see page 134) is well known.[39] That he was also instrumental in altering the mode of observing psychopathologies is less so. In an earlier nosological study which appeared in 1798, he had described somatic diseases in detail in order to classify them. His approach to medicine stood in the tradition of the Idéalogues, who, founding their philosophy of science on Condillac's sensationalism, developed a strictly empirical approach to scientific facts.[40] For Helvétius, Condorcet, Pinel, and the other Idéalogues, systematic description was an impossibility; only single cases could be observed and limited inferences made from them. This radical empiricism led directly to the use of illustrations of psychiatric patients in medical literature. The illustrations in Pinel's

study permitted the reader to observe the cases described, and this made possible the confrontation between the scientific observer and the observable fact.

Pinel interpreted the appearance of the idiot (the lower figures in the plate) in detail in the text:

On a first view of this idiot, what appears most striking is the extremely disproportionate extent of the face, compared with the diminutive size of the cranium. No traits of animation are visible in his physiognomy. Every line indicates the most absolute stupidity. Between the height of the head and that of the whole stature, there is a very great disproportion. The cranium is greatly depressed both at the crown and at the temples. His looks are heavy and his mouth wide open. The whole extent of his knowledge is confined to three or four confused ideas, and that of his speech to as many inarticulate sounds. His capacity is so defective, that he can scarcely guide the food to his mouth; and his insensibility so great, that he is incapable of attending to the common calls of nature. His step is feeble, heavy and tottering. His disinclination to motion is excessive. He is totally insensible to the natural propensity for reproduction;—a passion so strong even in the Cretin, and which gives him a deep consciousness of his existence. This equivocal being, who seems to have been placed by nature on the very confines of humanity, is the son of a farmer, and was brought to the hospital de Bicêtre about two years ago. He appears to have been impressed from his infancy with the above characters of fatuity.[41]

This analysis juxtaposes two ways of seeing the insane. Pinel describes a specific patient's physiognomy, stressing, as did Lavater, the facial characteristics, both the fixed (relative cranial size) and the movable. But he also supplies an abbreviated case study of the idiot, in order to justify his description. Pinel moved from physiognomy to etiology without question. Indeed he saw the perception of the physiognomy as the initial stage of diagnosis. While he centers his attention on the particularities of a single patient, implicit in his analysis is the application of the methodology of diagnosis to similar cases based on an equivalent interpretation of their physiognomies. He believed his image of the insane to be not abstract but strictly empirical.

Pinel goes on to contrast the idiot with the maniac (the upper figures). He contends that the maniac, who was subject only to sporadic attacks of insanity, had a skull better proportioned to the overall size of his body than the idiot. More importantly, the maniac's stature "approaches much nearer the proportions of the Apollo." Pinel continues his argument:

The ancient artists, who were equally remarkable for the delicacy of their touch and their acuteness of observation, could not fail to discover those proportions of the head which are the essential constituents of beauty. They have, consequently, divided those of the Apollo into four parts by horizontal planes at equal distances. One of those parts begins at the roots of the hair on the forehead, and extends to the crown. The form of the head of the maniac, figure 1, plate II, varies no more than well-proportioned heads in general from this standard, since the whole height of his head is twenty-three centimetres, and that of his face seventeen centimetres. Subtracting one from the other, we obtain a remainder of six centimetres, which, compared with the whole height, gives a proportion very nearly approaching that of one to four, as in the head of Apollo. The height of the head of the idiot, on the contrary, is eighteen centimetres, and his face fifteen. On subtraction we have a difference of three centimetres, which is only one sixth of the height, and which shews how much the vault of the cranium is flattened, and, consequently, its capacity diminished. This diminution is still more strikingly apparent if we examine the human skull in another point of view. In well formed heads, a horizontal section of the cranium made in the direction of the squammous margin of the temporal bones, gives an irregular ellipsis of such a form, that the double ordinate passing at the anterior portion of those bones, is much shorter than that passing through the posterior part. The head of the maniac approaches in those respects to the proper proportions, for the posterior double ordinate is longer by two centimetres than the anterior. On the contrary, those two lines are about equal in the head of the

idiot, as I have ascertained by a caliber compass; so that the section of this cranium would give a figure very nearly approaching that of a regular ellipsis.[42]

The analogy to the ideal proportions of the Apollo Belvedere and classical Greek sculpture in general placed the appearance of the insane on the plane of aesthetic perception. It provided the observer with a scale of normative appearance reaching from the ideal (the Apollo Belvedere) to the pathological (the idiot). Pinel supported this scale with drawings of the faces and heads, a mode of illustration which returns to the physiognomic studies of Lavater and the earlier craniological studies by anatomists such as Camper.[43]

A contemporary, early nineteenth-century work illuminates the understanding of the rela-

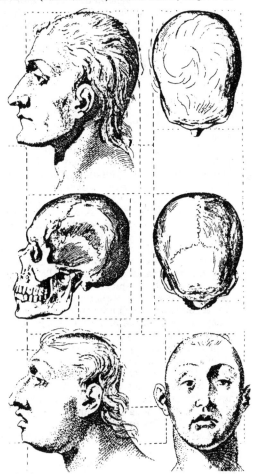

PLATE 89. A maniac and an idiot from Phillipe Pinel, *Traité médico-philosophique sur l'aliénation mentale, ou la manie* (Paris: Richard, Caille et Ravier, IX [1801])

tionship between Lavater's physiognomy and Pinel's psychiatry. Jacques Louis Moreau (de la Sarthe) was one of the most influential psychiatrists of his day, having written the essay "mental medicine" in the *Methodological Encyclopedia* (1816).[44] In 1807 he published a seven-volume translation of Lavater's work, supplemented by a series of appendices, the first of which covered the "physiognomy of madness."[45] In this appendix he presents and discusses in some detail two plates. One is Hogarth's Bedlam (see Plate 62), and Moreau de la Sarthe simply quotes Lichtenberg's description. In the other **[Plate 90]** he duplicates the idiot and maniac from Pinel's work but adds the head of Victor, the feral child of Aveyron, from Jean Marc Gaspard Itard's 1801 study.[46] Moreau de la Sarthe's comments reveal the further amalgamation of the medical and physiognomic views of the insane:

The physiognomy of the insane and of idiots constitutes, in the general pattern of morbid physiognomies, a clearly distinguished class, practically the only one differentiated by Lavater.

Let us add a few remarks to his observations. The configuration of the head and the character are more or less connected with insanity and idiotism, according to how intense and evident the physical alteration appears, which is the source of one or the other of these diseases of the mind. To avoid any mistake in research of this delicate and difficult type, M. Pinel has measured and compared a great number of skulls selected either from the collections of the Museum of Natural History or from the private collections of the school of medicine. He has taken, by means of a caliber compass, the dimensions of the heads of different persons of both sexes, who had been, or who were at the time in a state of insanity, without being able to observe a constant and exclusive connection between the elongated and spheroidal skulls on the one hand, and insanity on the other. The skulls number 1 and 2 of the opposite plate are taken from this famous professor's work. They are remarkable in their excessive elongation and rotundity, from which it is impossible to infer anything as to the nature of the intellectual faculties. "The lengthened cranium is that of a maniac, forty-two years old, who was completely cured about seven years ago." His state of insanity, severe and melancholic, cannot be ignored, but one can easily see that the features which indicate it are more evident in the physiognomy than in the configuration of the head.

The skull (No. 2) "contrasted with the portrait of the maniac, is that of a young

man who died at twenty-two" and who despite the excessive rotundity of his skull was endowed with a sound judgement.

A considerable lessening of breadth, a considerable elongation which contrasts with the smallness of the skull, and a lateral flattening of the head are the dispositions which are quite ordinarily observed among born idiots and which are attributed to almost all of the cretins of the pays de Vaud. It has also been observed that among born idiots, the head is much smaller. M. Pinel is in possession of a skull of an idiot girl who died at thirteen and the volume of whose skull scarcely equals that of a three-year-old child.

What appears extremely striking in the face view (No. 3) and the side-view (No. 4) of the head, is not only the stupid expression of the features, but the extreme disproportion of the extent of the face and that of the cranium. Everything about this head indicates the greatest intellectual fatuity. It is the portrait of an idiot who is, I believe, in the lunatic asylum of Bicêtre. This equivocal being, who seems to have been placed by nature on the very margin of humanity in regard to physical and moral qualities, is the son of a farmer. He was brought to Paris by a gendarme and is said to have been chained by the neck. This human-faced animal often and almost exclusively utters the words: bread, soldier, Paris, neck. He does not retain any memory of his family and does not give a sign of moral affection.

The physical defects which can be observed in the conformation of the skull and which seem to be connected with idiotism are, according to Pinel, a want of symmetry between the right and left side of the head, and the great thickness of the cranial structure which diminishes its capacity.

I was consulted some time ago about a seven-year-old child who was an idiot with the type of excessive mobility which makes any type of attention and rest impossible. I observed that in that child the forehead was, as it were, flattened, and surmounted above the eyebrows by irregular, eburnated protrusions which seem to indicate a very considerable development of the substance of the skull.

The physiognomy at rest, or the physiognomic characteristics of the insane vary with the type of insanity and the duration or intensity of the attacks. This physiognomy has nothing irregular about it and expresses but a usual state of either the exaltation of ideas or profound melancholy. In other cases the irregularity and disorder of the features correspond to the incoherence of the ideas and the want of harmony and homogeneity is generally an indication of dementia or of a predisposition to it.

Here (No. 5) is the portrait of the young savage of Aveyron: His moral treatment was undertaken some years ago by M. Itard, a doctor of medicine, and has enriched philosophy with infinitely curious results which have been published. . . . The portrait, I believe, speaks for itself. One cannot ignore the dominant expression of savagery, of astonishment mingled with uneasiness in it, and above all an expression of excessive mobility, lack of attention, and mental deficiency, which show in the extent, the protrusion and convexity of the upper lip. The marks which are seen on the head and the forehead are the scars of wounds received from the accidents and hazards of a life spent in the woods.[47]

Here the progression from the measurable (Pinel's measurement of relative skull size) to the impressionistic (the analysis of expression) is complete. Pinel's own scale of classical appearance has led to this alteration. The expressions perceived by Moreau de la Sarthe on the three faces portrayed are measured on a scale not unsimilar to the scale of the expression of the passions. There is a normal state, which is evidently viewed as immobile and passive, against which the other expressions of insanity are graded.

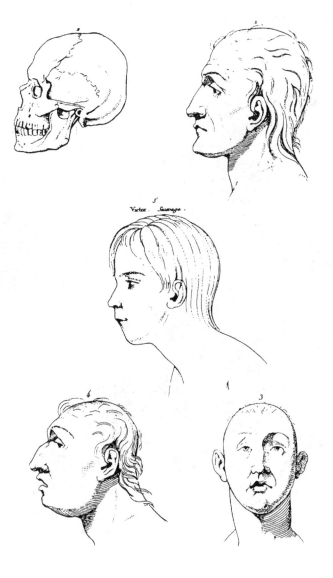

PLATE 90. Illustration from the chapter on the "physiognomy of madness" in Jacques Louis Moreau de la Sarthe's translation of Lavater (1807)

Pinel's focus on both the facial expression and the physical structure of the insane is carried forward in the plates illustrating a series of essays on psychopathologies in the *Dictionary of Medical Sciences* (1812-1822) by Pinel's pupil and co-worker Jean Etienne Dominique Esquirol.[48] Some of the illustrations concentrate on the facial characteristics, such as those of demonomania [Plate 91] and mania [Plate 92] in which Esquirol stresses the inquietude of expression but also describes the facial angle. Those of melancholy [Plate 93] and raging mania [Plate 94] reflect stereotypical views of these contrasting images, such as the hidden hands of the melancholic and the disheveled hair of the maniac. What is unique about all of these plates is that they are examples of specific cases rather than typical images of categories of insanity.

PLATE 92. "Mania," from Esquirol's essay on the topic in the *Dictionnaire*

PLATE 91. "Demonomania," drawn by Georges-François-Marie Gabriel for Esquirol's essay on the topic in the *Dictionnaire des sciences médicales* (1812-1822)

PLATE 93. "Melancholia," from the essay on "Madness" [*Folie*] by Esquirol in the *Dictionnaire*

PLATE **95**. "Lypemania" (melancholia) from the atlas
to J. E. D. Esquirol's *Des maladies mentales considérées
sous les rapports médical, hygiénique et médico-légal*
(Paris: J.-B. Baillière, 1838). This plate and the next are
a recutting of two of the engravings from Esquirol's
earlier work in the *Dictionnaire des sciences médicales*
(see plates 93 and 94), and show greater detail of line.

PLATE **96**. "Mania" from Esquirol's atlas

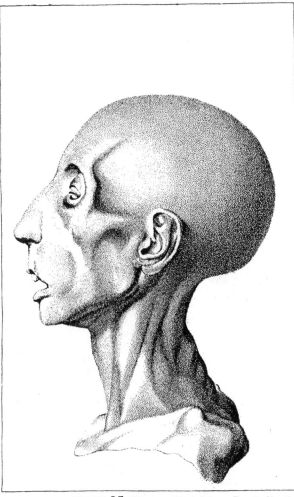

PLATE 97. "Demonomania" from Esquirol's atlas

PLATE 98. "Mania" from Esquirol's atlas

When Esquirol's collected papers appeared in an expanded version in 1838, the illustrations were appended in a full-fledged atlas, the first atlas of the appearance of the insane.[49] While it is not comprehensive, the twenty-seven plates provide a vivid and representative cross-section of the population of the Salpêtrière [Plates 95-100]. These were but a small fraction of the two hundred studies of the insane commissioned by Esquirol.[50] They reflect the detailed case work that had only been sketched in the earlier publi-

PLATE 99. "Dementia" from Esquirol's atlas

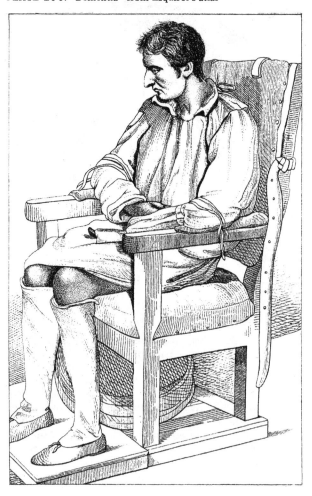

PLATE 100. "Dementia" from Esquirol's atlas

cation. A sample of this expansion can be seen in Esquirol's description of a case of melancholia [Plate 101]:

> In person, the lypemaniac is lean and slender, his hair is black, and the hue of his countenance pale and sallow. The surface over the cheek bones, is sometimes flushed, and the skin, brown, blackish, dry and scaly; whilst the nose is of a deep red color. The physiognomy is fixed and changeless; but the muscles of the face are in a state of convulsive tension, and express sadness, fear or terror; the eyes are motionless, and directed either towards the earth or to some distant point, and the look is askance, uneasy and suspicious. If the hands are not dried up, brown and earthy in their hue, they are swollen and livid.
>
> Mad'lle O. . ., twenty-three years of age, is brought to the Salpêtrière June 8th, 1812. In stature she is of medium size, her hair and eyes are black, the eyebrows very thick, and approximate closely at the root of the nose; her look is fixed upon the ground, her physiognomy expressive of fear, her aspect lean, and her skin brown. We observe some scorbutic spots on the lower extremities. The hands and feet, always very cold, are of a purplish red; the pulse is slow, and very feeble; constipation, which is ordinarily very obstinate, is sometimes replaced by a diarrhoea; secretion of urine scanty. She utters not a word, refuses every kind of movement, and persists obstinately in confining herself to bed. We have recourse to various means, to induce her to take nourishment. Affusions of cold water triumph over this repugnance, and she eats more readily. However, she manifests at times, her unwillingness to take nourishment, though with less obstinacy. For the four years that this woman has been in the house, but few words have escaped her, which however, have indicated to us, that fear absorbed all her faculties. She formerly lived in the country, and had been excessively frightened by soldiers. We have to oblige her to leave her bed, when, so soon as dressed, she sits down upon a bench, always in the same place, her attitude remaining the same: her head inclined to the left side of the chest, the arms crossed, resting upon the knees, and her eyes turned fixedly away from the sun. She remains thus, without moving, or uttering a word during the whole day. At meal time, she does not go for her food, but it is necessary to bring it to her, and press her to partake of it. She never changes her position to do this, and uses only the arm and hand of the right side. If any one approaches the patient, or speaks to her; if they interrogate or exhort her; her countenance becomes slightly flushed, and sometimes she turns her eyes aside, but never speaks. It is necessary to inform her when it is time to retire; when she is undressed, gathers herself up in bed, and envelopes her person entirely in the coverings. Menstruation is irregular and scanty; and is suppressed for six months. We never succeeded in overcoming the silence of this female, nor her aversion to motion. She never had an attack of fury, and died of phthisis at the age of twenty-nine years.[51]

The case study bridges the theoretical and the observable. The patient is perceived as a specimen. Esquirol stresses the physical appearance (both movable and immovable aspects, including skin color) as well as the patient's attitude in the asylum. The patient is seen, as in the illustrations, devoid of context. The stark portraiture in the engravings, the absence of any background, the detail of position and mode of treatment (where employed) create an image of the insane as the object of a Linnean study, categorizable by external appearance.

PLATE 101. "Lypemania" from Esquirol's atlas

The engravings in Esquirol's contributions to the *Dictionary of Medical Sciences* (see Plates 91-94) were based on drawings made in the asylum at the Salpêtrière by Georges-François-Marie Gabriel.[52] While the Gabriel originals for these particular plates have been lost, a book of sketches he did there during the 1820s has been preserved [Plates 102-105]. These figures, including that of Victor Hugo's brother Eugène, convey a sense of what the engraver, E. Lingée, used as sources for his plates. Ambroise Tardieu, the engraver for the atlas (see Plates 95-101), also used some of Gabriel's drawings, as well as sketches by Rouques, the teacher of Ingres, and Desmaison. Thus the illusion of objective observation underlying the use by the Idéalogues of illustrations of the insane was rooted in the highly impressionistic skill of these artists, subject in turn to further interpretation by the engravers.

PLATE 103. "Madman as priest" by Gabriel

PLATE 102. "Love madness" by Georges-François-Marie Gabriel (c. 1820)

Hugo, frere du poete, idiot.

PLATE **104**. "Idiot," Gabriel's portrait of Victor Hugo's brother Eugène

PLATE 105. "Melancholic" by Gabriel

In 1820, Etienne Jean Georget, a student of Esquirol at the Salpêtrière, published *On Madness,* one of the major studies to be produced by the school of psychiatry founded by Pinel. From Georget's point of view, direct observation was necessary to achieve understanding of the physiognomy of the insane because of the fleeting nature of their expression.

It is difficult to describe the physiognomy of the insane. One must observe this physiognomy, in order to retain an image of it. The ill are not to be recognized, their facial characteristics are disarranged, totally deformed. The physiognomies are as different as the individuals. They vary according to the passions, to the various ideas which dominate or drive them, to the character of the delirium, to the stage of the illness, etc. In general the face of the idiot is stupid, without meaning; the face of the maniac is as agitated as his spirit, sometimes distorted or cramped; the imbecile's face is cast down and without expression; the face of the melancholic is contracted, marked by pain or extreme preoccupation; the monomaniacal king has a proud, high facial expression; the religious maniac is meek, he prays, keeping his eyes fixed to the heaven or to the earth; the anxious patient flees, looking to the side, etc. I will leave this with this simple list, for only direct observation can give an impression of the rest.[53]

In this catalogue of the asylum inhabitants Georget stresses expression, and especially that of the eyes. While the madmen on his list can be found in Hogarth's Bedlam (see Plate 62), his emphasis on the ephemeral nature of the physiognomy of the insane and the need for immediate and constant observation places him in contrast to other clinicians following Pinel.

Georget was interested in capturing typical physiognomies for further study. To this end he requested his friend Théodore Géricault, one of the greatest of the French Romantic painters, to do portraits of ten patients at the Salpêtrière between 1821 and 1824 as potential illustrations.[54] Both men died before the project was completed and the illustrations were never published, but five of these paintings, representing five different psychopathologies, have been preserved [Plates 106-110]. These are posed portraits, whereas only one of Esquirol's plates is specifically referred to as having been posed for—a case of demonomania in which the patient believed, as part of her delusional state, that her portrait would be given to the archbishop. Following the views of the exponents of the face as the mirror of the passions, Géricault captures in each case the ha-

PLATE **106**. Théodore Géricault's *Monomania, The Assassin* (1821-1824). The titles of this and the following Géricault paintings are from Clement's 1879 catalogue of Géricault's works.

PLATE **107**. Géricault, *Monomania with Delusion of Military Grandeur*

PLATE **108**. Géricault, *Monomania, The Kidnapper of Children*

PLATE 109. Géricault, *Monomania, The Gambler*

PLATE **110**. Géricault, *Monomania of Envy*

bitual expression of the patient which represents the dominance of a single passion. His subjects are passive, reflecting as much the tradition of early nineteenth-century portraiture as the theories of the physiognomy of insanity.[55]

With Georget and Géricault the individuation of the insane, the reduction of the perception of the psychopathologies to the observation of individual patients, reached a new level. The concept of a portrait of a single insane individual embodies the new status of the insane as citizens within the state, not outcasts from it.

In Great Britain, in the meantime, the Scottish physician-anatomist Charles Bell had published one of the most influential studies on the portrayal of the insane. Included in his *Essays on the Anatomy of Expression in Painting* (1806) was his own illustration of "madness," which he completed after a visit to Bethlem Hospital in July 1805 **[Plate 111]**. Bell saw the insane in a manner which combines the qualities of many of the classic theories of the appearance of the mentally ill:

> If laying aside the peculiar expression of the features, I were to set down what ought to be represented as the prevailing character and physiognomy of a madman, I should say, that his body should be strong and muscular, rigid and free from fat; his skin bound; his features sharp; his eye sunk; his colour a dark brownish yellow, tinctured with sallowness, without one spot of enlivening carnation; his hair sooty, black, stiff, and bushy; or perhaps he might be represented as of a pale sickly yellow, with wiry red hair: yet in this I do not proceed upon the authority of the poet, for such I have seen.
>
>> His burning eyen, whom bloody strokes did stain,
>> Stared full wide, and threw forth sparks of fire,
>> And more for rank dispight than for great pain
>> Shak't his long locks, coloured like copper wire,
>> And bit his tawny beard to show his raging ire.
>
> I mean not here to trace the progress of the diseases of the mind, but merely to throw out some hints respecting the character of the outrageous maniac.
>
> You see him lying in his cell regardless of every thing, with a death-like fixed gloom upon his countenance. When I say it is a death-like gloom, I mean a heaviness of the features without knitting of the brows or action of the muscles.
>
> If you watch him in his paroxysm you may see the blood working to his head; his face acquires a darker red; he becomes restless; then rising from his couch he paces his cell and tugs his chains. Now his inflamed eye is fixed upon you, and his features lighten up into an inexpressible wildness and ferocity.
>
> The error into which a painter would naturally fall, is to represent this expression by the swelling features of passion and the frowning eyebrow; but this would only convey the idea of passion, not of madness. And the theory upon which we are to proceed in attempting to convey this peculiar expression of ferocity amidst the utter wreck of the intellect I conceive to be this, that the expression of mental energy should be avoided, and consequently all exertion of those muscles which are peculiarly indicative of sentiment. This I conceive indeed to be true to nature, but I am more certain that it is correct in the theory of painting. I conceive it to be consistent with nature, because I have observed (contrary to my expectation) that there was not that energy, that knitting of the brows, that indignant brooding and thoughtfulness in the face of madmen which is generally imagined to characterise their expression, and which we almost uniformly find given to them in painting. There is a vacancy in their laugh, and a want of meaning in their ferociousness.
>
> To learn the character of the human countenance when devoid of expression, and reduced to the state of brutality, we must have recourse to the lower animals; and as I have already hinted, study their expression, their timidity, their watchfulness, their state of excitement, and their ferociousness. If we should happily transfer their expression to the human countenance, we should, as I conceive it, irresistibly convey the idea of madness, vacancy of mind, and mere animal passion.
>
> The rage of the most savage animal is derived from hunger or fear. The violence of a madman arises from fear; and unless in the utmost violence of his rage, a mixture of fear will often be perceptible in his countenance. Often in lucid intervals, during the less confirmed state of the disease, they acknowledge their violence towards any particular person to have arisen from a suspicion and fear of their having intended some injury to them.
>
> This fact accounts for the collected shrunk posture in which a madman lies; the rolling watchful eye which follows you; and the effect of the stern regard of his keeper, which often quiets him in his utmost extravagance and greatest perturbation.
>
> I have thus put down a few hints on a most unpleasant and distressing subject of contem-

plation. But it is only when the enthusiasm of an artist is strong enough to counteract his repugnance to scenes in themselves harsh and unpleasant, when he is careful to seek all occasions of storing his mind with images of human passion and suffering, when he philosophically studies the mind and affections as well as the body and features of man, that he can truly deserve the name of a painter. I should otherwise be inclined to class him with those physicians who, being educated to a profession the most interesting, turn aside to grasp emoluments by gaudy accomplishments rather than by the severe and unpleasant prosecution of science.[56]

Bell's abstraction of "madness" follows the view that the depiction of insanity is related to the depiction of fear and terror. He also sees the appearance of the insane in terms of the animal analogies of Le Brun, in which madness reflects the baser appearance of man, and continues the Hogarthian manner of seeing the insane, for he argues elsewhere that when one portrays the insane "it is with a moral aim, to show the consequence of vice and the indulgence of passion."

In the light of Bell's wide audience it is not surprising that Esquirol's work was immediately popularly disseminated in Great Britain. As in Germany, it did not rely on publication of the complete atlas which accompanied the collected papers in 1838.[57] In 1817 the Scottish physician Alexander Morison visited Esquirol in Paris. Five years later Morison announced the first formal lectures in psychiatry held in Great Britain. The syllabus of these lectures, delivered at Edinburgh

PLATE 111. Charles Bell's "Madness" from his *Essays on the Anatomy of Expression in Painting* (London: Longman, et al., 1806)

University, appeared in 1825. A second edition followed in the next year, with thirteen engravings based on some of the drawings Esquirol had commissioned at the Salpêtrière. Morison's atlas was prefaced by a theoretical statement on the study of the physiognomy of insanity:

> The appearance of the face, it is well known, is intimately connected with, and dependent upon, the state of the mind. The repetition of the same ideas and emotions, and the consequent repetition of the same movements of the muscles of the eyes, and of the face, give a peculiar expression, which, in the insane state, is a combination of wildness, abstraction, or vacancy, and of those predominating ideas and emotions which characterize the different species of mental disorder, as pride, anger, suspicion, love, fear, grief, etc.
>
> Besides this moveable physiognomy, as it has been termed, other external signs, by which the different modifications of mental disorder might be ascertained, have been suggested. Some of those who adopt the phrenological ideas of Dr. Gall, conceiving mental disorder to proceed from disease in the departments of the brain exercising the functions disordered, allege that this disorder is marked, in recent cases, by increased heat in particular parts of the head, and in cases of long standing by external enlargement or diminution, and internal diseased structure in those parts.
>
> Masks of the insane have likewise been taken, to ascertain whether or not there exists any connection between what is termed the fixed physiognomy, or form and position of the bones of the face, and the different species of insanity.
>
> The following series of Plates is intended to convey an idea of the *moveable* physiognomy in certain species of mental disease.[58]

The illustrations [Plate 112] are strikingly similar to those of Esquirol for the *Dictionary of Medical Sciences*. The emphasis, however, is more on the movable facial features of the patient. Indeed, the bodies of the patients tend to vanish in the illustrations.

In 1829 Morison published a third edition of his *Outlines of Lectures on Mental Diseases*. It included seventeen illustrations [Plates 113-116] and departed from the aesthetics of portraiture found in Esquirol. The use of lithography, which had been developed in the late eighteenth century, permitted a more impressionistic sense of the mobility of the features than was possible in the earlier engravings, with their sharp, clearly delineated features.

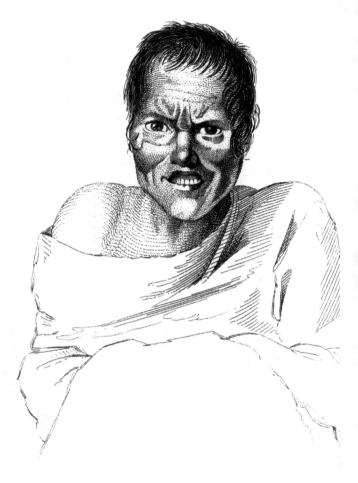

PLATE 112. "Dementia," from the second edition of Alexander Morison's *Outlines of Lectures on Mental Diseases* (London: Longman, et al., 1826)

PLATE 114. "Religious Monomania" from the 1829
edition of Morison's *Outlines*

PLATE 113. "Mania and Dementia," from the 1829
(third) edition of Morison's *Outlines*

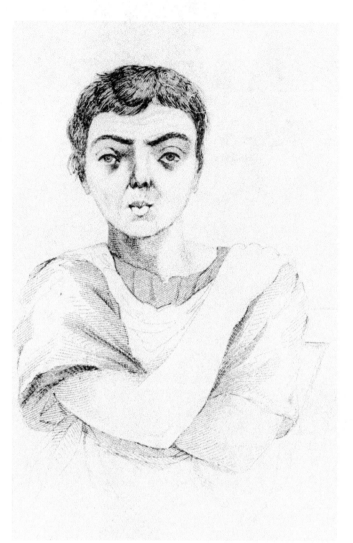

PLATE **115**. "Dementia," from the 1829 edition of Morison's *Outlines*

PLATE **116**. "Senile Imbecility," from the 1829 edition of Morison's *Outlines*

By 1840, Morison had commissioned enough new material to produce an independent atlas of mental illness. Morison's theoretical perspective had evidently not changed since the 1826 edition of his *Outline*, for he prefaced this atlas with the same introductory comments. However, the nature of the portraits had undergone a substantial alteration **[Plates 117 and 118]**. They still concentrate on the expression, but are even more impressionistic. A comparison of the 108 original drawings—by artists such as James Irvine, A. Johnston, and F. Rochard—with the printed reproductions shows how the lithographer copied the originals in such a manner as to emphasize the fleeting aspect of the expression **[Plates 119-132]**.

PLATES 117 and 118. "Mania, before" and "Mania, after" from the second edition of Alexander Morison's *The Physiognomy of Mental Diseases* (London: Longman, et al., 1840)

PLATE 119. "Puerperal Mania at Onset," from Morison's 1840 atlas

PLATE 120. "Puerperal Mania, seven months later"

PLATE 121. "Puerperal Mania, restored to reason"

PLATE **122**. Unpublished original drawing for Plate 119

PLATE **123**. Unpublished original drawing for Plate 120

PLATE **124**. Unpublished original
drawing for Plate 121

PLATE **125**. "Amatory Mania" from Morison's 1840 atlas

PLATE **126**. "Amatory Mania, recovered in about eight months"

PLATE **127**. "Insanity characterized by an irresistible propensity to steal"

PLATE **128**. "Periodical Attacks of Mania"

PLATE **129**. Unpublished original drawing for Plate 125

PLATE **130**. Unpublished original drawing for Plate 126

PLATE **131**. Unpublished original drawing for Plate 127

PLATE **132**. Unpublished original drawing for Plate 128

Morison's atlas, which was also later published in Germany,[59] was the first consistent attempt to create the illusion of transitoriness discussed by Georget. Yet this new scientificality did not divorce itself from the earlier British tradition of seeing the insane. Morison ends his atlas with six plates representing "some specimens of what has been previously done in this country; from an early period it had not escaped observation, that the expression of the countenance in the insane varied, according to the ruling ideas and emotions in the mind, as is manifest in the celebrated productions of Cibber and of Hogarth."[60] Morison reproduces Cibber's statues (see Plate 22) and figures from Hogarth's Bedlam (see Plate 62) and interprets these in the light of the expression of the figures. The last two plates bow to the interest in the "attitudes" of insanity, the gait and gesture, which had been stressed by Engel (see Plate 83). The cursory treatment of this aspect of insanity indicates Morison's avoidance of the question of physical posture.

While Morison's work was widely influential in England and Germany, the atlas by Matthew Allen, published in 1837, was all but ignored by his contemporaries.[61] Allen was superintendent of the York Asylum and had been involved in a court suit (*Allen* v. *Dutton*) in which he was accused of having made a false diagnosis. His nosological *Essay on the Classification of the Insane* was compiled as a result. Allen's work reflects the influence of the phrenologists. Unlike Morison, he stresses the fixed aspect of the patient's appearance as a part of his case presentation:

> This man is not more of an idiot than the one just described, yet there is much less appearance of mind about him; but his mental powers had not formerly been so much evolved and improved by education; and the mind, like the soil we tread on, once properly broken up and cultivated, will, in defiance of neglect, long retain traces of its former improved state. Besides his want of early culture, being one of the middle class of patients, he was wholly left without mental food or exercise. There was, under the old system, a complete sacrifice of the lower, utter neglect of the middle, for the sake of the higher class of patients; so that there was, with the middle class, for the most part, no intellectual interest excited by social converse and attention; nor, on the other hand, were the malignant passions kept alive by brutal treatment: and hence we now find amongst this class, the greatest proportion of those whose minds have sunk into torpid inactivity; and not so much because they are lost, but because, from their want of excitement, they have too long

continued in this motionless state. It is true, that their minds may, by the first attack, have undergone some great shock, to derange or paralyse the more perfect performance of its functions. . .[62]

Here the basic structure of description initiated by Esquirol becomes evident. The illustrations to Allen's case studies [Plates 133-135] indicate his preoccupation with the need to justify his diagnostic system. But Allen's influence on the psychiatric perception of the insane was minimal. By abandoning a general nosology (either implicit or explicit), Allen believed himself to be directly reflecting his clinical experience in describing the insane. This approach was not able to compete with the radical empiricism of Esquirol, which was combined with a specific nosology of insanity.

PLATE 133. "A mind sunken into a torpid state," from Matthew Allen, *Essay on the Classification of the Insane* (London: John Taylor, [1837])

PLATE 134. "A mind . . . of much greater activity than power," from Allen's *Essay*

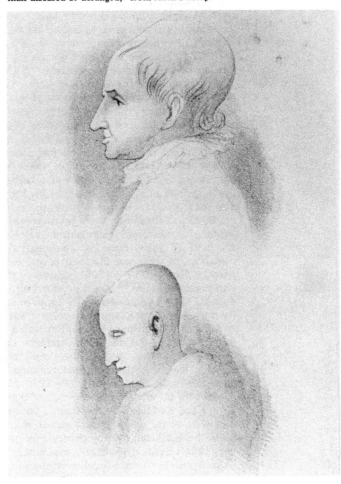

101

# the BIOGRAphy of madness

Recording the progress of psychopathologies in the form of descriptive case studies is as old as Galen. By the eighteenth century, verbal depictions were expanded into biographic sketches as scholars became more and more interested in the total structure of a madman's life as a potential explanation for his illness. This interest paralleled the development of the view that the passions were responsible for psychopathologies. Indeed, the standard German guide to correct behavior in society, Adolf Knigge's *On Intercourse with People* (1788), provided a segment on dealing with "melancholics, madmen and maniacs."[63] Knigge explained the need for a sane and civilized individual to understand the domination of weak individuals by strong passions. To illustrate this premise Knigge analyzed in detail two cases of insanity. Each began with the childhood of the individual and described how he was overcome by overpowering emotional conflict which led to his present state. Knigge's mode of relating the psychopathological development of his subjects was not atypical for the late eighteenth century.

Within this tradition there soon evolved collections of illustrated biographical sketches of the lives of typical madmen. The most widely circulated of these was the four-volume *Biographies of Madmen* (1795-1796), written by Christian Heinrich Spiess.[64] Spiess provided eighteen detailed histories representing the types of insanity caused by the passions. Each volume was prefaced with a frontispiece and an illustrated title page. Drawn by Johann David Schubert, the illustrator of Goethe's *Werther*, these capture incidents in the life stories recounted by Spiess. For example, in the frontispiece to the first volume [Plate 136] the artist depicts the case of Wilhelm M***r and Karoline W*g, in which a young soldier seduces the daughter of a pastor at whose house he is billeted. Her pregnancy precipitates her father's death. The girl goes mad and refuses to recognize her lover when he returns to claim

her and his child. He, in turn, sinks into melancholy and dies. The picture embodies the symbolic language of illustrations of madness. The melancholic and his sweetheart are divided by the stream of life. He is portrayed with a black countenance and bearing the bifurcated branch, the early icon of madness. The artist uses these traditional visual references to support the image of the lovers driven mad by their passions.

PLATE 136. The frontispiece to the first volume of Christian Heinrich Spiess, *Biographieen der Wahnsinnigen* (Leipzig: Voss, 1795-1796)

While Spiess's books were aimed at the general public and followed the format of the lives of famous criminals published in the various *Newgate Calendars* (in Germany as well as England), the work of Jean Louis Alibert stands at the forefront of the history of medical illustration.[65] Alibert, a student of Pinel, published the first medical text to have colored illustrations, *Description of the Illnesses of the Skin* (1806-1811). This was followed by his *Nosology of the Illness of the Human Body According to Classes* (1817), which included twenty-three color plates. Alibert's contribution to the study of internal medicine was substantial. His artists, Vaviel and Maurice, captured the visual presentation of illnesses such as scarlet fever through the medium of the colored copper etching.

When Alibert turned to the psychiatric biography in 1825, he employed a more traditional type of illustration. One of the case studies in his *Physiology of the Passions*,[66] which reflects his work with Pinel, is that of the "proud mad man at the Bicêtre" [Plate 137].

Among them was a most unique man. I promised myself to relate his story. It was Anselm, usually called Diogenes, who was in the institution for several years already, because he had been running around the streets of Paris in a Greek costume pretending that he had been charged with the philosophical mission to cure all people of ambition. The reading of the old classics had deranged his spirit to such an extent that he stood at public places and gave eloquent speeches to all people who passed him. Insane people have the special gift to collect everything that relates to their obsession. The majority among them manifest a surprising skill in making attributes of superiority and power, such as medals, sceptres, crowns. All things that can flatter their particular ambition. Anselm

PLATE 137. The portrait of Anselm from Jean Louis Alibert's *Physiologie des Passions* (2nd ed., Paris: Bechet Jeune, 1826)

dressed himself sometimes in a simple woolen blanket, but he draped it so skillfully that he gave the impression of being indeed one of the initiated men of the school of Portica or the Lyceum. He pretended to be a student of Socrates whose death he narrated sometimes in such a moving fashion that brought tears to his listeners eyes. For the rest he had identified with the teaching of the philosopher to such an extent that he could recite his doctrine and his opinions from memory.

Anselm was, as are all melancholic persons, very unbalanced in his moods. Sometimes he talked uninterruptedly, other times he had periods of several days of silence. One could see him spend entire months in meditative silence. But as soon as he had brought himself to speak, his facial features lit up like those of an enthusiast. His gestures were theatrical and lively; especially his voice which would attractively vary any modulation roused interest in his favor in an extraordinary manner. Nothing was more extraordinary than the speech he addressed to two mental patients who imagined themselves to be kings and who promenaded in the courtyard of Bicêtre while they were denying each other's precedence. "What fire consumes you," he shouted at them, "look how I conduct myself. Did you ever see me enraged? I could have reigned just as you, but I dedicated myself to philosophy." The amazing thing about this is the fact that the short address of this delirious man was sufficient to calm them. They took him for a wise man whose decisions one should respect.

What actually gave Anselm this great influence on his fellow sufferers was the incredible arrogance which made him indifferent toward everything, even toward the mockery directed against him. His glance expressed contempt, never impatience or rage.

He was the only one who rejected presents that one would offer during a visit at the asylum. I already mentioned that Anselm was given the nickname Diogenes. And he actually strove to imitate this philosopher in his laconic speeches, in the freedom of his judgments and the cynicism of his answers.

In the drawing by Marc François Perier, the singular figure of Anselm, called Diogenes, is in the foreground, seated in the melancholic's position and holding the lamp of Diogenes. Another seated melancholic and a figure with downcast eyes and hidden hands listen to his ruminations. Behind this group stands a king with his sceptre, indicative, according to Alibert, of the political upheavals which occupied the fantasies of many of the patients in the Bicêtre following the Rev-

olution. Peering into the courtyard is the manic face of an inmate, eyes bulging, hands spasmodically grasping the bars of his cell. This drawing, set in the openness of the courtyard of the Bicêtre, echoes the description of the asylum scene in the late eighteenth century. It is not so much an illustration of the individual as of the sense of madness portrayed by Alibert in his sketch:

One could always observe in Anselm a tendency to excel, which was a source of never ending torment. At every opportunity he talked about the successes which he had achieved in the world, and the obstacles he had encountered, about what he had done for his country, and the positions which had been denied him, about the rewards which were owed him, the ministers who had rejected him, and the incompetence of his rivals who had been preferred over him. Above all he complained that one had blocked his way which was to have led him to great results. He took care to add that—should the highest position in the country be offered to him—he would most certainly reject that offer. He thanked God who finally had delivered him from his unfortunate passion which had made his life so miserable.

In spite of this obvious conversion and Anselm's noble resolutions one could very quickly see that he slowly sank into deep melancholy. His gaze had a wild expression and the emotions in delirium were characterized by distorted facial features. During the time of which I speak it was not Diogenes anymore who brightened up his face through the biting irony of his flashes of genius. He had grown as gloomy as Timos, the unhappy philosopher in Athens who heaped curses on mankind and died of contempt for man. We will see that our poor Anselm suffered almost the same fate.

I already mentioned that he was working on a codex of law which he wanted to send to all ruling powers. When this great project was completed he did not lose time to send it to the various sovereignties of whom none accepted it. This rejection humiliated him to an unspeakable degree. Despair overpowered him and a sudden stroke ended his life unexpectedly.

Thus this man who believed to be totally cured of all old passion, who pretended to despise all fame and greatness experienced the most intense sorrow because he would not receive an answer to his letters which carried the stamps of the mental hospital. These beautiful rules which he presented day after day to the imagined kings without thrones who could be seen daily in the courtyards of Bicêtre, were of no use to himself. He died the death of the ambitious in an asylum to which he had limited his existence but which had not succeeded in curtailing his desires.

This then is the terrible effect of this passion that nothing can satisfy and that almost always devours him who is stopped by obstacles: it will devour the heart it has set on fire. As soon as it is ruling over a heart the person will try in vain to change. In vain he will seek the company of the wise, follow the way of Socrates, feed on the doctrine of Epictetus: ambition is present in the Portica as it is in the Lyceum, and the slaves it drags behind itself can only hope for peace when they go down into their grave.

Here the nosological function of the illustration, so important to Alibert in his work on internal medicine, is lost, and it serves a purpose not very different from that in Swift's *Tale of A Tub* (see Plate 61), to provide a visual sense of the asylum as a microcosm.

In 1838 Esquirol's atlas appeared, and the influence of this volume on the illustrated case study became immediately apparent. Two years later Jean Baptiste Lautard followed Esquirol's model in his "historical and statistical essay" on *The Madhouse at Marseilles.*[67] The following is typical of Lautard's case histories in its psychological portrait of the individual [**Plate 138**]:

Case study of Rose B., age 16. She became insane over the preference her older sister received from a young man, her husband, so that she had to be put into an institution. Her mania was definitely of periodic character, i.e., always from three to six in the afternoon, the rest of the day she behaved completely normally. Starting at 12 noon she became serious, retreated into solitude and finally sank into deepest melancholy. Following that she would become lively and exactly at three in the afternoon she would get fits of rage during which she would smash everything she could put her hands on. She tore her clothes and attacked the attendants. She also drank enormous quanities of cold water. Starting at six she was perfectly calm again. This intermittent rage had lasted in its astounding regularity for 30 months already, when Rose one morning at about five o'clock —it was her namesday—tried to strangle herself with a silk cord. Prompt help called her back to life. She complained bitterly about it and within one year made three attempts to kill herself. After her last attempt, however, she was found unconscious. Her lips were black already and her extremities had begun to turn cold. In spite of this she could be saved from death. She regained the use of her senses, but extremely slowly so. This was

PLATE **138**. The case of Rose B. from Jean Baptiste Lautard's *La Maison des Fous de Marseille* (Marseille: D'Achard, 1840)

—unexpectedly however—the triggering factor to a—seeming or real—recovery of her mania which recurred with great regularity which up to now had withstood every treatment. From this time onward the formerly critical hours of the day remained without effect. It is noteworthy that this young girl never tried suicide in any other way than by strangulation, although one had found poison hidden in her straw mattress. After the condition of her intellectual capacity had not given rise to suspicion over a period of six months and she also did not seem suicide prone anymore, she was released. Her family received her with joy after almost four years of her absence. Signs of repentance and piety made her recovery seem stable, so that one was thinking of marriage for her. Then she suddenly disappeared from home without the slightest trace of where she had gone and why. Months after this flight her anxious parents learned that Rose had suddenly become so enthusiastic about the theatre that she was moving with a group of actors from village to village and that she had appeared as an actress several times already. It also was said that she had the reputation of a distinguished artist among these buffoons and the fanciers of this crude genre. Unwavering in her resolution she rejected all her family's exhortations, all begging and all threats. This life of scandal, misery, and debauchery had not opened her eyes yet to the repulsiveness and the debasement of it. And yet, such evils often bear the germs of healing in them.

There was a change in her insanity. Suddenly she burns her glittering dresses, wraps herself in coarse woolen cloth, takes the crucifix, and the long pilgrim staff, decorated with shells. She joins a group of pilgrims on their way to Rome. For the most part those pilgrims were not guided by religious motives, but they wanted to satisfy their curiosity, a life without work and some also wanted to make people forget their past transgressions.

As soon as she arrived in Rome, Rose threw her outfit into the Tiber and fled, utterly exhausted, into the Cathedral of St. Peter from where the guards could hardly induce her to move when they were about to close the gates for the night. Still in ecstasy she spent the night under the arches of the Colosseum. A respected church official wished to make her acquaintance. She told him her life's story and her precarious situation at present. Her openness touched him and he placed her in a convent for poor orphans, where she was to teach French. She fulfilled her duties with great care and was well liked. After a year of testing she was ready to renounce the world. She disappeared without a word and went to Ancone where she embarked on a run-down ship together with an Italian improvisor who was on his way to Sicily. They were shipwrecked near Messina. Rose and several sailors were washed ashore in a bay where shepherds gave them food to eat, let them dry their clothes in the sun, and showed them the road to the city. Rose was admitted to the hospital for strangers; her feet were bleeding and her body was bruised. A young doctor felt compassion for her and provided her with the most loving care. He felt so strongly attached to her that he could never find her well enough to discharge her. In order not to be separated from her they embarked together on a Greek ship which set them ashore near Maina in the region of former Laconia after they had been robbed of everything.

In Maina they were treated like runaway slaves; only the sign of the cross and the language they spoke saved them. It was there that the Sicilian doctor had to flee into the mountains when a murderer threatened him and overpowered Rose. She was left alone soon afterwards, though, and was taken in by a priest of the Greek church who bestowed the most generous hospitality on her. At the time when we saw her she had lost all recollection of the various regions in Greece through which she had wandered, partly in the company of a pirate captain who was interested in her and partly with merchants who had

pity on her in her misfortunes. She also did not remember how long her wanderings had lasted. Her spirit found no rest. Her adventures came in such close succession that she lost track of the details. But she remembered well that she had been sold as a Turkish woman in a village ransacked by those who had defeated the Turks. She had been sold for a large sum of money to a captain from Marseille who could save her life that way and remove her from the excesses of a soldatesca intoxicated by debauchery and wine. She followed her liberator, but the journey from the Archipelago to Marseille which was full of deplorable incidents, found an end when the captain died of a brain hemorrhage. Without any concern about news from her family, Rose, who by now was not known under her real name anymore, went straight to Saint-Baume. She lived off roots and fruit for a while. Finally she went to the Trappist who in the meantime retreated from that rough and harsh place. There she confessed, received communion and two hours later threw herself off the cliff that towers over the chapel. She fell at the foot of the grotto of St. Magdalena.

The illustration accompanying this lengthy exposition provides the only visual clue to the nature of the subject, serving as an uninterpreted physiognomic study paralleling the case history.

The complexity of the illustrated case study reached its height with the publication of the first volume of Karl Wilhelm Ideler's *Biographies of the Mentally Ill in Their Psychological Development* (1841). Ideler introduces his study with a critique of the short commentaries in Morison's *Atlas*, and states that "the physiognomy of the mentally ill is a true mirror of their soul. It expresses many of the deeply hidden processes in a way impossible for the pen, and makes the portrait an essential element of its description."[68] The eleven plates accompanying the detailed and extensive biographical profiles of the patients were drawn from life by the medical illustrator Carl Resener and reproduced as lithographs. Unlike Lautard, Ideler not only provides a detailed background for each case, but incorporates some discussion of the relationship of the madman's appearance to his illness. In the third study, the case of R. [Plate 139], a young student who had tried to murder his landlady's mother, Ideler observes that:

He did not respond to the repeated question as to what he had done to be arrested. Then he raised his fist to hit the interrogator on the head. When he was energetically pushed off, R. retreated, and again raised his hands in

PLATE 139. The case of R. from Karl
Wilhelm Ideler's *Biographieen Geisteskranker* (Berlin: E. H. Schroeder, 1841)

a threatening manner toward the interrogator and shouted: "I need not deny my faith,
I will not deny it." Saying this he moved his
hand in order to grab a pair of paper scissors
that were lying there.

Q. "What did the woman do to you?"

A. "Well, we are not talking about doing
here, since I do not have to suffer anyone
who denies his faith."

Q. "What did you do to the woman?"

A. "Well, I don't need to tell you that again
since I already stated that she denied the faith
and that I will defend the faith against anyone who denies it."

Q. "Had you spoken to the woman before?"

A. "We are not dealing with 'speaking'
here, but with the denial, in that case I can
use force that is self understood."

Q. "Do you have any complaints about
your last landlords?"

A. "I don't. However I have much to lament about, because they deny the faith
which I don't have to tolerate, and which I
have tolerated long enough. But since I saw
that they did not treat me as a human being,
and didn't give me the respect I demand from
them, and since they wanted to force me into denying my faith, I couldn't tolerate it
any longer and I need not tolerate it any
longer etc."

It is noted that at this fit of rage a deep
red flushed his face which then suddenly
blanched again. His brown eyes were fixed
and piercing, and the gaze from his deep
seated eyes expressed as much fear as rage.
His posture was negligent and his head remained bowed throughout.

Since all the reported facts and his own
utterances showed beyond doubt that he
had been afflicted with a fully developed
mental illness for some time, he could not be

imputed for the deed committed in this condition. He was, therefore, on July 7, sent to the insane asylum in the Charité, where he remained until April 24, 1838. The following general comment may suffice here: his small but well proportioned body manifested the habit of a melancholic temper. There were no conspicuous disorders in his physical functions whatsoever. He also was spared any kind of sickness during his entire stay at the sanitarium.

This impression of illness is heightened by the downcast eyes in the appended portrait. Even in these quasi-scientific illustrations some symbolic references are introduced. The portrait of G. accompanying the fourth study, an instance of puerperal depression [Plate 140], employs the image of the melancholic to characterize the figure.

The illustrated case study, influenced by Esquirol, continued as an important subcategory of presentations of insanity in the nineteenth century. The biographies of typical (or atypical) cases, with their portraits, reappeared in many forms, but the illustrations were always intended to provide physiognomic or pathognomic proof of the illness portrayed.

PLATE 140. The case of G. from Ideler's *Biographieen*

# the phrenology
# of madness

In 1801, the same year that Pinel published his illustrated textbook on insanity, Frans Josef Gall was forced to flee Vienna because of opposition to his theories of the material nature of the mind. Settling in Paris, Gall published an extensive, four-volume study, *Anatomy and Physiology of the Nervous System in General and the Brain in Particular, with Observations on the Possibility of Understanding the Various Intellectual and Moral Dispositions in Men and Animals Based on the Shape of their Skulls.*[69] In 1819 an atlas appeared which illustrated Gall's analysis. Many of the illustrations of psychopathologies in these volumes were borrowed from Moreau de la Sarthe's translation of Lavater. In addition to

these, Gall incorporated eighteen original plates of studies of the skull and facial structure of the mentally ill [**Plate 141**].

Gall's illustrations of the insane stand in the tradition of cranial studies of the eighteenth century typified by Haller's work on the physiognomy of mental illness.[70] In his discussion of the relationship between skull structure and mental illness Gall paralleled Pinel, but he propounded a complex set of generalizations based on the anatomy of the brain. He was primarily interested in understanding the localization of emotion and intellect in the segments of the brain. His discussion of mental illness ranged from the physical characteristics of idiocy (relying heavily on Hal-

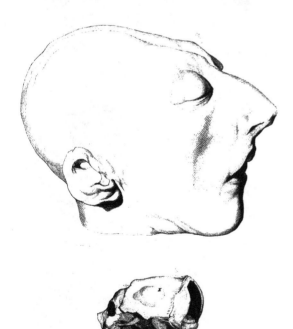

PLATE **141**. Skull of a twenty-five-year old idiot from the *Atlas* to Franz Josef Gall's study of the relationship between the brain and the mental and moral dispositions of men (1819)

ler) to the complicated interrelationship between poetic expression and mania. Gall saw all psychopathologies as stemming from alterations in brain structure. He emphasized, however, the tangential relationship of the external appearance of the skull to diseases of the brain. While some relationship might exist, other factors (especially those of inheritance) could confuse aspects of the individual's appearance with changes in the nature of the brain.

Even with this caveat, Gall's system was seen as a way of extrapolating the diagnosis of insanity based specifically on cranial structure. Johann Gaspar Spurzheim, Gall's Viennese colleague and the first to use the term "phrenology," presented a systematic exposition of the phrenologist's approach to seeing the insane.[71] Spurzheim had settled in London, where in 1817 he published his *Observations on the Deranged Manifestations of the Mind, or Insanity*.[72] Spurzheim's monograph,

with two illustrations representing psychopathologies [Plate 142], is built on Gall's hypotheses. Spurzheim, however, takes specific exception to Pinel's attack on the phrenologists in terms of Pinel's interpretations of illustrations representing the insane:

> There are persons who suppose that we maintain the possibility of knowing by the external shape of the head whether any one is predisposed to insanity or not. Pinel was of that opinion; and, in order to show the erroneousness of the assertion attributed to us, he caused two skulls to be drawn of nearly the same size and shape. One of these skulls belonged to a madman, and the other to a person of sound senses.
>
> That this is our opinion is merely imaginary, and no one will find it in any part of our writings. The contrary is easily understood from our general considerations with respect to the brain. We continually repeat that the

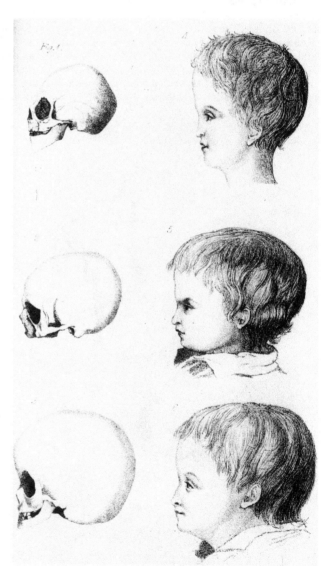

PLATE 142. An illustration from Johann Gaspar Spurzheim's *Observations on the Deranged Manifestations of the Mind, or Insanity* (London: Baldwin, Cradock and Joy, 1817) representing (1) the skull of an idiotic child of eight years; (2) the skull of an old person idiotic from birth; (3) a skull and (4), (5), (6), three heads, distended by water in the interior of the brain

brain is an organic part, and, as to anatomy, physiology, and pathology, subject to the same considerations as any other organ. Now, every part of the body, whatever its configuration may be, can become diseased. The eyes, for instance, of every size, form, and colour, may be inflamed; the respiration of small and large lungs may be disturbed; and the same may happen with any other part of the body, and with the brain and its parts; I say, that brains of all sizes and forms can be disordered. As, however, certain eyes are more disposed to inflammation than others, and certain lungs more to consumption; and in the same way as medical men speak of an apoplectic configuration of the neck, a consumptive habit of the thorax, so we find that certain brains are more disposed to disease, and certain configurations more liable to insanity. This is particularly the case with idiotism from birth, and partial insanities, called hallucinations. Pinel, however, though he refuted the above-mentioned opinion, thought it worth his attention and labour to measure the skulls of insane people in all their dimensions, to compare both sides with each other, and the whole with the proportions of the head of Apollo de Belvedere, which he considered as the model of perfection. But Pinel does not dare to draw any inference, not even from the small heads of idiots. "I must be," says he, "on my guard against too hasty conclusions. I confine myself to historical facts, without pronouncing that there is a connexion between idiotism and the defect of organization."[73]

For Spurzheim there is no question as to the validity of the illustration as a proof. Indeed he argues that Pinel's illustrations overly emphasize the correlations drawn between fixed appearance (size and shape of the skull) and mental state. In Spurzheim's own illustrations, as in Pinel's plate, there is a clear parallel between the expression of the faces presented and the comprehension of these images as representations of the pathognomy of the mentally ill. The phrenologists assume that, in many cases, anomalous size and shape of skull are related to expression. While the latter conclusion is never explicit in the works of Gall and Spurzheim, the use of physiognomic illustrations such as those of Lavater and Engel permitted the incorporation of physiognomic and pathognomic criteria in the phrenologist's discussion of the insane.

The visualization of the insane radiates even from the barest bones of the skull. In 1829, in a series of lectures on psychology, Goethe's friend Carl Gustav Carus discussed the etiology of insanity in the disruption of the mind-body identity. In 1841 he illustrated this theory in his "cranioscopy."[74] His views mirrored those of Gall and Spurzheim in that he constructed a spectrum of human types based on skull development. For example, in presenting the skull of a twenty-four-year-old idiotic girl [Plate 143], he concludes his description with the comment that "it is striking how similar the pronounced jaw line is to the skull of a Black. For it is evident that decadent structures among civilized peoples are often similar to the typologies of uncivilized peoples." The Black and the insane shared a similar position on the spectrum of humanity. Here the association of blackness and madness seen in the Middle Ages reappears in a quite identifiable form.

This nineteenth-century perpetuation of humorial theory was repeated by Carus in his classic work on the *Symbolism of the Human Form* and his study of *Physis*. According to these writings, all variations of human character evolve from the four classic types. Such scholarly continuations of humorial theories extended the concept of a scale of mankind, positing the inferior position (and appearance) of the Black and the madman. This is little more than a conflation of images of the "other" perceived through a specific cultural bias.

PLATE 143. Skull of an idiotic girl from Carl Gustav Carus, *Cranioscopie* (Stuttgart: Balz, 1841)

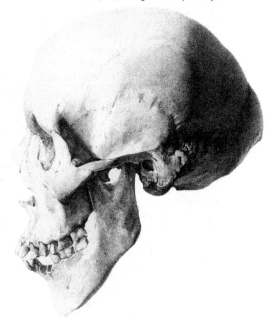

In the case of William Freeman, who attacked and murdered a family in upstate New York in 1846, the reality of a Black madman reinforced and was reinforced by the parallels established between the two categories of otherness. Freeman's image in the local papers [Plate 144] was actually that of an unremarkable individual. It was indicative of the parallel between madness and blackness in the public's imagination that his crimes were the subject of a traveling panorama which catalogued them in every detail. The intense expression on Freeman's face [Plates 145 and 146] in the representations of both the commission of the crime and his peering through the window at his victims recalls the traditional view of the expression of mania. Here the image of the murderer is not only the image of the madman, but it reflects the phrenologist's scale of appearance which equates the Black and the madman. Thus Black, murderer, and madman become interchangeable, incorporating the negative image of the Black as "the ignoble savage," the counterweight to the idyllic world of the noble savage with its lack of all illness.

In the United States during this period the myth, bolstered by the sixth national census of 1840, was used as an argument for the perpetuation of slavery. Published in 1841, the results of the census showed the total of insane and feeble-minded to be over 17,000, of whom 3,000 were Black. The statistics were staggering. The census purported to show that the incidence of mental illness among freed Blacks was eleven times higher than for slaves and six times higher than for the white population. This presented the anti-abolitionist forces with major "scientific" proof that Blacks were congenitally unfit for freedom. The Vice-President of the United States, John C. Calhoun, perhaps the most vocal spokesman for the slaveholding states during the 1840s, incorporated this argument as his mainstay in a letter to the British ambassador defending the "peculiar institution":

It deserves to be remarked, that in Massachusetts, where the change in the ancient relation of the two races was first made (now more than sixty years since), where the greatest zeal has been exhibited in their behalf, and where their number is comparatively few (but little more than 8,000 in a population of upwards of 730,000), the condition of the African is amongst the most wretched. By the latest authentic accounts, there was one out of every twenty-one of the black population in jails or houses of correction; and one out of every thirteen was either deaf and dumb, blind, idiot, insane, or in prison. On the other hand, the census and other authentic sources of information establish the fact that the condition of the African race throughout all the States, where the ancient relation between the two has been retained, enjoys a degree of health and comfort which may well compare with that of the laboring population of any country in Christendom; and it may be added, that in no other condition, or in any other age or country, has the negro race ever attained so high an elevation in morals, intelligence, or civilization.[75]

Even more interesting than Calhoun's political use of the 1840 census to justify slavery was the medical literature spawned by the statistical association of blackness with madness,[76] in spite of the fact that Edward Jarvis had rebutted the statistics by showing that there were gross errors in the compilation of the census (for example, there were 133 black insane paupers listed in the town of Worcester, Massachusetts, which had a total black population of 151).[77]

As late as 1851 the *American Journal of Insanity* cited the 1840 census as proof of the inferiority of the Blacks:

It is obvious. . . . that there is an awful prevalence of idiocy and insanity among the free blacks over the whites, and especially over the slaves. Who would believe, without the fact, in black and white, before his eyes, that *every fourteenth colored person in the State of Maine is an idiot or lunatic*? And though there is a gradual improvement in their condition, as we proceed west and south, yet it is evident that the free States are the principal abodes of idiocy and lunacy among the colored race.[78]

In that same year Samuel Cartwright published a paper in the *New Orleans Medical and Surgical Journal* which attempted to substantiate the association of blackness and madness by specifically identifying those psychopathologies to which Blacks alone were prey.[79] He pinpoints two "illnesses" which he labels "Drapetomania, or the diseases causing slaves to run away" and "Dysaesthesia aethiopis or hebetude of mind and obtuse sensibility of body—a disease peculiar to negroes—called by overseers, 'rascality.' " Mental "illnesses" ascribable to the rejection of the institution of slavery by Blacks were thus fitted into a medical model of insanity. Cartwright's views, which were quite widely disseminated and sub-

PLATE 144. Portrait of the murderer William Freeman from the *Cayuga Tocsin*, April 9, 1846

# THE MURDERER, WILLIAM FREEMAN.

PEASE. SC. Albany.

ter an ineffectual attempt to get in at the window, she then went round to the hall door, where she was let in by Miss Holmes, and conducted through Mrs. Wyckoff's room one through which the negro first entered the house was then open, she went and fastened it, and, in doing so, she had to pass and re-pass over the dead body of Mr. Van ately, and brought the first intelligence to the village.

After passing Mr. Williamson, the negro pursued his way till near New Guinea, when

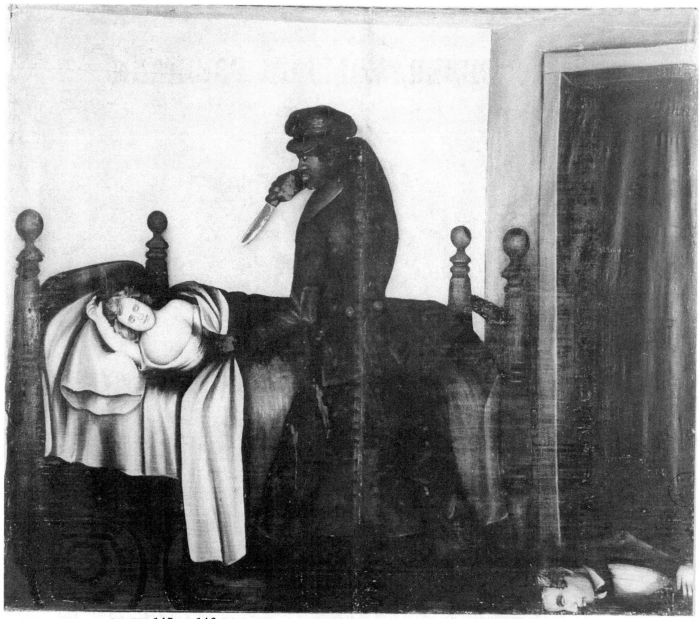

PLATES 145 and 146. Panels from a contemporary diorama chronicling the Freeman murders

jected to attack as well as defense, were couched in a medical vocabulary but had a clearly political thrust, as can be noted in his description of the etiology of "dysaesthesia aethiopis":

According to unalterable physiological laws, negroes, as a general rule, to which there are few exceptions, can only have their intellectual faculties awakened in a sufficient degree to receive moral culture, and to profit by religious or other instruction, when under the compulsatory authority of the white man; because, as a general rule, to which there are

but few exceptions, they will not take sufficient exercise, when removed from the white man's authority, to vitalize and decarbonize their blood by the process of full and free respiration, that active exercise of some kind alone can effect. A northern climate remedies, in a considerable degree, their naturally indolent disposition; but the dense atmosphere of Boston or Canada can scarcely produce sufficient hematosis and vigor of mind to induce them to labor. From their natural indolence, unless under the stimulus of compulsion, they doze away their lives with the

114

capacity of their lungs for atmospheric air only half expanded, from the want of exercise to superinduce full and deep respiration. The inevitable effect is, to prevent a sufficient atmospherization or vitalization of the blood, so essential to the expansion and the freedom of action of the intellectual faculties. The black blood distributed to the brain chains the mind to ignorance, superstition and barbarism, and bolts the door against civilization, moral culture and religious truth. The compulsory power of the white man, by making the slothful negro take active exer-

cise, puts into active play the lungs, through whose agency the vitalized blood is sent to the brain to give liberty to the mind, and to open the door to intellectual improvement. The very exercise, so beneficial to the negro, is expended in cultivating those burning fields in cotton, sugar, rice and tobacco, which, but for his labor, would, from the heat of the climate, go uncultivated, and their products lost to the world. Both parties are benefitted—the negro as well as his master—even more. But there is a third party benefitted—the world at large. The three millions of bales of cotton, made by negro labor, afford a cheap clothing for the civilized world. The laboring classes of all mankind, having less to pay for clothing, have more money to spend in educating their children, and intellectual, moral and religious progress.

The wisdom, mercy and justice of the decree, that Canaan shall serve Japheth, is proved by the disease we have been considering, because it proves that his physical organization, and the laws of his nature, are in perfect unison with slavery, and in entire discordance with liberty—a discordance so great as to produce the loathsome disease that we have been considering, as one of its inevitable effects—a disease that locks up the understanding, blunts the sensations and chains the mind to superstition, ignorance and barbarism. Slaves are not subject to this disease, unless they are permitted to live like free negroes, in idleness and filth—to eat improper food, or to indulge in spirituous liquors.[80]

It is specifically the physiology of the Black that predisposes him to mental illness. Here the association of blackness and madness is made to appear incontrovertible. Inherent in the nature of the Black is a greater potential for madness.

The special relationship between the Black and insanity remained a theme long after the issue of abolition was resolved. In 1896, J. F. Miller observed the radical increase in the number of Blacks in lunatic asylums since emancipation, and attributed this to the nature of the Black who could live in comfort "under less favorable circumstances than the white man, having a nervous organization less sensitive to his environments; yet it is true that he has less mental equipoise, and may suffer mental alienation from influences and agencies which would not affect a race mentally stronger."[81] In 1908, William F. Drewry, in a paper presented to the Thirty-Fifth National Conference of Charities and Correction, used the more modern scientific vocabulary of eugenics when he attributed "the causation of insanity" among Blacks to the "hereditary deficiencies and unchecked constitutional diseases and defects."[82] In 1916 a scholarly presentation of the relationship between madness and blackness argued that the "simple nature" of the Black, his "childlike essence," does not permit him to function well in the complexities of the modern world and predisposes him to insanity.[83]

The strength of this association is quite overwhelming and has permeated racist thinking to this day. As recently as 1964, Benjamin Pasamanick felt called on to refute the "myths regarding prevalence of mental disease in the American Negro." He concluded that if all data were taken into consideration "the total Negro mental disorder rate would not exceed that of the whites."[84] Pasamanick pinpoints the historic origin of the association of blackness and madness in the Enlightenment:

The dogma of the inferiority of the Negro begins largely with the beginnings of the Age of Reason in the eighteenth century and has been reinforced from all sources since. A corollary dogma which arose almost simultaneously stated that slavery was the ideal state for such inferior and inadequate persons and indeed that freedom resulted in their decay and degradation. The nineteenth-century political, sociological and anthropological literature is filled with the demonstration of these allegations. During our century, the scientific evidence and tools have been sharpened and these dogmas fiercely applied.[85]

Pasamanick clearly recognizes the growing politicization of the concept of blackness in the late eighteenth and the nineteenth centuries. With the merging of the concept of "Black" and the concept of "Slave," special criteria evolved for dealing with the status of the Black as slave in western consciousness. This alteration in perspective incorporated the existing model of the nexus between madness and blackness to achieve its varied ends.

The image of the madman came, through the influence of the phrenologists, to encompass a wide spectrum of visual stereotypes. If all behavior was determined by brain structure, antisocial behavior was the result of defective brain structure. Thus the phrenologists argued for the concept of criminal insanity as a means of explaining sociopathic behavior. This view was held by many of the liberal phrenologists of the early nineteenth century, including Eliza W. Farnham, the matron of Mount Pleasant State Prison in New York State, who wrote an introduction to the American edition of M. B. Sampson's study of criminal insanity and added an atlas of criminal types.[86] The basis for the woodcuts illustrating the Sampson-Farnham volume was a series of daguerreotypes by Matthew Brady.[87] The commentaries on the illustrations provide a range of racial and national types found in the various New York prisons. Just as Brady's plates were reduced to simplified woodcuts, Farnham's commentaries reflect an equally simplistic reduction of the image of the criminally insane to its phrenological parts. Farnham comments on one of the illustrations [Plate 147]:

S. S. is a vagrant, and inmate of what is termed the Luna House, on Blackwell's Island. He is an Irishman; was formerly a prize-fighter; was sent to the State Prison for five years for assault and battery, with intent to kill, and since his liberation, a period of some six or eight years, has spent most of his time in the city and county prisons of New-York. Before his mind became deranged, he exhibited great energy of passion and purpose, but they were all of a low character, their sole bearing being to prove his own superiority as an animal. He was both vain and selfish.

The drawing shows a broad, low head, corresponding with such a character. The moral organs are exceedingly deficient, especially benevolence, and the intellect only moderately developed. The whole organization, indeed, indicates a total want of every thing like refined and elevated sentiment. If the higher capacities and endowments of humanity were ever found coupled with such a head as this, it would be a phenomenon as inexplicable as that of seeing without the eye, or hearing without the ear.

The expansion of the concept of insanity to include sociopathic individuals illustrates how visual stereotypes of the insane permeated the perception of other social and psychological categories. Criminality was seen as insanity, and the criminal as insane.

The introduction of photography permitted phrenologists to diagnose the individual from his fixed image as well as from life. Samuel R. Wells, for example, was prepared to read a person's character "from a good daguerreotype, the 3/4 pose preferred" for four dollars.[88] Wells, a long-time associate of the Fowler brothers, was one of the most vociferous American proponents of phrenology. Wells began his study of the "physiognomy of insanity," published in 1883, with Bell's illustration of mania (see Plate 111) and a recapitulation of Bell's views.[89] Like Lavater he saw insanity as the discordance of appearance. Rejecting skull malformation as the sole sign of insanity, he saw in both fixed aspect and expres-

PLATE 147. Woodcut for the case of S. S., based on a photograph by Matthew Brady; from M. B. Sampson, *Rationale of Crime and Its Appropriate Treatment* (New York: Appleton, 1846)

117

PLATE 148. "Malice," from Samuel R. Wells,
*New Physiognomy; or, Signs of Character* (New
York: Fowler & Wells, 1883)

PLATE 149. "Deserted," an echo of the
Ophelia-motif, from Wells' *New Physiognomy*

PLATE 150. "Raving," from Wells' *New Physiognomy*

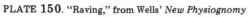

PLATE 151. "Lost," from Wells' *New Physiognomy*

sion clues to the inner being of the insane. Wells supplied a mini-atlas of visualizations of the insane [Plates 148-151] and concluded his discussion with an original interpretation of the figures represented in Kaulbach's asylum scene (see Plate 174). Wells' discussion of idiocy also emphasizes the correspondence between the totality of physical appearance, including expression, and mental capacity. Along with a picture of an idiot [Plate 152], Wells provides a contrasting image of the normal physical appearance which parallels the normal mental state [Plate 153]. The ethnocen-

tric image of the normal places the image of the insane into a specific context, for the normal figure is a stereotypical middle-class white Anglo-Saxon schoolboy while the idiot appears not only idiotic but of a lower economic class, as can be seen by his dress.

The influence of the phrenologists' discussion of madness added to the visual image of the madman. They expanded the image, including other groups such as the sociopath and incorporating much of the physiognomists' interpretation of the appearance of the insane.

PLATE 152. "Total idiocy," from Wells' *New Physiognomy*

PLATE 153. "A sound mind in a sound body," from Wells' *New Physiognomy*

# the aesthetics of madness

The first British edition of Lavater's works was Thomas Holloway's translation of the 1781 French edition, for which Lavater himself had contributed additional material. The Holloway edition is of special interest because two major British artists, Henry Fuseli and William Blake, were involved with it and their contact with the theories of the physiognomy of insanity caused the image of the madman in their work to develop in a specific direction. This contact altered the earlier British visualization of the insane in a manner which was indicative for the late eighteenth and early nineteenth centuries, especially in Great Britain.

Henry Fuseli, a close friend and correspondent of Lavater, contributed a "real scene" [Plate 154] from the asylum of St. Spirito in Rome to the 1781 French edition which was, in turn, reprinted in Holloway's 1789 English translation.[90] Lavater (or his French editor) used only the fragment of the plate that showed the fleeing patient and his captors, and it was described as follows:

> Fury and force, an energy uniformly supported, and ever active—this is what distinguishes most of the figures and compositions of the masculine genius. Spectres, Demons, and madmen; fantoms, exterminating angels; murders and acts of violence—such are his favourite objects; and yet, I repeat no one loves with more tenderness. The sentiment of love is painted in his look—but the form and bony system of his face characterize in him a taste for terrible scents, and the energy which they require.[91]

Fuseli's scene, referred to as "the horrible and the pathetic" in the introduction to this translation, incorporates the detailed physiognomy of fear and terror discussed by Lavater in a context that relies heavily on Hogarth's image of the asylum (see Plate 62). The figure in prayer at the far left parallels the religious melancholic in Bedlam, while the triangular group in the background

reflects the groupings in the Hogarth plate.[92] The central figure is raving and half-draped, strongly reminiscent of Rakewell. Unlike Rakewell, however, his contorted face reflects the physiognomists' impression of the expression of the insane as fearful, horrible, or terrified, to use Parsons' categories. Fuseli had earlier used the traditional positions of his figures as indications of psychopathology, as in his portrait of the mad Ajax. There is a meshing of the earlier image of the insane in the context of confinement with the new emphasis on the facial expression of the passions.

William Blake's involvement with the Holloway edition was as designer and engraver.[93] This work and his close friendship with Fuseli exposed him to Lavater's theories. In 1795 Blake issued one of his "printed drawings," a portrait of the Biblical monarch Nebuchadnezzar, the quintessential madman as wild man [Plate 155]. Blake drew on an earlier design from *The Marriage of Heaven and Hell* illustrating the mechanistic concept of the unity of all things, the "one law for both the lion and the ox."[94] Man is not a beast, as had been suggested by the visual parallels of human and animal analogies from della Porta via Le Brun to Lavater. Each aspect of creation is unique, except when man conceives of himself as part of a mechanistic universe. Such madmen, symbolized by the figure of Nebuchadnezzar, then become like beasts. Blake saw this process of becoming mad as a quality of the contemporary world. He wrote in 1804 to William Hayley: "Nebuchadnezzar had seven times passed over him; I have had twenty; thank God I was not altogether a beast as he was; but I was a slave bound in a mill among beasts and devils; these beasts and devils are now, together with myself, become children of light and liberty, and my feet and my wife's feet are free from fetters."[95]

Blake's imagery is related to Jacob Boehme's conception of madness as the domination of the devil through the temperaments, a view known

PLATE **154.** Henry Fuseli's illustration for Lavater "drawn from memory after a real scene in the Hospital of S. Spirito at Rome"

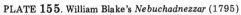

PLATE **155.** William Blake's *Nebuchadnezzar* (1795)

PLATE **156**. John Brown's *Head of An Insane Woman* (c. 1770)

PLATE 157. An unpublished page from the Blake-Varley Notebook of 1819 with "Types of Insanity"

to Blake.[96] In interpreting the appearance of Nebuchadnezzar, Blake consciously merged two traditions. The first is that of the madman as wild man, which goes back to the early Middle Ages; the second, that of the physiognomy of insanity, tempered by the matched images of animals and men found in the physiognomies that appeared through the early nineteenth century.[97] In addition Blake employed the expression of fear, horror, and terror attributed to the insane in the handbooks on the passions. It is striking to note the parallel between the facial expressions of Fuseli's madman and Blake's Nebuchadnezzar.

A hitherto unpublished drawing by Blake reveals another tradition of representing the insane incorporated and altered by the artist. Earlier, in the 1770s, the Scottish artist John Brown had sketched an insane woman [Plate 156] with protruding eyes, weak chin, and disheveled hair, an apparent version of the physiognomists' concept of insanity. In 1819, Blake provided for his colleague John Varley a strikingly similar portrait of the insane [Plate 157]. Varley had asked Blake to draw in a notebook the figures he saw in his visions, and Varley used at least one of these in his *Treatise on Zodiacal Physiognomy* in 1828.[98] On a leaf of the notebook, with illustrations similar to others in the existing sketchbook, an early nineteenth-century hand has inscribed "See Murdoch on Insanity." John Murdoch's *Pictures of the Heart, Sentimentally Delineated in the Danger of the Passions*[99] presented a detailed allegory on the struggle between Reason and the Passions, a theme Blake often embodied in his work. If indeed Murdoch's work was the inspiration for these two heads, they represent insanity as the result of the passions. At the same time they are strongly reminiscent of Lavater's heads. This merger of two traditions is complementary to Blake's image of madness in the figure of Nebuchadnezzar, itself a fusion of older traditions with the new manner of seeing the insane.

PLATE 158. Thomas Rowlandson's *Doctor and Lunatic*, a wash drawing

PLATE 159. Thomas Rowlandson's *The Maniac*

Thomas Rowlandson, the most famous British caricaturist after Hogarth, was another late eighteenth-century artist who merged the older views of expression with contemporary concepts of physiognomy. In 1800 Rowlandson produced and engraved the plates for G. M. Woodward's *Le Brun Travestied, or Caricatures of the Passions* and in 1820, under the influence of the phrenologists, a volume entitled *Comparative Anatomy, Resemblances between the Countenances of Men and Beasts.*[100] Earlier Rowlandson had captured images of insanity in two unpublished drawings [Plates 158 and 159]. In both there is a striking depiction of the insane based on the older images of the raving maniac. In Plate 158 the passive doctor observes his patient. The chains and the barred window as well as the position and the expression reflect the state of mania. This drawing is very close to many of the late eighteenth-century renditions of George III as the mad king (see Plate 63). The other drawing relies on the Hogarthian image of succor found in the figure of Sarah Young, who hovers over Rakewell in Bedlam (see Plate 62). Rowlandson's characters are not human beings. They are lumps of animal horror or stupidity. Rowlandson sees the human race as cattle or swine, "a reeking fat-stock done up in ribbons or breeches, which has got into coffee houses, beds, and drawing rooms."[101] As in Blake's *Nebuchadnezzar*, the older tradition of della Porta and Le Brun, a tradition which never completely vanished in the eighteenth century, returns, and the madman is seen in terms of his equation with the bestial. The juxtaposition of the mad figures with those surrounding them makes this even more apparent.

In the works of Fuseli, Blake, and Rowlandson the image of the madman blended various traditions. A parallel point of departure for observing the fusion of such traditions is the interpretation of the same image of the insane by various artists. Indeed, one could provide a manual of images of the insane by simply chronicling illustrations of Ophelia and Hamlet. In the late eighteenth century, however, the most popular prototype of the madwoman was that presented by William Cowper in *The Task* (1785):

> There often wanders one, whom better days
> Was better clad, in cloak of satin trimm'd
> With lace, and hat with splendid ribband
> bound.

A serving maid was she, and fell in love
With one who left her, went to sea, and died.
Her fancy follow'd him through foaming
waves
To distant shores; and she would sit and
weep
At what a sailor suffers; fancy, too.
Delusive most where warmest wishes are,
Would oft anticipate his glad return,
And dream of transports she was not to
know.
She heard the doleful tidings of his death—
And never smil'd again! And now she roams
The dreary waste; there spends the livelong
day,
And there, unless when charity forbids,
The livelong night. A tatter'd apron hides,
Worn as a cloak, and hardly hides, a gown
More tatter'd still; and both but ill conceal
A bosom heav'd with never-ceasing sighs.
She begs an idle pin of all she meets,
And hoards them in her sleeve; but needful
food,
Though press'd with hunger oft, or comelier
clothes,
Though pinch'd with cold, asks never.—
Kate is craz'd![102]

PLATE 160. Henry Fuseli's *Crazy Kate* (1806)

PLATE 161. Thomas Barker of Bath's Romantic *Crazy Kate*

126

"Crazy Kate" became a standard image of love melancholy. Fuseli's *Crazy Kate* [Plate 160] reflects the influence of Lavater. Her face forms the central focus of the painting. Her physical condition matches Cowper's description, but her eyes are the center of the work. The expression of the insane dominates the portrait. In Thomas Barker of Bath's version [Plate 161] the hidden hands of the melancholic are added to an image in which the features and coloration of the face demonstrate the adaptation of the classic view of the melancholic by the physiognomists. Her position is, however, typical of the genre picture of the time. How the traditional image of the melancholic continued into the late eighteenth century can be seen in another, related work by Barker [Plate 162]. Here the genre stance of the earlier image of Kate is replaced with the seated posture of melancholy, hands hidden, accompanied by two bifurcated trees as symbols of madness. George Shepheard's *Crazy Kate* [Plate 163] also employs the seated position of melancholy. In these four portraits we see the standard body position combined with the facial expression of the melancholic as representative of the images of the passions seen in Parsons and later in Lavater.

PLATE **162**. *Crazy Ann*, the heroine of a British folk ballad, by Thomas Barker of Bath

PLATE **163**. George Shepheard's *Crazy Kate* (1815)

PLATE 164. Francisco Goya, *The Madhouse at Saragossa* (1794)

On the continent, in the meantime, Francisco Goya also exemplified in his work the transition from the late eighteenth to the early nineteenth century manner of seeing the insane.[103] Goya's depiction of madness during the eighteenth century is heavily indebted to earlier portrayals of insanity, including classic icons of melancholy[104] and images of exorcism such as his portrait of San Francisco de Borja (1788) with attendant demons.[105] Indicative of his view of the insane in this period is a portrait of the "courtyard of lunatics, two of them fighting nude, with their overseer beating them and others wearing sacks," as he notes in a letter dated January 7, 1794.[106] This scene **[Plate 164]** was witnessed by Goya at the madhouse in Saragossa and was cast in the Hogarthian manner of representing the insane. The wrestlers, echoing Rakewell (see Plate 62), stand disrobed in the center of the composition, with the warder actively attempting to restrain them. On one side stands the melancholic, with gaping mouth and hidden hands; on the other sits a grinning figure with hands clasped about his knees. Behind him, in the position of Cibber's recumbent melancholy (see Plate 21), lies another patient. The seated, grinning patient seems to

be a version of the succubus figure in Fuseli's famous painting *The Nightmare*, which Goya had used as the basis for the image of the demonic in his portrait of San Francisco de Borja mentioned above.[107] Like Hogarth, Goya provides his own iconography of the madman in the structure of the asylum scene. The bright openness above the walls and the crowd of patients barely delineated in the background convey a stultifying image of the asylum as a place of horror as well as confinement. The blackness of madness is translated into the blackness of the asylum.

This is also true in a later work by Goya, *The Madhouse*, painted in the early nineteenth century **[Plate 165]**. Here again a Hogarthian image of insanity is in evidence. The figures, from raving mania on the left, through melancholy, religious melancholy, love melancholy (with the cuckold's horns), to the seated kings with their sceptres and straw crowns, inhabit a world of half-light. An undifferentiated mass of patients huddles behind the madman with his feathered crown, his hand being kissed by one of his insane subjects. Here the light streaming through the barred window is dissipated in the unlit recesses of the cell. Goya's image of the asylum as a world of dark-

PLATE 165. Goya's *Madhouse* (c. 1810)

PLATE 166. Goya, *The Mad Picaro* (c. 1824)

PLATE 167. Goya, *The Mad Man* (c. 1824)

to the world of light is in keeping
...iasis on the soul as the dark hiding
...108

...'a was forced to leave Spain, how-
...siognomic tradition of portraying
...his land of exile, France, was quite
...i the tradition of Hogarth and La-
...iad known in Spain. Exiled in Bor-
...ept notebooks from 1824 to 1828
...ketched a series of madmen at the
...These ranged from a "raging luna-
...adman made through scruples."109
...aro" [Plate 166] and the madman
...ublished) [Plate 167] reflect the
...physiognomy as well as the older
...avater.110 Stripped of any context
...it immediately surrounding the fig-
...wings depict the fixed appearance,
...tance of the insane in the manner

...of the madman in the asylum had
...like the artists who based their ver-
...:y Kate" on Cowper's poem, many
...ic artists found inspiration in liter-
...the most complex of these is the
...sso by Eugène Delacroix, who was
influenced by Byron's depiction of the insane
poet. Delacroix was fascinated with the figure of
the mad Tasso as early as 1819 but, in a letter
to his friend Pierret in September of that year,
he noted that he had not yet read Byron's "fine
elegy." He had, however, his own specific visualization of the poet in the asylum:

> How indignant one feels with those shameful
> patrons who oppressed him under pretext of
> protecting him against his enemies, and de-
> prived him of his beloved manuscripts! What
> tears of rage and indignation he must have
> shed on seeing that in order to make sure of
> keeping them from him, his patrons declared
> him mad and incapable of creating! How ma-
> ny times must he have struck his head against
> those shameful bars, thinking of the baseness
> of men and blaming for her lack of affection
> the woman he has immortalised through his
> love! What a slow fever was to consume him!
> How his days must have dragged by, with
> the added pain of seeing them wasted in a
> lunatic's cell!111

The vision of the raving maniac in this letter was
replaced by Byron's picture of Tasso's "repose"
in the frenetic world of the asylum, for by 1824,
the date of the first version of his portrait, Delacroix had read Byron's description of the asylum
in "The Lament of Tasso" (1817):

> Above me, hark! the long and maniac cry
> Of minds and bodies in captivity.

And hark! the lash and the increasing howl,
And the half-inarticulate blasphemy!
There be some here with worse than frenzy
    foul,
Some who do still goad on the o'er-laboured
    mind,
And dim the little light that's left behind
With needless torture, as their tyrant Will
Is wound up to the lust of doing ill:
With these and with their victims am I
    classed,
'Mid sounds and sights like these long years
    have passed.
'Mid sights and sounds like these my life
    may close:
So let it be—for then I shall repose.[112]

The contrast of passive acceptance and raving madness is present in Delacroix's paintings.
This contrast is bound together with the image
of the asylum as parallel to that other Western
image of confinement, the prison. Tasso is the
victim of the state, his madness a reaction to it.

In the third and final version of his work,
painted in 1839 [Plate 168], Delacroix uses elements from the standard vocabulary of madness
to depict Tasso.[113] The poet sits in the classic
position of the melancholic, half-nude, his hair
disheveled. On the floor are strewn sheets of paper, an indication of his inability to write, to undertake creative activity. Three inmates, mouths
agape, stare at the poet through the barred window. He sits in a stream of light. Even the other
inmates, unlike those in Goya's paintings (see
Plates 164 and 165), are clearly illuminated. The
introduction of light into the asylum scene miti-
gates the despair, and provides a potential resolution.

Thus we find in the art of the late eighteenth
and early nineteenth centuries an amalgamation
of various manners of perceiving and portraying
insanity. No small debt was owed to the resur-
gence of interest in physiognomy and the wide
proliferation of English and French editions of
Lavater's work. The new physiognomy was for
the most part merely a resuscitation of the old
with a veneer taken from some of the newer theories of human expression. It was the artists who
themselves transmuted this tradition into new
manners of seeing insanity and influenced the
public view of the insane as well as being influenced by it.

PLATE 168. Eugène Delacroix, *Tasso
in the Asylum* (1839)

131

# the reform of madness

# the population
# of the reformed asylum

Rakewell's shadow dominated the image of the insane in the asylum scenes of the eighteenth century. Even in a caricature of Hogarth [**Plate 169**], Paul Sandby placed the artist in the position of the mad cartographer in the final plate of *A Rake's Progress*[1] (see Plate 62). Sandby was satirizing the publication of Hogarth's *Analysis of Beauty* (1753), with its emphasis on the serpentine "line of beauty." In his engraving Sandby introduces the staff of madness in the form of a serpentine artist's staff. This is paralleled by the fool's staff so prominently displayed underneath by the fool in asses' ears threatening the British lion. This image of the madman in Bed-

PLATE **169**. Paul Sandby's *The Author Run Mad* (1753)

lam is not far removed from Hogarth's own image. The mad, useless labor undertaken by the caricatured Hogarth points to the isolation of the madman from the real world. While this is Sandby's view of Hogarthian aesthetics, it also encompasses a basic eighteenth-century vision of the asylum.

In October 1793, Phillipe Pinel, following the lead of certain British and continental reformers, publicly struck off the chains of the inmates at the Bicêtre. This was a political action, restoring the insane to the status of human beings possessing implicit rights. In Paris some thirty years later, Charles Aubry published his *Comic Album of Picturesque Pathologies*, which continues older visual traditions but also illustrates the positive movement toward an altered image of the insane in the light of their new political standing.[2] In addition to a nightmare scene based on Fuseli's famous painting, the volume includes an asylum scene [**Plate 170**], and a scene representing possession [**Plate 171**]. In the asylum scene a madwoman brandishes the staff of madness in the form of a witch's broom, the mad king reclines, and the prideful dandy struts, his hair disheveled. In the scene of possession the erratic movements of the dancers are also set off by the image of the staff, in this case the pilgrim's staff indicating the pilgrimage to Molenbeek (see Plate 41). What is striking about both these plates is that the symbolic language of the older images of the insane has been moved outside the walls of the asylum. There is no sense of the claustrophobic limits of the traditional images of confinement. This may account for the inclusion of the pilgrimage scene as a counterpoint to the asylum scene in the album, for the procession of pilgrims moves freely across the countryside, stopping at a roadside shrine. The image of openness associated with the movement of the insane through the world in Breughel's sketch is reintroduced into the world which had been dominated by a closed image of the asylum.

PLATE **170**. Charles Aubry, "An Asylum Scene," from his *Album Comique de pathologie pittoresque* (Paris: Tardieu, 1823)

PLATE **171**. "Saint Guy's Dance" from Aubry's *Album Comique*

The anonymous British lithograph *The Mad House* [Plate 172], from the early years of the nineteenth century, uses older images of insanity in a new context. The stress is placed on the expression and gesture of both the seated madman and the despairing visitor. But the madman is directly illuminated by a beam of light whose source seems to be a window, and its symbolic significance is emphasized by the figures above the main scene. Here the angelic spirit protects the madman, restored to his senses, while the demons of madness are being exorcised. Thus the light and openness of the asylum represent potential salvation from madness. Inherent in the attempts to reform the manner of treatment as well as the position of the insane in the asylum was the altered view of the treatability of insanity. The insane could be cured, could be restored to their earlier civil state, could be returned to the light of sanity.

The use of symbols of madness was not limited to works originating outside the madhouse. In the 1850s Richard Dadd, a patricide, the most famous artist inmate of nineteenth-century Bed-

PLATE **172**. *The Mad House*, a British lithograph from the early nineteenth century

lam, portrayed the passions in a series of drawings.[3] His "Agony-Raving Madness" **[Plate 173]** introduced a new symbolic reference taken from Charles Bell (see Plate 111). Bell's work on expression had a wide audience, especially among those interested in the fine arts. Dadd adopted Bell's imagery even though it had no basis in the reformed asylum of the period, but it is not the actual patient, whom he knows intimately, that Dadd is representing. It is a symbolic equation of madness with the exaggerated expression of the passions—here, agony—that Dadd wishes to achieve. His figure sits, tearing his hair in a gesture of despair. The chains, no longer representing actual restraint, refer to the nature of madness itself which restrains the individual from returning to the world of sanity. Indeed, Dadd's image of the madman reflects the general conflation of symbols of insanity during the Romantic period. William Wordsworth writes in his poem *The Prelude* of "Bedlam, and those carved maniacs at the gates, / Perpetually recumbent" (XII, 132-133), seeing both states of madness as one, summarized, as in Dadd's figure, by their posture.

PLATE **173**. Richard Dadd,
*Agony-Raving Madness*
(c. 1850)

The early nineteenth-century interest in the expression of the insane was incorporated into the portrayal of the world of the reformed asylum. In Wilhelm von Kaulbach's 1835 *The Mad House* [Plate 174] the movement of the inmates to the outside has been accomplished,[4] but the plate relies on the expression and gesture of the inmates to characterize them. Kaulbach's illustration, in the engraving by H. März, was an immediate success throughout Europe. Indeed, as had happened with Hogarth's rendition of Bedlam, a literature concerning the image of the insane grew up based on its interpretation.

To understand Kaulbach's view of the madman, it is important to note that Kaulbach visited the aylum in Düsseldorf in 1826 when his teacher, Cornelius, was commissioned to paint a series of murals in the asylum chapel. It was not until 1835, however, that he created the work of art, now lost, upon which the famed engraving was based. The time that elapsed between the initial impression and the actual creative act gave the artist the perspective needed to reinterpret what he saw in the light of the reformed asylum and the new physiognomy of expression. When his contemporaries turned to his work they saw a verisimilitude that closely reflected their own stereotypical concept of the appearance of the insane.

In 1836 Guido Görres, a Bavarian critic and historian, published a lengthy pamphlet in which he based his analysis of the relationship between madness and art on Kaulbach's plate. Görres emphasized that this was the first time the image of the insane was presented with absolute accuracy, stressing that "these are not invented images of phantasy, but individuals who have been treated by doctors, who have described them. It would be easy to increase these examples by hundreds, for the kingdom of the mad is inexhaustible."[5] These patients formed a cross-section of the categories of the insane. Görres also stressed the rationale for the aesthetic portrayal of the imperfect as a manner of better presenting the abstraction of perfection.[6]

The aesthetics of representing the insane in art were further stressed by the neo-Hegelian Karl Rosenkranz in his mention of Kaulbach's plate.[7] In fact, Rosenkranz places Kaulbach as the only artist among the select few, including Shakespeare, Goethe, George Sand, who have successfully portrayed the concept of madness.

In 1863 the psychiatrist Johann August Schilling devoted a hundred pages of his *Psychiatric Letters on the Insane, Insanity and the Asylum* to a detailed explication of Kaulbach's plate.[8]

Not only did Schilling stress the reality implicit in Kaulbach's images, but he provided a mock case study, relying in part on Görres's comments, for each of the figures. It quickly becomes apparent that Schilling could identify each of the figures because of Kaulbach's use of the symbolic language of insanity inherent in the physiognomy of the characters. Beginning with the warder on the right, the entire population of the asylum is presented. Only the mad mother cradling her child, a swaddled log, is unfamiliar. It was the introduction of infanticide as a theme in European letters in the late eighteenth century, the "Storm and Stress" period, that made the infanticide a commonplace image of the madwoman,[9] culminating in *Faust I* with the madness of Gretchen caused by the murder of her child. Gretchen becomes the prototype for the mad mother among the dramatis personae of the madhouse.

The other characters are easily identifiable. The three figures of religious melancholy, praying with crucifix and rosary, are placed against a second triad, two women fighting over an individual in top hat. Both Görres and Schilling see in this figure the image of the critic gone mad. Most probably, however, it is the hatter, driven mad by exposure to the lead used in the manufacture of beaver-felt hats. The face of the old woman knitting stands as an example of senile dementia based on Lavater's physiognomy. The seated figures are easier to place in the symbolic mode: the mad philosopher, with his books and manuscripts; the Napoleonic warrior gone mad, seated in the classic position of melancholy with his wooden sword; the mad king, with his bifurcated sceptre; two figures seated in variations of the melancholic pose; and the raving madman, indicating through the grass he holds in his hand his relationship to the animal-like Nebuchadnezzar.

Yet Kaulbach also stresses the need for a reform of the asylum, greater than the implication of the "nonrestraint" movement, for although the inmates are unchained, they are still the prisoners of an asylum which attempts to deal with them by violent means. The madman's staff is paralleled by the billy-club peeping from the pocket of the warder. This weapon is not merely decorative, as is shown in the image within the image in this portrait, for very faintly drawn on the wall next to the warder are two stick figures. One is the inmate, with raised arms, the other, the warder, truncheon raised against the first, characterized by a key jingling from his pocket and a stocking cap upon his head. The violence present in the asylum, even in the reformed asylum, the asylum without chains, is emphasized

PLATE 174. The engraving by H. März of Wilhelm von Kaulbach's *The Mad House* (1835), the nineteenth-century counterpart of Hogarth's representation of Bedlam

by this drawing, assumed, from its childlike simplicity, to have been done by an inmate. Kaulbach underlines the potential for darkness by his use of the barred window, here viewed from the outside, with opaque bottleglass.

This engraving so dominated the representation of the asylum during the nineteenth century that as late as 1883, when Samuel Wells, the outstanding American phrenologist, needed an asylum scene, he too turned to the Kaulbach plate.

PLATE 175. Amand Gautier, *A Princess
of the Salpêtrière*, an 1855 lithograph

140

PLATE 176. Gautier's *The Madwomen of the Salpêtrière* (1855)

In 1854 Paul Gachet, a young and influential psychiatrist at the Salpêtrière, invited his artist friend Amand Gautier to sketch the inmates to capture their gesture, position, and expression. A series of works resulted from Gautier's visit.[10] One was a lithograph, *A Princess of the Salpêtrière* (1855) [Plate 175], portraying a case of megalomania. More famous is the outdoor asylum scene, *The Madwomen of the Salpêtrière* [Plate 176], completed at the same time, depicting representative cases of dementia, lunacy, mania, imbecility, and hallucination. The original Gautier painting was exhibited in the 1857 Salon in Paris but later destroyed during the Franco-Prussian war. Charles Baudelaire saw in it a major step forward in portraying the insane:

> It represents the courtyard of an asylum for female lunatics—a subject which he treated not according to the philosophic, Germanic method (that of Kaulbach for example, which makes one think of the categories of Aristotle) but with the dramatic feeling of the French, combined with a faithful and intelligent

amount of observation. The painter's friends claim that everything in the work—heads, gestures and physiognomies—was minutely exact and copied from nature. I do not agree, first because I detected symptoms to the contrary in the organization of the picture, and then because what is positively and universally exact is never admirable.[11]

Gautier's "cour des agitées," the courtyard in the asylum, is, as Baudelaire points out, an interpretation of the new asylum rather than a literal image. Gautier emphasizes, as did Kaulbach, the openness of the asylum with an indication of restraint present in the barred gate. Where Kaulbach stands mostly in the Hogarthian tradition, exhibiting a cross-section of figures from the contemporary world, Gautier abandons any attempt to present a microcosm. Rather, since he shows only female inmates, his is a one-sided view of the asylum without Kaulbach's attempt at a balance. Gautier aims at depicting case studies, using recognizable historical models of expression and position to indicate the various afflictions.

141

Paul Gachet, who enabled Gautier to sketch in the Salpêtrière, had made his own preliminary pen and chalk studies of the patients. His images [Plates 177-188], which convey the "lasciviousness" of the posture of the insane, captured little more than abstractions of their momentary, fleeting movements. Gautier translated these into the "dance" of the insane in his asylum scene, in which the figures assume differing and indicative poses. In the tradition carried forward by Esquirol, Gachet and Gautier added the posture of the insane to the study of their expression.

PLATES **177-183**. Sketches by Paul Gachet of manic and excited patients (c. 1850), reproduced from *Histoire de la médecine* (1958)

PLATES 184-187. Paul Gachet's sketches of melancholic and restrained patients (c. 1850)

PLATE 188. Gachet's portrait of a woman in a straitjacket (c. 1850)

PLATE 189. Thomas Rowlandson and Augustus Pugin, "St. Luke's" from their
*Microcosm of London* (London: T. Beasley, 1809)

The reform of the asylum also involved a revival of emphasis on rehabilitation through meaningful activity. While it is difficult to separate the "work house" concept from a more modern "work therapy" view in perceiving the activities of the insane, it is clear that images of the insane reflect purposeful, rather than useless or meaningless, activity only after the beginning of the nineteenth century. This alteration is striking in Thomas Rowlandson and Augustus Pugin's rendering of St. Luke's in 1809 **[Plate 189]**. Here the asylum is a well-illuminated, open space. In the foreground are the standard images of Bedlam, raving mania and melancholy. On the left side are other stereotypical inhabitants of the asylum, including love melancholy, presented through posture and expression. This aspect of the scene is not very different from Hogarth. However, the right half of the plate, with the inmates shown working at ironing and washing, is unique, demonstrating the new concept of constructive work in the reformed asylum.

Johann Konrad Fäsi-Gessner's images of the Zurich asylum present similar examples of activity. The meal scene **[Plate 190]** and the chapel scene **[Plate 191]** show the influence of genre paintings, as they provide a commentary on an action. Other scenes, such as that illustrating the pounding of fibers **[Plate 192]**, are more closely related to the creative and meaningful activity at St. Luke's, activity mirroring the actions of the outside world rather than caricaturing them.

PLATE 190. *Festive meal in the Oberpfründerstube at the Zurich Asylum,* an etching by Johann Konrad Fäsi-Gessner (c. 1840)

PLATE 191. Fäsi-Gessner's *Hymn hour in the Oberpfründerstube*

PLATE 192. Fäsi-Gessner's *Pounding linen fibers*

The concept of the reformed asylum permeated many of the images of the madman during the first half of the nineteenth century. On January 17, 1852, Charles Dickens published in his periodical, *Household Words*, an anonymous article entitled "A Curious Dance Round a Curious Tree," intended to make the readers appreciate their bounty during the holiday season. The essay was substantially by Dickens, as the manuscript shows, with, however, some passages by Dickens' subeditor, William Henry Will.[12] The "Curious Dance" was the Boxing Day festivity held annually at St. Luke's Hospital for the Insane (Old Street, London); the "Curious Tree," the Christmas Tree, the lighting of which ends the piece. The essay was felt to cast such a positive light on the asylum that the directors of St. Luke's reissued it as a pamphlet, with Dickens' permission, in 1860.[13]

The essay, certainly appropriate as a moral lesson on counting one's blessings, begins with a description of the reformed asylum at the close of the eighteenth century. It had replaced the proverbial Bedlam, Bethlem Hospital, where "lunatics were chained, naked, in rows of cages that flanked a promenade, and were wondered and jeered at through iron bars by London loungers." The benevolence of the new asylum was, however, "mixed, as was usual in that age, [with] a curious degree of unconscious cruelty." Dickens proceeds to quote at some length and in detail from John Haslam's *Observations on Madness and Melancholy, including Practical Remarks on Those Diseases* of 1809. Haslam, after a Parliamentary inquiry in 1815 revealed such practices at Bedlam, was dismissed from his post there. Dickens sees the forced feeding of patients who refuse to eat and the manacles shackling the violent as evidences of the older model of dealing with insanity. "These practitioners of old would seem to have been, without knowing it, early homeopathists; their motto must have been, *Similia similibus curantur*; they believed that the most violent and certain means of driving a man mad, were the only hopeful means of restoring him to reason."

The asylum that Dickens enters bears little resemblance to a "chamber of horrors." Vestiges of the old manner of treating the inmates are visible only in the alcoves where "the chairs, which patients were made to sit in for indefinite periods, were, in the good old times, nailed." This sign of the "good old times" is contrasted with "a niche [in which] . . . stood a pianoforte, with a few ragged music-leaves upon the desk. Of course, the music was turned upside down." Dickens made

these observations while walking through the asylum toward the "Curious Dance" to be held in a farther hall: "As I was looking at the marks in the walls of the Galleries, of the posts to which the patients were formerly chained, sounds of music were heard from a distance. The ball had begun, and we hurried off in the direction of the music." The polar structure of the essay can be seen in these passages. The past is the age in which torture dominated the asylum; today, the asylum is the world of civilization. Dickens has consciously chosen the image of music and the dance as his metaphor for the new asylum.

By the time Dickens reaches the gallery in which the dance is taking place, he and his readers have passed through the length of the asylum. Casting his eye about the "brown sombre place, not brilliantly illuminated by a light at either end, adorned with holly," he fastens his attention on the dancers:

There were the patients usually to be found in all such asylums, among the dancers. There was the brisk, vain, pippin-faced little old lady, in a fantastic cap—proud of her foot and ankle; there was the old-young woman, with the dishevelled long light hair, spare figure, and weird gentility; there was the vacantly-laughing girl, requiring now and then a warning finger to admonish her; there was the quiet young woman, almost well, and soon going out. For partners, there were the sturdy bull-necked thick-set little fellow who had tried to get away last week, the wry-face tailor, formerly suicidal, but much improved; the suspicious patient with a countenance of gloom, wandering round and round strangers, furtively eyeing them behind from head to foot, and not indisposed to resent their intrusion. There was the man of happy silliness, pleased with everything. But the only chain that made any clatter was Ladies' Chain, and there was no straiter waistcoat in company than the polka-garment of the old-young woman with the weird gentility, which was of a faded black satin, and languished through the dance with a love-lorn affability and condescension to the force of circumstances, in itself a faint reflection of all Bedlam.

This description by Dickens of the dance at St. Luke's is matched in two contemporary publications. In 1848, Katharine Drake produced a lithograph entitled "Lunatic's Ball" [Plate 193] which conveyed her impression of the asylum as a place where "Harmony" reigns through the social activity of the dance.[14] Likewise, an article on the "Lunatic's Ball" in *Frank Leslie's Illustrated Newspaper* for December 9, 1865, presented a similar scene [Plate 194]:

PLATE **193**. Katharine Drake, *Lunatic's Ball*, a lithograph depicting the event at the Somerset County Asylum (1848)

Not a few visitors were present to enjoy the novel spectacle of a dance, in which nearly all the participants were among the most justly commisserated of the human species.

Their delusions forgotten, many of the patients whirled about in glee, which, though wild, did not exceed the bounds of common-sense propriety; others were merely roused from their apathetic state, and gazed with a slight smile upon the scene.

Although the majority of the dancers preferred original variations from the various approved figures, quadrille parties were formed which did credit to the institution.

A break-down jig seemed, however, the favorite style of showing delight at the violin's screechings and twiddlings. Some sixty people were present.

Balls are an item that has been but lately added to the list of amusements for patients in the Blackwell's Island Asylum. Music, with magic lantern exhibitions, have hitherto been mainly employed in enlivening them, but perhaps the ball, in its power of withdrawing the

maniac from the fancies which oppress him, surpasses both.[15]

The asylum becomes the extension of society through the dance. Among the dancers were to be found not only the patients but also the staff, who no longer consisted of the sadistic torturers of the old asylum but had become an extended family. The master, Thomas Collier Walker, and his wife are described as the parents of this family. Charlotte Eliza Walker is one "whose clear head and strong heart Heaven inspired to have no Christmas wish beyond this place, but to look upon it as her home, and on its inmates as her afflicted children."

In Dickens' account, his visit to St. Luke's is climaxed by the lighting of the tree. In this moment the shades of Christmas past are once and forever exorcised from the asylum:

The moment the dance was over, away the porter ran, not in the least out of breath, to help light up the tree. Presently it stood in the centre of its room, growing out of the floor, a blaze of light and glitter; blossoming in that place (as the story goes of the American aloe) for the first time in a hundred years. O shades of Mad Doctors with laced ruffles and powdered wigs, O shades of patients who went mad in the only good old times to be mad or sane in, and who were therefore physicked, whirligigged, chained, handcuffed, beaten, cramped, and tortured, look from

> Wherever in your sightless substances,
> You wait—

on this outlandish weed in the degenerate garden of Saint Luke's!

Dickens concludes his essay with a hope for future Christmases at St. Luke's:

> To lighten the affliction of insanity by all human means, is not to restore the greatest of the Divine gifts; and those who devote themselves to the task do not pretend that it is. They find their sustainment and reward in the substitution of humanity for brutality, kindness for maltreatment, peace for raging fury; in the acquisition of love instead of hatred; and in the knowledge that, from such treatment improvement, and hope of final restoration will come, if such hope be possible. It may be little to have abolished from mad-house all that is abolished, and to have substituted all that is substituted. Nevertheless, reader, if you can do a little in any good direction—do it. It will be much, some day.

For Dickens the ultimate goal of the asylum is the "restoration" of its inmates to the community, which can be achieved only through "love."

The substitution of one model of insanity for another which Dickens experienced in his own lifetime, and which is reflected in his essay on St. Luke's, focused on the introduction of "non-restraint." Nonrestraint as a basis for the management of insanity implies the ability to reform the individual to conform with the social strictures of the society in which he or she must function. Thus Dickens deemphasizes the hopelessly insane in his essays, ignoring the more grotesque or horrifying symptoms of insanity and pointing up the comical or endearing ones. The first inmate described in any detail in the essay sits "sewing a mad sort of seam, and scolding some imaginary person." What disturbs Dickens is the absence of meaningful activity ("work"): "No domestic articles to occupy, to interest, or to entice the mind away from its malady. Utter vacuity." While he sees progress made in "the large amount of cures effected in the hospital, (upwards of sixty-nine per cent. during the past year)," he argues that if "the system of finding the inmates employment . . . were introduced into St. Luke's, the proportion of cures would be much greater."

Dickens' goal is a productive restructuring of the insane, and for that purpose the insane must be viewed as very close to sanity. According to *The Times* of July 22, 1853:

> In strictness, we are all mad when we give way to passion, to prejudice, to vice, to vanity; but if all the passionate, prejudiced, vicious and vain people in this world are to be locked up as lunatics, who is to keep the key of the asylum? As was very fairly observed, however, by a learned Baron of the Exchequer, when he was pressed by this argument, if we are all mad, being all madmen, we must do the best we can under such untoward circumstances.[16]

If the sane are in fact so closely related to the insane then our rejection of the image of insanity is indeed a repression of our own inner fear for our own stability.

PLATE **194**. "Ball of Lunatics at the Asylum, Blackwell's Island, East River, N.Y."
from *Frank Leslie's Illustrated Newspaper*, December 9, 1865

# the individual
# in the reformed asylum

The image of the madman as the passive recipient of treatment dominates the representation of psychiatric care throughout the ages. In Bernard Picart's engraving showing the treatment of the possessed at St. Médard **[Plate 195]**, published in 1735, the passivity of the patients being beaten under religious supervision is indicative of the early eighteenth-century attitude.[17] The use of beatings as a means of treatment was not atypical. William Cullen observed in the 1780s: "This

awe and dread [of the physician] is therefore, by one means or other, to be acquired; in the first place, by their being the authors of all restraints that may be occasionally proper; but sometimes it may be necessary to acquire it even by stripes and blows."[18] In Picart's plate the figure "C" lies completely prostrate while being beaten. The fact that his face is cast into the shadow, combined with his position, is indicative of his illness, melancholy. In the center of the plate, figures "B"

PLATE 195. Bernard Picart's depiction of the possessed of St. Médard (1735)

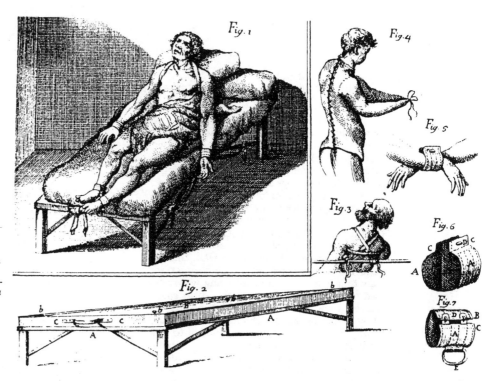

PLATE 196. The "maniac's bed" and the "English camisole" (straitjacket) from Vincenzo Chiarugi's *Della pazzia in genere* (Firenze: Luigi Carlieri, 1794)

and "D" illustrate the *arc de cercle* extreme of tension. Figure "A" is being restrained prior to the beginning of treatment. The plate is dominated by a strongly religious tone (represented by the various figures labeled "E"). The earlier religious images of treatment, such as Christ curing the insane, and medical treatments, whether real or fantastic, merge in such a presentation. The passivity of the patients assures their domination by the Christ surrogate, the priest or the doctor, and thus their cure.

The representation of the insane as inferior to those treating them has a long history and has had a long-lasting effect. Even in the psychiatric literature of the late eighteenth century, which attempted to reform the treatment of the insane, aspects of this tradition are still to be observed. Vincenzo Chiarugi's *Medical Treatise of Insanity, with one hundred observations* (1793-1794)[19] contains two plates depicting the insane. One is a study of brain structure; the other, a representation of two methods of restraint [Plate 196]. This illustration is of particular historical significance because it is the first to show the "English camisole" or straitjacket (Figure 4). Figure 1 depicts the "maniac's bed" with details of how its restraints operated.

While both of these devices were major improvements over chains, the figures created to illustrate them are, in addition, of special interest as innovations in the depiction of the insane, for they represent the passive nature of those under treatment. While some of the older vocabulary symbolizing the insane, such as the nakedness of the figure on the maniac's bed, covered with a blanket, is also present, the major difference between Picart's and Chiarugi's images is the total absence of violence in the later illustration and thus a heightened sense of passive acceptance of treatment or restraint. The restraints portrayed by Chiarugi were intended to control the most violent patients, yet the image of the insane as a wild beast is not present. In the Picart engraving the madmen are clearly out of control, thus the treatment is perceived as in keeping with this return to the animal state. By the end of the century this view was being modified to conform to the perception of the etiology of insanity as what Chiarugi called "an impairment of the physical structure of the sensorium commune."[20] The appearance of the insane is unaltered, but the image of treatment and restraint portrays the madman as an unexceptional figure, passively accepting his lot.

The image of the insane as perceived by the nineteenth-century reformers continued the direction away from that of the madman as beast exemplified in Sir Charles Bell's portrayal of the maniac (see Plate 111). One illustration, drawn from life at Bethlem, as was Bell's, was in fact a major impetus toward the reform of that institution. In May 1814, Edward Wakefield, a member of Parliament, on an inspection tour of the asylum, found William Norris, an American seaman, who had been chained in a lower gallery for over ten years:

> In one of the cells on the lower gallery we saw William Norris; he stated himself to be 55 years of age, and that he had been confined about 14 years; that in consequence of attempting to defend himself from what he conceived the improper treatment of his keeper, he was fastened by a long chain, which passing through a partition, enabled the keeper by going into the next cell, to draw him close to the wall at pleasure; that to prevent this, Norris muffled the chain with straw, so as to hinder its passing through the wall; that he afterwards was confined in the manner we saw him, namely a stout iron ring was rivetted round his neck, from which a short chain passed to a ring made to slide upwards or downwards on an upright massive iron bar, more than six feet high, inserted into the wall. Round his body a strong iron bar about two inches wide was rivetted; on each side of the bar was a circular projection, which being fashioned to and inclosing each of his arms, pinioned them close to his sides. This waist bar was secured by two similar bars which, passing over his shoulders, were rivetted to the waist bar both before and behind. The iron ring round his neck was connected to the bars on his shoulders, by a double link. From each of these bars another short chain passed to the ring on the upright iron bar. We were informed he was enabled to raise himself, so as to stand against the wall, on the pillow of his bed in the trough bed in which he lay; but it is impossible for him to advance from the wall in which the iron bar is soldered, on account of the shortness of his chains, which were only twelve inches long. It was, I conceive, equally out of his power to repose in any other position than on his back, the projections which on each side of the waist bar inclosed his arms, rendering it impossible for him to lie on his side, even if the length of the chains from his neck and shoulders would permit it. His right leg was chained to the trough; in which he had remained thus encaged and chained more than twelve years.[21]

Wakefield asked George Arnald to sketch Norris. This documentation was quickly circulated as a colored etching [Plate 197] as well as a broadside calling for reform [Plate 198]. Dickens' description of the barbarity of the older manner of treatment reflected this public exposure of Norris's condition.

Norris's case played a vital role in supporting the ideal of the reformed asylum. Whereas Bell's image provided visual evidence of the need for chains to hold the violent maniac in check, the sad, passive figure of Norris seems overwhelmed

PLATE 197. George Arnald's portrait of William Norris at Bedlam (1814)

by the mechanism that secures him to the bar next to his bed. Treated in a manner totally out of keeping with his apparent harmlessness, Norris seems the ultimate victim. Both Arnald's image of Norris in chains and Chiarugi's of the patient under more modern restraint (such as the straitjacket) draw on the same rhetoric of passivity. Here the insane are shown to be desirous only of treatment, and do not warrant their denigration as animals.

# PORTRAIT OF WILLIAM NORRIS,

SKETCHED FROM THE LIFE, BY G. ARNALD, A.R.A, ON THE SECOND OF MAY, 1814, WHEN HE WAS VISITED BY

C. C. WESTERN, Esq. M. P. Messrs. ROBERT CALVERT, JAMES BEVANS, EDWARD WAKEFIELD, FRANCIS PLACE, Sen. AND FRANCIS PLACE, Jun.

This unfortunate Man was confined about Twelve Years, in the Manner represented in this Engraving, in Bethlem Hospital. Of which Hospital Dr. MUNRO is the Physician, and Mr. JOHN HASLAM the Apothecary.

EXTRACTS relating to WILLIAM NORRIS, taken from the Minutes of Evidence before the COMMITTEE of the HON. THE HOUSE OF COMMONS ON MAD HOUSES, in 1815.

EDWARD WAKEFIELD, Esq.

" William Norris stated himself to " be 55 years of age, and that he had " been confined about 14 years. He " was confined by a stout iron ring, ri- " vetted round his neck, from which a " short chain passed to a ring, made to " slide upwards or downwards on an " upright massive iron bar, more than " six feet high, inserted into the wall. " Round his body a strong iron bar, " about two inches wide, was rivetted ; " on each side the bar was a circular " projection, which being fashioned to " and inclosing each of his arms, pi- " nioned them close to his sides. This " waist bar was secured by two similar " bars, which, passing over his shoul- " ders, were rivetted to the waist bar, " both before and behind. The iron " ring round his neck was connected " to the bars on his shoulders by a " double link. From each of these " bars another short chain passed to " the ring on the upright iron bar. We " were informed, he was enabled to " raise himself, so as to stand against " the wall, on the pillow of his bed in " the trough bed in which he lay ; but " it is impossible for him to advance " from the wall in which the iron bar " is soldered, on account of the short- " ness of his chains, which were only " TWELVE INCHES LONG. It was, " I conceive, equally out of his power " to repose in any other position than " on his back. The projections which " on each side of the waist-bar inclosed " his arms, rendering it impossible for " him to lie on his side, even if the " length of the chains from his neck " and shoulders would have permitted " it. His right leg was chained to the " trough in which he had remained, " THUS encaged and chained, MORE " THAN 12 YEARS."

WM. SMITH, Esq. M. P.

" I was informed that he had been " chained down in his wooden bed- " stead for above nine years, which did " then, and has ever since appeared to " me, as a most rigorous and unneces- " sarily cruel mode of restraint. The " cruel and constant coercion in which " he was kept, and which, when conti- " nued unremittingly for such a length " of time, I should think far better " calculated to drive away the reason " of a sane man, than to restore a " madman to his senses."

C. C. WESTERN, Esq. M. P.

" The description of the irons in " which Norris was incased is perfect- " ly correct. At the time I saw Nor- " ris, it was impossible to believe the " continuance of all his irons was in " any degree necessary, if they ever " were so."

THE HON. H. G. BENNETT, M.P.

" From what I have seen of furi- " ous maniacs in other Hospitals, and " places of confinement, I should " have no hesitation in saying, that it " was a mode of restraint unnecessary " and unwarranted. It has always ap- " peared to me, from what I have seen " of Bethlem, that the restraint was " used THERE more from feelings of " revenge, than for purposes of medical " cure."

MR. JOHN HASLAM.

The drawing from which the above Portrait has been etched, being shewn by the Committee to Mr. Haslam, he was asked—" Do you admit it as a " correct representation of the manner " in which Norris was confined?"—he replied,

" I think the apparatus is all cor- " rect."

Being asked the reason for the mul- tiplied means of restraint contrived for Norris, he answered,

" I can give no reason for the con- " trivance at all, not having contrived " it."

" Standing Rules and Orders for the GOVERNMENT of the Royal Hospitals of Bridewell and Bethlem, with the DUTY OF THE GOVERNORS, and " of the several OFFICERS AND SERVANTS.

" LONDON :—PRINTED BY H. BRYER, BRIDEWELL-HOSPITAL, BRIDGE STREET.

" GENERAL ORDERS, 8th Clause.——No Patient is to be confined in Chains without the previous Knowledge and Approbation of the Apothecary, nor released from such Confinement without his Consent.

" The Bethlem Sub-Committee is to view the House and Patients at least once a Month, and to minute down any thing of moment in a Book."

NORRIS IS DEAD.

PRINTED BY J. M'CREERY, BLACK-HORSE-COURT, FLEET-STREET, LONDON ;

AND PUBLISHED BY G. ARNALD, No. 2, WESTON STREET, PENTONVILLE.

PLATE 198. A broadside condemning the treatment of the insane at Bedlam (1815)

The image of total restraint also accompanies the treatment of one of the nineteenth century's favorite etiologies for insanity, masturbation. The hypothesis that masturbation was a cause, if not the prime cause, of insanity was first promulgated in the anonymous English moral tractate *Onania; or, The Heinous Sin of Self-Pollution.*[22] But not until the publication in 1758 of Samuel Auguste André David Tissot's *Onanism or the Illnesses Produced by Masturbation* (translated into German in 1785) did the idea of masturbatory insanity become commonplace in the lay as well as the medical community. By 1784 Germany's most respected educator, Christian Gotthilf Salzman, had published for the broadest possible audience his essay *On the Secret Sins of Youth*, which appeared in a fourth edition in 1819.[23]

According to the eighteenth-century view, masturbation dissipated the vital essence of the natural spirit and therefore led to insanity. Benjamin Rush reports the following case study in 1812: "A. B. aged seventeen, of a cold pflegmatic temperament of body, of a sedentary life, and studious habits, in consequence of indulging in the solitary vice of onanism, has lately become very much diseased. His vision is indistinct, and his memory much impaired, and he now labours under much muscular relaxation, prostration of strength, atrophy, and depression of spirits."[24] This "weakness of the whole body" is described by G. W. Becker in *On the Prevention and Cure of Masturbation with its Results in Both Sexes* of 1803.[25] Indeed the very mode of treatment of the patient leads the reader to understand the nature of his illness. Totally catatonic, sewn into restraints which fix his hands behind his back to prevent further masturbation, he sits in a " tranquillizer," a chair which, among other things "relieves him, by means of a close stool, half filled with water, over which he constantly sits, from the foetor and filth of his alvine evacuations." The restrained masturbator also appears in D. M. Rozier's *Secret Habits or the Illnesses Produced by Onanism in Women* (1825)[26] **[Plates 199 and 200]**.

The practice of restraint reaches its apogee in Benjamin Rush's "tranquillizer" of 1811[27] **[Plate 201]**. Here the patient vanishes into the apparatus. He is faceless, his every movement blocked. But the madman in the restraining chair is only one of the representations of treatment in the early nineteenth century.[28] The plethora of devices for treatment depicted in the various handbooks all present the patient as passive. Most of these methods continued or revived older shock treatments for insanity. Ernst Horn, in his self-

PLATE **199**. The image of the masturbator from D. M. Rozier's *Des Habitudes secrètes* (Paris: Audin, 1830)

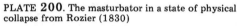

PLATE **200**. The masturbator in a state of physical collapse from Rozier (1830)

PLATE 201. Benjamin Rush's "Tranquillizer" from the *Philadelphia Medical Museum* (1811)

justificatory account of his directorship of the Charité in Berlin, included illustrations of treatment by steam and shower baths[29] **[Plate 202]**. These approaches, many originating in the seventeenth century, reappear in later versions such as William Saunders Hallaran's "circulating swing" **[Plate 203]**, from his *Practical Observations on Insanity* (1818), and Peter Joseph Schneider's textbook of 1824.[30] Horn, Hallaran, Schneider, and Joseph Guislain,[31] the reformer of the asylum at Ghent, presented active modes of treatment through the image of the passive patient. Guislain's shock and water treatments **[Plates 204 and 205]** seem to have been used only on totally willing, unresisting patients, grateful for treatment. In the images of the reformed asylum the idea of aggressive, violent, or obscene behavior is missing. Indeed a comparison of the straitjacket illustration in Horn's work **[Plate 206]**, or that of Guislain **[Plate 207]**, with those in Esquirol's atlas (see Plate 94) makes clear the new attitude which saw only the curable aspect of the insane.

PLATE 202. "Water Treatment" from Ernst Horn, *Oeffentliche Rechenschaft über meine zwölfjährige Dienstführung* (Berlin: Realschulbuchhandlung, 1818)

PLATE 203. Hallaran's "Circulating Swing" from Peter J. Schneider's *Entwurf zu einer Heilmittellehre gegen psychische Krankheiten* (Tübingen: Heinrich Laupp, 1824)

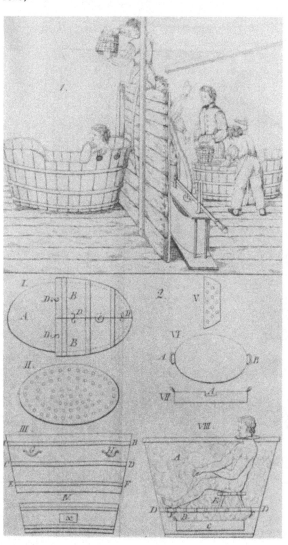

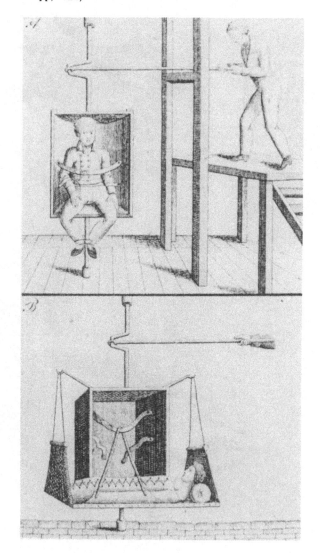

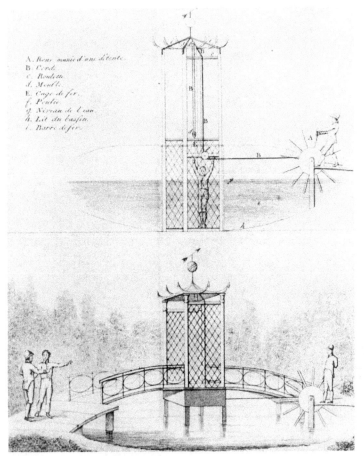

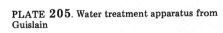

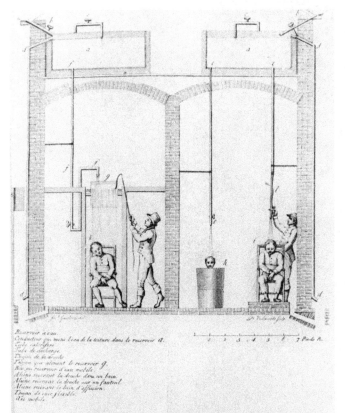

PLATE **204**. One form of water treatment from
Joseph Guislain's *Traité sur l'Aliénation mentale*
(Amsterdam: J. van der Hey et fils, 1826)

PLATE **205**. Water treatment apparatus from
Guislain

PLATE **206**. Standing restraint first depicted by
Horn in 1818, as reproduced in Schneider's work
of 1824

PLATE **207**. Restraints used in conjunction with
a circulating swing, from Guislain (1826)

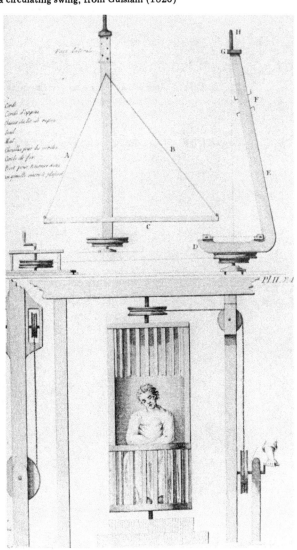

159

PLATE 208. Pulling a heavy wagon as exercise in the asylum, from Horn (1818)

PLATE 209. Military drill in the asylum courtyard, from Horn

The idea of the potential restoration of sanity is embodied in two of the most striking plates in Horn's study. The return of sanity means a return to the world outside of the asylum; and one manner of achieving this return is through physical activity mirroring the outside world. Horn depicts a group of inmates exercising by pulling a heavy wagon [Plate 208]. This mode of activity harks back to the idea of the madman as beast, but on a somewhat more esoteric plane. The second illustration [Plate 209] is equally revealing. On the asylum's parade ground, with its covered area and swing, a group of female inmates is drilling with large and cumbersome wooden guns. This most Prussian of activities in the Berlin asylum seems a parody of the world outside the institution. The meaninglessness of the activities suggested for treatment becomes apparent. It is only activity for its own sake.

In all the images of treatment and restraint in the reformed asylum the visual impression of the passive patient is dominant. In no case is the patient either through appearance or gesture typified as mad. Indeed the overwhelming normalcy of the individuals depicted in these plates is striking. As long as the focus is on the mode of treatment this remains the case. Once consideration is given to the etiology of the illness, as in the case of masturbatory insanity, the pathognomic and physiognomic signs of illness reappear, even in the depiction of treatment or restraint. Thus, hidden within the reformed perspective of the new asylum lurked parallel traditions of seeing the insane.

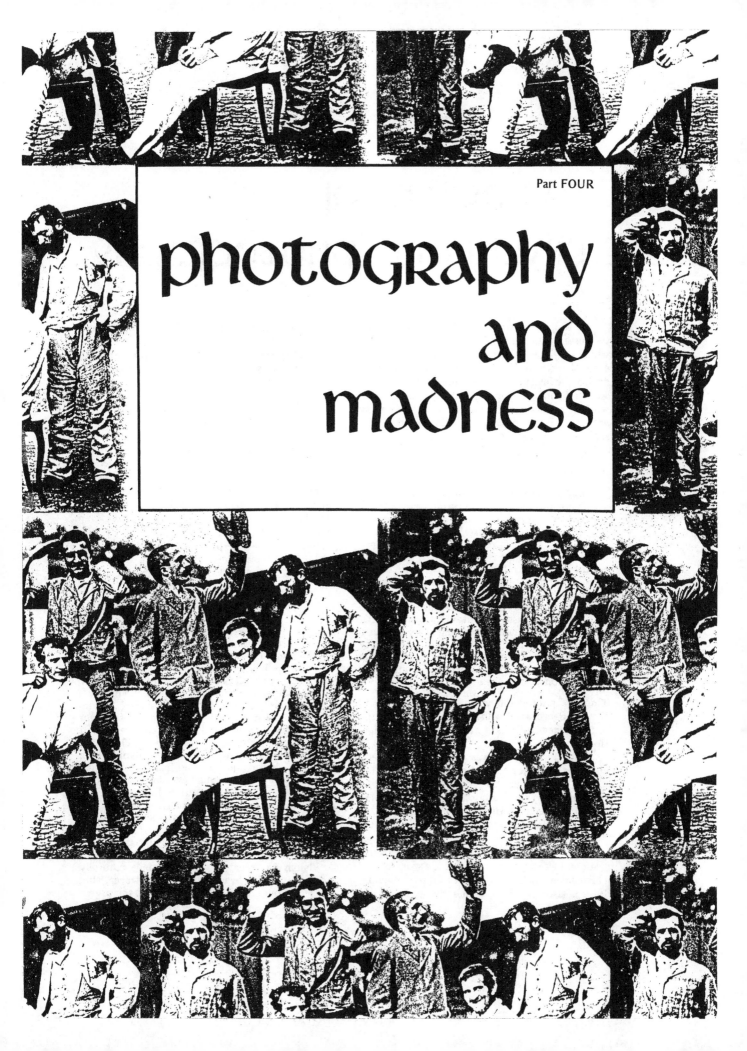

Part FOUR

# photography and madness

# the ORIGINS of
# psychiatric photography

In 1839 the introduction of photography into Western Europe radically changed the way in which the insane were seen. The photograph became the key to the new scientific physiognomy during the latter half of the nineteenth century.[1] Arthur Schopenhauer, for example, opened his work on physiognomy published at mid-century with a discussion of the illustrations used for the study of this subject:

> That the outer man is a graphic reproduction of the inner and the face the expression and revelation of his whole nature, is an assumption whose *a priori* nature and hence certainty are shown by the universal desire, plainly evident on every occasion, to *see* a man who has distinguished himself in something good or bad, or has produced an extraordinary work; or, failing this, at least to learn from others *what he looks like*. Therefore, on the one hand, people rush to the places where they think he is; on the other, newspapers, especially the English, endeavour to give minute and striking descriptions of him. Thereafter, painters and engravers give us a graphic representation of him and finally Daguerre's invention, so highly valued on that account, affords the most complete satisfaction of that need.[2]

Thus the photograph was perceived, at least in the first decades following its introduction, as the ultimate means of creating an objective reproduction of reality.

The new medium was used almost immediately for recording scientific data. It was not until the early 1850s, however, that photography was applied to the study of the insane. On May 22, 1856, Hugh W. Diamond presented his findings to Britain's Royal Society in a paper entitled "On the Application of Photography to the Physiognomic and Mental Phenomena of Insanity."[3] Diamond was superintendent of the women's department of the Surrey County Lunatic Asylum. He was also one of the most active exponents of

the new technique and a founding member and early officer of the Royal Photographic Society. His paper was the first attempt to present a systematic discussion of depicting the insane in this new medium.

Diamond argued that the photograph could have three important functions for the psychiatrist and his patient. First, it could record "with unerring accuracy the external phenomena of each passion, as the really certain indication of internal derangement, and [it] exhibits to the eye the well known sympathy which exists between the diseased brain, the organs and features of the body." This exact parallel between mind and body, between the appearance of the insane and his mental state, is a continuation by Diamond of Lavater's physiognomy. Second, the photograph could serve to facilitate treatment, especially in the light of its uniqueness and relative rarity:

> There is another point of view in which the value of portraits of the Insane is peculiarly marked. — viz. in the effect which they produce upon the patients themselves — I have had many opportunities of witnessing this effect — In very many cases they are examined with much pleasure and interest, but more particularly in those which mark the progress and cure of a severe attack of Mental Aberration — I may particularly refer to the four portraits which represent different phases of the case of the same young person [Plate 210] commencing with that stage of Mania which is marked by the bristled hair, the wrinkled brow, the fixed unquiet eye, and the lips apart as if from painful respiration, but passing, not to a state in which no man could tame her, but happily through less excited stages to the *perfect* cure — In the third portrait the expression is tranquil and accompanied with the smile of sadness instead of the hideous laugh of frenzy — The Hair falls naturally and the forehead alone retains traces, tho' slight ones, of mental agitation. In the fourth

PLATE 210. A lithograph based on Hugh W. Diamond's photographs of the four stages of a case of puerperal mania (c. 1856)

there is a perfect calm — the poor maniac is cured. This patient could scarcely believe that her last portrait representing her as clothed and in her right mind, would even have been preceded by anything so fearful; and she will never cease, with these faithful monitors in her hand, to express the most lively feelings of gratitude for a recovery so marked and unexpected . . .

Third, besides recording the appearance of the insane for study and treatment, the photograph of the patient could serve to facilitate identification for readmission as "the portraits of the insane. . . give to the eye so clear a representation of their case that on their re-admission after temporary absence and cure, I have found the previous portrait of more value in calling to mind the case and treatment, than any verbal description I may have placed on record." Diamond's stress throughout the paper is on the new objectivity made possible by photography and he ends on this note:

> In conclusion I may observe that Photography gives permanence to these remarkable cases, which are types of classes, and makes them observable not only now but for ever, and it presents also a perfect and faithful record, free altogether from the painful caricaturing which so disfigures almost all the published portraits of the Insane as to render them nearly valueless either for purposes of art or of science.

For Diamond the advantages of the new medium outweighed the difficulties. One of the substantial technological problems he faced was the long exposure time necessary in the wet collodion process. While Diamond cites Esquirol in his paper and uses Esquirol's images as one of the visual models for his photographs of the insane, there are no representations in his work of violent behavior parallel to those in Esquirol's atlas (see Plates 91-101). Diamond's photographs are in fact much more closely related in their studied formality to the photographic portraits made by his friend Lewis Carroll.[4]

In spite of the technical difficulties of photography, its use in asylums became widespread. Both Henry Hering at Bethlem Asylum and T. N. Brushfield at the Chester County Lunatic Asylum photographed the inmates of their institutions. As Brushfield commented:

> I have not had an opportunity of reading or knowing the contents of Dr. Diamond's paper on photography as applied in the treatment, &c. of lunacy, beyond the ordinary newspaper article; but I have found, notwithstanding my imperfect attempts, that patients are very much gratified at seeing their own portraits, and more particularly when associated with a number of others on a large sheet of Bristol board, framed, and hung up as an ordinary picture in the ward. In our worst female ward I have had a positive (on glass) framed and hung up for nearly eighteen months, and it has never yet been touched by any of the patients, although nearly all know whom it represents. Last week a patient, who was formerly one of our most violent cases, begged for a portrait of herself, that she might send to her son, who was in Ireland, to show how much better she was.
>
> In the case of *criminal* lunatics, it is frequently of great importance that a portrait should be obtained, as many of them being

originally of criminal disposition and education, if they do escape from the asylum are doubly dangerous to the community at large, and they may frequently be traced by sending their photographs to the police authorities (into whose hands they are very likely to fall), from some act of depredation they are likely to commit; the photographs would thus cause them to be identified, and secure their safe return to the asylum.[5]

The use of the photograph for recording the appearance of the insane raised questions about the access of the photographer to patients. While artists were permitted to sketch in the asylum during the eighteenth and early nineteenth centuries, with the reform of the asylum the patient was no longer seen as the legitimate object of curiosity seekers; rather, new emphasis was placed on the patient's privacy. Esquirol cites only one patient who was specifically asked whether she was willing to have her portrait drawn. Her consent sprang, however, from her dementia, as she believed herself possessed and wanted her portrait presented to the Archbishop for his blessing. Of a photograph taken by Sir William Charles Hood at Bethlem during the early 1850s [**Plate 211**], there is a more detailed description of the patient's reaction:

> After being several weeks at Bethlem it became practicable to take her portrait; and she was very willing to have it done. In fact, the taking of portraits has become one of the pleasures of which the patients cheerfully partake in our lunatic asylums; and helps, in combination with the various other alleviations studied by humane superintendents, to diversify and cheer the days passed in necessary seclusion from the busier, but scarcely happier world, without. One incidental effect of these artistical amusements is to draw the attention of the patients themselves to their own costume, and sometimes also to their general appearance, as to face and figure; and this direction of their notice may lead to salutary results. In the case in question, the patient made some objection to her own dress, which she evidently thought not very becoming; and she at length made it a condition of her sitting quiet that she should be represented with a book in her hand. The book, indeed, was held upside down; but it did quite as well. Her sense of propriety was gratified, and her face shows that she required no printed page to suggest thoughts to her yet busy mind.[6]

Diamond's innovation served as the basis for a series of essays titled "The Physiognomy of Insanity" (1858) by John Conolly, one of the ma-

PLATE 211. A lithograph based on Sir William Charles Hood's photograph of a case of "religious mania" from Bethlem Hospital (c. 1858)

jor reformers of the British asylum.[7] Diamond had claimed that the student of physiognomy could use the fixed aspect of the photograph as an accurate substitute for the presence of the patient. Conolly undertook precisely such a task. He saw in the photograph the ultimate means of presenting a clinical description and for distinguishing between "the ordinary expression of the passions and emotions" and "its exaggeration in those whose reason is beginning to remit its control, and whose wits are just beginning to wander away from the truthful recognition of things." The goal was to determine the fine line between the normal and the abnormal so that a more effective restoration to normality could be achieved.

For example, he made these comments on a photograph of a patient suffering from senile dementia [Plate 212]:

In this Illustration we fancy that we see represented an individual on whom the oblivion of years has crept gently: one who has gone on day after day, for a great part of his life, with occupations demanding talent and accuracy, but of which he was perfectly master. By slow degrees he grew incapable of continuous attention to minutiae, now and then became puzzled, now and then forgetful, and dreamy and drowsy; wondering, meanwhile, what soporific influence was overshadowing him, and comparing himself to a man in a kind of mesmerised sleep. The figure represents a venerable ruin. In the finely-developed head we seem to read an equally well-balanced mind; without extravagance, without extremes. The eye is large and meditative, the nose well pronounced, the lower jaw indicative of steadiness and strength. In the upper lip there is, perhaps, a want of compression, belonging to the approaching dementia. . . . To find the sight less acute, and the ear blunted and treacherous, and the limbs heavy, and the voice tremulous; and, worse than all, the glorious faculties of the mind gathering some strange dimness, the reflection faulty, and the imagination fickle and flighty, is to be

sensible to the approaches of death; and actually to feel how gradually and yet how surely "this sensible warm motion" is becoming "a kneaded clod."

Although Conolly's comments were aided by a detailed knowledge of the patients' case records, he claimed to focus on the impressions made by the photographs:

There is so singular a fidelity in a well-executed photograph that the impression of very recent muscular agitation in the face seems to be caught by the process, which the engraver's art can scarcely preserve. This peculiarity seems to produce part of the discontent often expressed when people see the photographic portraits of their friends or of themselves. It gives, however, peculiar value when, as in the portraits of the insane, the object is to give the singular expression arising from morbid movements of the mind; and thus, instead of giving pictures which are merely looked at with idle curiosity, furnishes such as may be studied with advantage; helping the observation of the Medical student, illustrating the lectures of a teacher, and suggesting some not unproductive reflections to all who examine them.

The difficulty with Conolly's and Diamond's analyses is not merely their assumption of the

PLATE 212. Hugh W. Diamond's photograph of a case of senile dementia (c. 1856)

PLATE 213. A lithograph made from the photograph at the left (1858)

objectivity of the photograph but the additional problem, in this transitional phase of psychiatric photography, inherent in the reproduction of the illustrations by the printing techniques then available. For example, when the photograph of the case of senile dementia (see Plate 212) was redone as a lithograph to accompany Conolly's essay [Plate 213], the process involved transformations viewed unfavorably even by their contemporaries:

> The late Dr. Conolly, the highest authority on this subject, not only studied attentively numbers of photographs of different forms of insanity brought under his notice, but actually wrote a valuable series of papers in which the varieties of insanity were described by reference to photographs. These were taken by Dr. Diamond from cases then under his care, and are comprised in the collection now laid on the table for your inspection. I have also placed a work containing a lithograph of one of these cases. It is entirely destitute of all those minute points of expression which alone could give any value to such an illustration. But it was the best thing of its kind; and comparison of it with the photograph by Dr. Diamond of the same case will indicate, better than words can tell, the great intrinsic value of photography in thus reproducing minute characteristics of expression.[8]

The differences between photograph and reproduction can also be seen, although in another context, in the illustration for Conolly's case of "chronic mania" [Plate 214]:

> Comical as this picture of an old woman appears at the first view, it tells a somewhat lamentable tale of long mental vexation. . . . The apparently careless air, the reversed bonnet, and a sort of drollery lurking in the cheeks and chin, are largely mixed with traces both of former agitation and excitement, and also with some shadows of lost hope and joy.

Some twenty years later, in 1874, Diamond's portrait reappeared in J. Thompson Dickson's *The Science and Practice of Medicine in Relation to Mind*,[9] in which a number of Diamond's photographs were reproduced by the new process of photolithography. Dickson used these, however, to illustrate only the anomalies of the external aspect of the insane. Thus "chronic mania" became merely an example of the "incongruity of dress" [Plate 215].

Although such impressionistic reproductions caused consternation among the advocates of psychiatric photography, Diamond's work had international ramifications. In the first general

PLATE 214. A lithograph of "chronic mania" based on a photograph by Diamond (1858)

PLATE 215. A photolithograph from the original of Diamond's portrait at the left (1874)

169

PLATE **216**. One of Hugh W. Diamond's photographs from the Surrey Asylum (c. 1856), depicting a case of "religious melancholy"

history of photography, written in 1856, Ernst Lacan, a leading member of the Parisian Photographic Society, commented:

I have before me a collection of fourteen portraits of women of various ages. Some are smiling, others seem to be dreaming [Plate 216]. All have something strange in their physiognomy: that is what one sees at first glance. If one ponders them for a longer period of time, one grows sad against one's will. All these faces have an unusual expression which causes pain in the observer. A single word of explanation suffices these are portraits of the insane. These photographs are part of the masterly work of Dr. Diamond, who practices at the Surrey County Asylum near London. In the interest of his art, and to serve the study of mental diseases, Dr. Diamond, one of the most skillful amateur photographers, has had the courage to reproduce the features of the unfortunate women placed under his care. It is with a painful interest that one follows in these portraits, taken at various times, the stages of the disease. . . .

If Dr. Diamond's example is followed, as we hope it will be, how many such valuable collections can be formed, how many scientific treasures will be added to those already in our museums and medical schools.[10]

Lacan proselytized Diamond's views throughout France, where photographs of the inmates of the Parisian asylum had already been made. In 1857, B. A. Morel incorporated lithographic reproductions of photographs in the atlas to his classic treatise on degeneration.[11] The tenth illustration is a lithograph of two cretins based on a photograph taken by Baillarger at the Salpêtrière [Plate 217]. Morel provided these images to substantiate his opinion that the insane formed a category representing "the invariable, distinct and immutable characteristics which distinguish the natural race from its degenerate variants." The insane are visually set apart from the totality of humanity as a subspecies marked by their appearance. Morel chose a form of idiocy caused by physiological variables as his iconographic sign of the physiognomy of insanity. Goiter had long served this function. Morel thus joins this tradition in his search for visual documentation of the degenerate appearance of the insane.

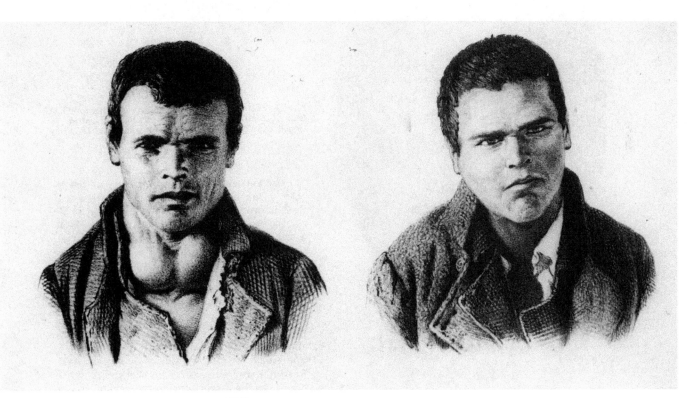

PLATE 217. Two cretins, based on a photograph taken by Baillarger, from B. A. Morel's *Atlas* of 1857

PLATE 219. "Eva H.," a case of "melancholia attonita" from Dietrich Georg Kieser, *Elemente der Psychiatrik* (Breslau and Bonn: Kaiserliche L.-C. Akademie, 1855)

PLATE 218. "Beckie and Bessie" from Isaac Kerlin's *The Mind Unveiled* (Philadelphia: U. Hunt and Son, 1858)

The appearance and physiognomy of the insane as mirrored in the early photographs and their interpretations were not the only rationale for the use of the new medium. In 1858, Isaac Kerlin of the Philadelphia Asylum provided a series of tipped-in photographs for his volume *The Mind Unveiled*.[12] It was the purpose of the book to raise funds for the asylum, and these novel illustrations conveyed a sense of the immediacy of the inmates. However, Kerlin's photographs stress the normalcy of the subjects' appearance [Plate 218]. None of the more evident forms of idiocy generally associated with institutionalization (such as Down's syndrome) are portrayed. Rather, Kerlin emphasizes his charges' ability to return to the world outside the asylum, to be normal as well as to appear normal.

PLATE 220. "Christoph S.," a case of "religious melancholia" from Kieser

PLATE 221. "Friedrich S., a case of "melancholia attonita" from Kieser

While Kerlin aimed at the public's sympathy for the mentally ill, medical handbooks on psychiatry, following the lead of Pinel and Esquirol, were incorporating mini-atlases of photographs as teaching aids. The paucity of institutions at which the insane could be studied as part of a regular medical education led to the use of psychopathic physiognomies in textbooks. The first textbook illustrated with photographs, reproduced as lithographs, was Dietrich Georg Kieser's *Elements of Psychiatry* in 1855.[13] Kieser, who had been instrumental in founding the Jena Asylum in 1816, used a number of photographs taken there during 1854-1855 by Carl Schenk

and Dr. J. Schnauss [Plates 219-221]. Like Esquirol and Ideler, Kieser supplied detailed case studies, including micro-anatomical reproductions of brain specimens. As he observed in his introduction, "The photographic portraits are complementary to the living physiognomy, showing what the case study reveals in words." Kieser therefore did not discuss the implications of the patients' appearance, as this was assumed to be completely explicable from the illustrations.

The idea of the photograph as mute witness was echoed in 1865 by Max Leidesdorf, who appended to his *Textbook on Psychiatric Illness*[14] five engravings based on photographs but accompanied them with only the most skeletal information about the patients depicted. These photographs were taken at the asylum at Hall and, according to the author, presented "the major psychopathologies, from melancholia to idiocy" [Plates 222-226]. What is striking about Kieser's and Leidesdorf's illustrations are the poses chosen for inclusion in these volumes. In many cases they reflect the older iconographic tradition of portraying the insane, including the image of the hidden hands.

PLATE 223. "Mania," from Leidesdorf

PLATE 222. "Melancholia with fearful delusions" from Max Leidesdorf, *Lehrbuch der psychischen Krankheiten* (Erlangen: Ferdinand Enke, 1865)

PLATE 224. "Madness with epilepsy," from Leidesdorf

PLATE 225. "Insanity," from Leidesdorf

PLATE 226. "Apathetic idiocy," from Leidesdorf

175

PLATE 227. The frontispiece to the third American edition of John Charles Bucknill and Daniel Hack Tuke, *A Manual of Psychological Medicine* (Philadelphia: Lindsay and Blakiston, 1874). The lithographs, made from photographs taken in the Devon County Lunatic Asylum, depict (clockwise from top): Acute Mania; Acute Suicidal Melancholia; Secondary Dementia; Congenital Imbecility; Primary Dementia; General Paralysis; and (center) Monomania of Pride

Unlike the use of photographs of the insane in Germany in the 1850s and 1860s, the British tradition, in the footsteps of Diamond and Conolly, emphasized the need to provide guidelines for interpreting the images. This accounts for the discussion of physiognomy in the most influential textbook of the mid-nineteenth century, *A Manual of Psychological Medicine*, published in 1858 by John Charles Bucknill and Daniel Hack Tuke. Bucknill and Tuke see the physiognomy of the insane, typified by the subjects in their frontispiece [**Plate 227**], as consisting of three distinct aspects.[15] The first, the intellectu-

al sphere, is indicated by "a certain fixedness of the features." Here they assume a direct correlation between fixed features and the patient's mental and intellectual state. For example, "an ample brow, a clear and steadfast eye, a firm and well-proportioned mouth" are signs of "a high degree of intelligence." In the second, they divide "the emotional expression of the physiognomy" into "expansive" and "contracted" states. Finally, "the expressional impress of strong animal propensities often profoundly degrade and brutalize the human face." Here the bestial undercurrent that can surface in insanity is again seen. Bucknill and Tuke consider the outward expression of the insane, such as the play of the lines of the forehead, meaningful and purposeful for diagnosis:

> The physician who is a good physiognomist (and no physician can practise his art satisfactorily and successfully unless he is so), when introduced to a patient suspected to be insane, must diligently study the features in conformity with the above principles. He will very frequently find his opinion strongly biassed by the impression which the looks of the patient make upon his experienced judgment; and upon this ground alone he will, in numerous instances, be able to pronounce with accuracy, not only that the patient is insane, but the general form of the insanity under which he labors; at least this will be the case in numerous instances of incipient mania, in dementia, and paralysis. The cases in which the looks of the patient will often defy the scrutiny of the physician are those of monomania or partial insanity, and of melancholia. In cases of partial insanity, where the delusion or delusions are not of a kind strongly to implicate the feelings, the mental disease frequently leaves no trace whatever on the physiognomy, and the looks of the patient are exactly those of a sane man. In the earlier and middle stages of melancholia, also, the physiognomical expression of sadness is not be be distinguished from that of natural and healthy grief. The extreme anxiety and wistfulness of acute melancholia, and the dark shadows of the severer forms of chronic melancholia, are, however, not be be mistaken. With the above-named exceptions, the physician will derive invaluable aid from the physiognomical study of his patient. The information thus derived he must immediately turn to account, in the conduct of his interrogation and conversation.

Thus the appearance of the insane, down to the "darkness" inherent in melancholy, is taken as clinical verification of diagnosis.

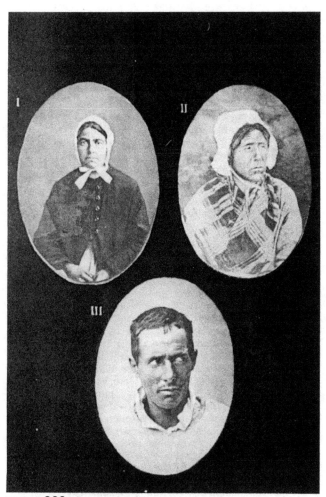

PLATE 228. Three studies of "impulsive insanity" from Henri Dagonet, *Nouveau traité élémentaire et pratique des maladies mentales* (Paris: J.-B. Baillière, 1876)

PLATE 229. Three cases of "mania" from Dagonet

The photographs in the Bucknill and Tuke frontispiece were printed lithographically. It was not until 1876 that the first textbook appeared which made extensive use of the newer photogravure process to reproduce photographs directly. Henri Dagonet's *New Elemental and Practical Treatise on Mental Illness* included eight plates of photographs taken in the Strassburg asylum by Drs. Hildenbrand, Cayre, and Bonnet [Plates 228-230]. These were accompanied by only the most impressionistic comments, such as "quiet, chronic mania, with extravagant acts" [III, Plate 229]. For the 1894 edition, Dagonet's brief remarks were expanded to much lengthier descriptions of the pathognomy of insanity:

The physiognomy of the manic patient reveals, at first glance, the disturbed order of his thoughts, the lack of association of his ideas and the excitement of his emotions. To a certain degree they reflect the various stages and specific forms of the illness. The face is of a lively color, often however of a noticeable paleness. Often the facial characteristics are distorted. The hair is disordered; the clothing torn, dirty, the gestures like the

PLATE 230. Three studies of "megalomania" from Dagonet

language indicate a type of shamelessness and brutality that betrays the destructive tendencies and negative drives which dominate the patient. The glance of the maniac is characteristic: while excessively mobile it is vague, unsure, often fresh; it does not focus on anything, does not pause.[16]

Moving from Diamond's initial experiments with photographing the insane to the clinical use of photographs for analysis of the physiognomy of insanity, we can sense the objectivity implied by the new medium. This revitalization of Lavater's physiognomy, to which positive reference is made by Conolly as well as Bucknill and Tuke, was forecast in 1861:

It is equally true that with such portraits and engravings of portraits as we have had, it has been utterly impossible to get beyond the nebulous science of a Lavater. We required the photograph. Certainly it looks a hard thing to say that the great portrait-painters are not to be trusted. Is it to be supposed that these masters did not know their business, and have failed to give us correct likenesses of the persons who sat to them? It must be remembered that to give a general likeness is one of the easiest strokes of art. With half-a-dozen lines the image is complete, as anyone may see in the million wood-engravings of the day; while at the same time it would be difficult to gather from these rough sketches, where two dots go for the eyes and a scratch for the mouth, what is the precise anatomy of any one feature. So while we can accept as in the main truthful the portraits that have come down to us, it is impossible to place perfect reliance on any particular lineament.[17]

Here the beginning of a new "science" of the physiognomy of insanity through the introduction of "objective" photography was postulated. The positivism inherent in such a view paved the way for the first major scholarly attempt to provide a psychology of expression which rested to no little extent on the psychiatric photograph.

# CHAPTER 15

# Darwin's Influence on Seeing the Insane

A year after publication of *The Descent of Man*, Charles Darwin presented his seminal study of *The Expression of the Emotions in Man and Animals* (1872). In this work, richly illustrated with photographs, Darwin attempts to reinforce his theory of the development of the species by demonstrating a continuum in the modes of expression of emotion throughout the animal kingdom.[18]

In documenting his sources for the evidence used to support his view, Darwin notes that "in the first place" he recorded the development of emotions in infants, including his own children. "In the second place, it occurred to me that the insane ought to be studied, as they are liable to the strongest passions, and give uncontrolled vent to them."[19] This study by Darwin of the expression of the mentally ill reveals itself only upon a careful reading of the text, for although he had collected and examined hundreds of photographs of insane subjects, only one of these appears in the book (see Plate 240). Nevertheless, his interest in the mentally ill and his reliance on photographs of their expressions in his researches marked a turning point in the attitude toward the nature of empirical evidence for behavioral studies. This is related to technological developments in both neurology and photography and their effect on the nineteenth-century understanding of visual documentation.

For his observations on the insane, Darwin relied primarily on Sir James Crichton Browne, "an excellent observer" who, in the course of their unpublished correspondence, "has with unwearied kindness sent me copious notes and descriptions."[20] Browne was one of the most distinguished psychiatrists of the late nineteenth century.[21] Not only Darwin but other behaviorists such as Henry Maudsley consulted him concerning the most modern research in neurology and psychiatry. Trained in Edinburgh, Browne became medical director of the West Riding Asy-

lum at Wakefield in 1866. He founded the first pathological department in a British asylum, as well as a house journal, the *West Riding Lunatic Asylum Medical Reports*. These annual volumes, the first of their kind in Great Britain, combined psychiatric and neurological case studies with theoretical essays.

Browne, like Diamond, was also an amateur photographer of considerable talent. In his journal he accompanied the case studies with striking photographs of his patients which, in his estimation, provided an objective portrayal of the signs and symptoms of specific classes of illness. Darwin approached Browne to obtain photographs of the insane as well as for help in understanding the nature of their mode of expression, and the two became involved in an ongoing debate as to the relationship between the means of perceiving the insane and the validity of interpreting what was seen.

It was generally assumed at that time that definable categories of expression, if not of physiognomy, existed for the various types of mental illness. Using models such as cretinism and paresis, nineteenth-century psychiatrists considered themselves able to recognize these categories and use them for diagnostic purposes. Contemporary research into localization of brain function gave promise that alterations in expression would be concomitant to specific brain diseases,[22] which were in turn perceived as the ultimate etiologies for all mental illness. Browne served as Darwin's expert on the most recent findings in this area.

Darwin's interest in the physiognomy of insanity, heightened by Browne's many lengthy and detailed communications, spurred his search for photographic evidence. In 1869, when Browne sent him a "packet of photographs . . . out of my album" [Plates 231-238], Darwin wrote him that "sometime ago I went into several shops in London to try to buy photographs of the insane, but failed; so you may believe with how much

PLATES **231** and **232**. Two cases of "Euphoria Mania" photographed by Sir James Crichton Browne

interest I have carefully looked at your excellent ones." A year later, Darwin again wrote Browne of his wish to observe, if only indirectly, examples of cases he hoped to study: "I have been trying to get a London photographer to make one of a young baby screaming or crying badly; but I fear he will not succeed. I much want a woodcut of a baby in this state. I presume it will be hopeless, from constant movement, to get an insane person photographed, whilst crying bitterly." Darwin understood the difficulty of his request. He needed to capture a fleeting emotion at one point during its expression so that the totality of the emotion could be extrapolated from that instant. This was beyond the technical capability of photography in the early 1870s.

A few years earlier, Duchenne de Boulogne had published a volume of photographs illustrating the effect of electrical stimulation on the facial muscles.[23] Duchenne's results are themselves quite problematic, for he posed an actor miming various expressions and then used electric stimulation to recreate them. While Duchenne was in most cases able to document what muscles or group of muscles caused each expression, there was no attempt to verify their universality. Rather, the theatrical grimaces of the French actor were taken to be an accurate reflection of the scale of all human expression.

Darwin sent Browne a copy of the Duchenne volume, requesting his opinion and noting that: "In order to test Duchenne's plates I have shown the most characteristic (hiding any indication of what they were meant to express) to between 20 and 30 persons of all kinds, and have recorded their answers: when nearly all agree in their answer, I trust him." By requesting numerous interpretations, Darwin was able to see whether a consensus of opinion could be found as to the emotion expressed. Darwin ignored the evident

PLATES 233 and 234. Two cases of "Melancholia" photographed by Browne

ethnocentricity of such interpretations as well as the difficulty of interpreting passing emotions based on static representations. Browne's lengthy but highly impressionistic comments proved to be "exactly the things which I am anxious to hear."

After all these investigations, Darwin finally reported to Browne his successful discovery of a source for useable photographs to illustrate his book. "I have received the photographs and am greatly obliged for all your never-ceasing kindness. They are not expressive enough for my purpose. I am, however, now rich in photographs for I have found a photographer in London, Rejlander, who for years has had a passion for photographing all sorts of chance expressions exhibited on various occasions, especially by children, and taken instantaneously."

Darwin's "discovery" of Oscar Rejlander, perhaps London's most popular photographer, added a new dimension to his study. In his book

he reproduced twenty-eight of Rejlander's photographs. But these were not in fact "instantaneous." Because of technical limitations, Rejlander posed his subjects and directed them to react on cue. His photographs were conscious works of art, not unlike the carefully posed "assemblages" for which he was justly famous.[24] Indeed several of the photographs Darwin used were of Rejlander himself in a series of posed expressions. While Duchenne's posed photographs had set a precedent for this method, the empirical value of such material is slight. That Rejlander's photographs had more aesthetic appeal than scholarly value is evidenced by the fact that the public purchased some 60,000 copies of the image of a howling child, entitled "mental distress," within a short time after it was offered for sale.

By 1873, after publication of his book on expression, Darwin had occasion to indicate that his views on the use of visual material as empiri-

PLATE 235. A case of "Melancholia" by Browne

PLATE 236. A case of "Imbecility" by Browne

cal proof of the nature of expression had undergone a substantial change. Browne sent Darwin fifteen photographs of his wife, who "voluntarily assumed the expressions which she believed to be indicative of certain emotions and frames of mind of which I had given her a list." Darwin replied that "the photographs are very curious and show great power of acting; but still I think I should have known that the expressions were acted, if I had not read your letter first." Darwin exhibits in this polite comment a caution lacking in his own search for photographic material.

How careful Darwin had become in evaluating the photograph as proof in behavioral studies can be judged in his final exchange with Browne on the subject. Browne requested that Darwin contribute to a volume on the "pathology and treatment of general paralysis covering every aspect of the disease. . . . Now it occurred to me that you might immensely aid us in our work if

you would consent to give us a few remarks on the Physiognomy of the Disease. I could submit to you a series of photographs illustrating its various stages, and a very few words of yours would I am certain embody the true significance of the whole."

What Browne here was asking Darwin to do was very much like Darwin's earlier interpretations of the expression of the insane based on Browne's photographs. In declining participation, Darwin summed up his revised views:

But I really think it will be impossible for me to write even a short essay on the subject. I have had a good deal of experience, and am convinced that the utmost that I can do is to give you the impression which each produces on my mind; and I doubt whether any one could *safely* do more. Though photographs are incomparably better for exhibiting expression than any drawing, yet I believe it is

PLATE 237. "Happy, Hilarious Mania" by Browne

PLATE 238. "Intense Vanity" by Browne

quite necessary to study the previous appearance of the countenance, its changes, however small, and the living eyes, in order to form any safe judgement. I suspect moreover that our judgement is in most cases largely influenced by accessory circumstances. From your being able to study the living patients, and more especially from your various letters to me, I am fully convinced that you could do *well* that which I could effect only in the most imperfect manner. Nevertheless I shall be very glad to give you the impression a careful inspection of any photographs which you may send me produces on my mind.

Darwin never wrote his interpretation and the scholarly correspondence concluded on this note except for an exchange of publications and pleasantries.

In examining Darwin's understanding of the insane and the means through which this understanding was achieved, it becomes evident that

Darwin's position in the history of observing the insane was a pivotal one. On the one hand he was indebted to the earlier physiognomic tradition of Lavater as well as to the older theories on expression of Bell; on the other, he was able to postulate expression as a physiological rather than a purely cultural phenomenon. How he achieved these ends is of interest. Darwin's reliance on data provided by others is certainly known, but his extensive use of visual material to buttress his arguments has been little appreciated. This research device becomes extremely important when the question of Darwin's perception of insanity is involved. What was Darwin looking for in the photographs of the insane? What did he see? What he sought was proof that the expression of raw, uncontrolled emotions in man parallels forms of expression in the higher mammals. The insane, for Darwin, were those individuals who, through their illness, had lost the protective structure by

PLATE 239. Browne's photograph of a case of "Monomania of Pride: Homocidal Impulses"

The arrogant man looks down on others, and with lowered eyelids hardly condescends to see them; or he may show his contempt by slight movements . . . about the nostrils or lips. Hence the muscle which everts the lower lip has been called the *musculus superbus*. In some photographs of patients affected by a monomania of pride, sent me by Dr. Crichton Browne **[Plate 239]**, the head and the body were held erect, and the mouth firmly closed. This latter action, expressive of decision, follows, I presume, from the proud man feeling perfect self-confidence in himself. The whole expression of pride stands in direct antithesis to that of humility; so that nothing need here be said of the latter state of mind.

This is the first attempt in his study to extrapolate the relationship between the state of mind and the mode of expression of the insane based on visual material, but Darwin does not supply the photograph for the reader. His unqualified comments relate to his own interpretation of the nature of the medium as well as to Browne's clinical notes. Darwin would have been aware that the exposure time of such a photograph was so long as to preclude the instantaneous freezing of an emotion. Nevertheless he believed he could extrapolate one feature, the function of the lower lip, from the complexity of fixed structures in the photograph. Actually he sought out exactly those photographs which supported his view by presenting an unwarranted and exaggerated aspect of pride. He followed the same procedure for his discussion on fear.

In a later chapter, Darwin discusses the "erection of the hair in man and animals." Browne had supplied him with numerous cases of the insane who exhibited this symptom. However, these patients were probably suffering from myxedema, a form of hypothyroidism of which mania may be an auxiliary manifestation. It is in this context that the sole illustration of a mentally ill patient is presented in the book **[Plate 240]**. "I have had one of these photographs copied," Darwin notes, "and the engraving gives, if viewed from a little distance, a faithful representation of the original, with the exception that the hair appears rather too coarse and too much curled." There is indeed a noticeable difference in the appearance of the hair in the engraving when compared to that in Browne's photograph **[Plate 241]**. Here, for the first time, Darwin comments on the difficulties inherent in this medium of reproduction. However, he in no way calls into question his own ability to interpret the visual material presented to him, even when drawing a totally false analo-

which man controls his expression of emotion. In a way the insane and idiotic form a "missing link" to our emotional past. It is not surprising that Darwin found what he sought in Browne's photographs.

In his book, Darwin discusses the expression of the emotions in the insane under several headings, such as the nature of grief, inappropriate affect, and anger. In the latter context he cites Henry Maudsley's *Body and Mind* (1870) to the effect that the idiot is the arrested form of man at an earlier (and more primitive) stage of development. Darwin does not seem to have subscribed completely to Maudsley's view that all insanity is a form of genetic reversion, but his interpretation of the expression of the emotions in the insane was greatly influenced by Maudsley's formulation.

The first emotion among the mentally ill actually "seen" by Darwin is pride:

PLATE 240. The engraving "from a photograph of an insane woman, to show the condition of her hair," the only illustration of an insane subject in Darwin's *The Expression of the Emotions in Man and Animals* (London: John Murray, 1872)

PLATE 241. The photograph by James Crichton Browne on which the Darwin engraving was based

gy between erection of the hair in animals and in the insane.

The idea that the photograph supplied an objective source from which observations could be made, the underlying concept of scientific photography in the nineteenth century, had been unquestioningly transferred to psychiatric photography. Darwin, once his initial enthusiasm waned, came to see the innate subjectivity of such photographs, for even a strictly phenomenological description of the action of the various muscles in the expression of certain emotions presupposes that the emotions can be elicited and registered in an uncontaminated manner. Darwin ultimately avoided this problem, as had Duchenne, by employing posed photographs through which a common denominator could be used to delineate the various expressions of emotion. Such an ethnocentric procedure could have little or no scientific validity. Darwin became aware of this in the course of his researches on expression, and made his conclusions clear in the final letters to James Crichton Browne.

185

Darwin had built upon the work of a number of diverse thinkers. Alexander Bain had promulgated a complex theory of mind-body interaction in *The Senses and the Intellect* (1855) and *The Emotions and the Will* (1859) and Herbert Spencer had discussed expression in "The Physiology of Laughter" (1860).[25] From Duchenne, Darwin borrowed the importance of the role of the photograph in documenting as well as studying expression, and from Pierre Gratiolet (1865) and Theodor Piderit (1866) some implications of the photograph for theories of pathognomy.[26] Even the concept of a continuum of expression across the animal kingdom can be traced as far back as the Aristotelian physiognomy.

It was Darwin, however, who integrated all these strands and first postulated a "scientific" theory of expression. Darwin's conclusions were held to be "scientific" because they were the end result, not of impressionistic interpretation of selected data, but of the objective unification of a broad range of data. One of the keystones of this approach was Darwin's study of the expression of the insane, and here the contribution of Crichton Browne and the use of photography as a means of scientific proof should not be underestimated. When, for example, Piderit selected the photograph (or at least the line drawings extrapolated from photographs) as the means of proof for his study of human physiognomy, he did so to support the scientific verifiability of his argument. However, for his brief discussion of the physiognomy of insanity, in connection only with the lines of the forehead, he drew upon Kaulbach's mad king (see Plate 174) for his illustration. Insanity, for Piderit, was somehow more truthfully seen through the eye of the artist than through the viewfinder of the photographer.[27]

After the publication in 1872 of *The Expression of the Emotions in Man and Animals*, most scholarly investigations of the expression of the insane included reference to Darwin. Hermann Oppenheim, in one of the most intelligent analyses of the implications of Darwin's work for psychiatry, surveyed this question in a lecture to the Organization of Berlin Psychiatrists in 1884,[28] and followed Darwin in stressing the universality of human expression and its unfettered appearance in the insane.

Oppenheim's presentation of the "expression of the insane" did not (and, after Darwin, could not) avoid discussion of the nature of the images used to study human expression. Just as Piderit felt it necessary to justify his use of line drawings based on photographs as more objective than original drawings, Oppenheim felt a need to explain

the analysis of static representations of expression as a means of examining and discussing the total spectrum of expression. To support such interpretations of nineteenth-century scientific photographs, Oppenheim turned to eighteenth-century aesthetics, as exemplified in Lessing's *Laoköon*, for his rationale. Freezing the action of the muscles, whether in the sculpture or in a photograph, provided a cross-section which could serve as the basis for study of the expression. What is of interest is that Oppenheim did not stress Lessing's basic thesis that there is an inherent difference between literary description, as in a case study or in Virgil's depiction of the death of Laocöon, and a visual representation, in which the entire action must be extrapolated from a single moment. The fragility of this moment does not concern Oppenheim or, indeed, any of the other scholars who regularly called upon photographic evidence to document their discussion of the expression of the insane.

The strong linkage between photography and the scientific study of the expression of the insane can be judged from an essay in the first volume of the *International Medical-Photographic Monthly*. From work done at the Armenian Hospital in Constantinople, Luigi Mongeri provided a sweeping overview of the pathognomy of insanity based upon photographs of his patients.[29] As with many other late nineteenth-century works of this type, such as Augusto Tebaldi's atlas of 1884,[30] photographic evidence was perceived as complete documentation of the uniqueness of the insane.

While Mongeri's essay provided summaries of the muscular play which results in the expression of the insane, John Turner[31] supplied a neurological rationale for the seemingly mechanical relationship between expression and affect. Pathology of expression and impaired brain function are linked inexorably. Turner, who was interested in studying the asymmetry of the expression of the insane, saw this factor as a sign of damage to brain structures [Plate 242]. Here the study of expression becomes part of the late nineteenth-century drive to apply Griesinger's dictum that all mental diseases are brain diseases and thus to pinpoint the localization of expression.

Such an attempt to integrate the study of expression of the insane into the general trend of neurology and psychiatry during this period, in order to see all psychiatric problems as neurological, rests on an analogy. Sir Charles Bell, at the beginning of the century, had shown the complexity and specificity of neural interaction and its relationship to the brain.[32] The linkage of expression and neural stimulus, stressed by Darwin, was an expansion of this model. The stimulus generated motor innervation, which in turn created mimetic expression via the pathway of the muscles. Damage to the circle of expression through an alteration of the brain's structure resulted in a pathology of expression. Indeed psychiatrists such as Theodore Ziehen chose examples, such as paresis, where a basic organic alteration of the brain was mirrored by physiognomic signs, such as unequal pupils.[33]

Turner, Ziehen, and others extrapolated from this neurological model a general association between brain disease and the pathology of expression. For Ziehen, especially in his 1894 textbook, expression became a diagnostic tool for evaluating all psychopathological states [Plate 243]. This principle was nowhere more elegantly expressed than by Richard Krafft-Ebing in his textbook of psychiatry (1879): "It may be stated that every psychopathic state, like the physiologic states of emotion, has its own peculiar facial expression and general manner of movement which, for the experienced, on superficial observation, make a probable diagnosis possible."[34]

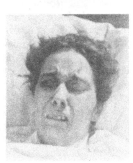

PLATE 242. An illustration accompanying John Turner's essay on the faces of the insane in *The Journal of Mental Science* (January, 1892)

PLATE 243. Photographs of a patient suffering from bipolar depression, in the manic state on the left, in the melancholic state on the right, from Theodor Ziehen's *Psychiatrie für Ärzte und Studierende bearbeitet* (Berlin: Friedrich Wreden, 1894)

187

The corollary to such a view was that it must be possible to capture on the photographic plate not merely individual expression revealing individual aberrations, but general visual categories reflecting specific patterns of expression. Such an attempt was undertaken in 1887 by William Noyes, based on the work of Francis Galton.[35] Galton had evolved the use of composite photographs of groups of subjects, from criminals to generals, to provide visual, "scientific" proof for his theory of eugenics. Noyes, photographing the insane, used the technique to catalogue a generalized appearance of the specific pathologies. By taking a series of multiple exposures of paretics and melancholics, Noyes believed himself able to prove the existence of a particular physiognomy of insanity which did not rest upon the interpretation of the appearance of a single individual: "The accompanying composite photograph of general paresis [Plate 244] is made from the portraits of eight patients, three females and five. males. . . The percentage of females is higher than in the natural ratio of the two sexes in the disease. The cases are all in the second stage of the disease, and their individual portraits show the marked characteristics of general paresis."[36]

For Noyes the use of cumulative evidence for specific modes of appearance provided a key to the general sense of the physiognomy of insanity as perceived by Bucknill and Tuke or Krafft-Ebing's trained observer. The eye of the camera became the unblinking surrogate for the scientific expert, providing visual documentation for the disruption of the normal paths of expression through brain disease. Noyes' adaptation of Galton's composite portrait illustrates how closely linked the studies of the pathognomy of the insane were to the idea of decadence and insanity.

James Shaw, in a series of essays beginning in 1894,[37] attempted to provide a comprehensive study of the appearance of the insane which, in many cases, such as his discussion of the color of melancholy, was indebted to older models:

> The patient, after his attitude and general demeanour have been observed, should be placed in a good light, in order clearly to see the complexion, slight changes of colour, fine lines, delicate movements, fibrillary tremor, and pupillary alterations. The patient should, if possible, be made to face the light squarely, so that the observer may detect any asymmetry of the head or face, or any inequality of the facial lines or in the size of the pupils. . . . A description of the patient's appearance (or, better still, a good photograph of him) before his illness ought to be obtained where procurable. The family physician has the

PLATE 244. Composite portrait of a paretic by William Noyes (1888) from John B. Chapin, *A Compendium of Insanity* (Philadelphia: W. B. Saunders, 1898)

great advantage of having known the patient when sane. Friends often perceive the alteration in physiognomy, but cannot always accurately describe it.

More relevant to the late nineteenth-century concern is the seemingly easy transition Shaw makes from such observations to a detailed discussion of "the physiognomy of degeneracy" [Plate 245], in which he catalogues the physical anomalies which characterize the insane:

> The indications of degeneracy are known as stigmata-hereditatis or *stigmata of degeneration*. They may be defined as anatomical or functional deviations from the normal, which in themselves are usually of little importance as regards the existence of an organism, but are characteristic of a marked or latent neuropathic disposition.
> These stigmata are vices of functional and organic evolution—excesses or arrest of development—and must be distinguished from the deficiencies or deformities produced by accidents at birth, by imitation, or by disease.
> The functional stigmata may be divided into physiological and psychical. From the physiological point of view the anatomical stigmata are, of course, the most important.

Shaw's sense of the relationship between the physical signs of insanity (the "stigmata") and the psychopathological state reveals the inherent identity of mind and body found in the various models for the appearance of the insane in the late nineteenth century.

By the close of the century the connection

188

between seeing and photographing the insane was so closely made that a theoretical framework for the use of the photograph in the scientific study of insanity was developed. Robert Sommer, the professor of psychiatry at Giessen, published a lengthy discussion of this question.[38] Sommer argued that the photograph must replace the written case record (or at least supplement it) as the photograph was a totality, uncontaminated by the interpretative problems inherent in language. Sommer saw in the photograph a more objective recording of signs and symptoms of insanity, a record which incorporates all visual representations of insanity:

> In principle it is important that the representation of a symptom which was recorded verbally or graphically in the older medical history be given in a manner which corresponds to the nature of the expression, i.e., in a visual manner. From this it followed that the drawing was introduced. Since this skill was available to only very few, the photograph was then used. Through the medium of the drawing a great number of psychiatric impressions have been captured which were more able than mere words to introduce us to certain psychiatric symptoms. This is the case even when these impressions have been subject to artistic interpretation. I call special attention to the works of Chodowiecki, Hogarth, and Kaulbach, which, in spite of sub-

jective aspects, are of great value for the history of culture, and specifically, for psychiatry. In any case the artists showed us the correct manner of optical presentation of visible symptoms.

The appreciation of photography is only another step in this direction. The significance for psychopathology was recognized in wider circles only through the *Iconography of the Salpêtrière*. In this collection, outstanding results have been reported in the techniques of photography in the areas of neurology and psychiatry, which were then encouraged to improve their methods even further.

It is not our task here to discuss the general techniques of photography. We will only indicate some facts which make it important for the photographing of psychiatric patients.

I will establish the following guidelines for this purpose: 1. The patient should not be especially prepared for the photographic session. 2. The patient may not be disturbed by the act of photographing him. According to the first point one would generally prefer those methods which would allow for snapshots of the patient in all circumstances. Unfortunately the ordinary snapshot is dependent on lighting. If this method is chosen, one will have to forgo a great many clinically important situations which occur exclusively indoors, particulary in the dayroom, the isolation cell, the bath.

PLATE 245. "Male epileptic, with glabrous face and chin, and facial asymmetry," left, and "Female imbecile, with hypertrichosis," right, from James Shaw, *The Physiognomy of Mental Diseases and Degeneracy* (Bristol: John Wright, 1903)

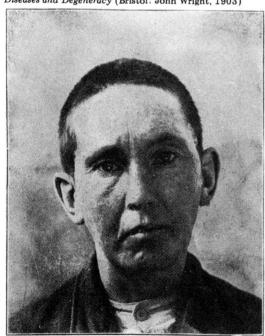 

Sommer stressed the unposed photographing of the subject, for indeed the textbooks of the period had become warehouses of posed photographs indicating the appearance and positions of the insane. Emil Kraepelin, for example, introduced photographs into the fifth edition of his textbook in 1896 only because of the publisher's demands for a product that could compete with the other illustrated manuals and handbooks[39] [Plates 246 and 247].

Because Sommer saw the limitations of such photographs, he introduced the illusion of three-dimensionality into his portraits of the insane by supplying the reader with a series of stereopticon cards [Plates 248 and 249]. A further step was taken by his pupil, A. Alber,[40] with the use of sequential photography [Plates 250 and 251].

Sommer noted that these were major additions to the depiction of insanity, but he felt that still photography nevertheless limited the objective representation of the insane.

At the close of the nineteenth century a new technological advance occurred, and Sommer was quick to decide that the true salvation of psychiatric photography must lie in the work of Edison and the Lumière brothers, in what he called "serial photography," the motion picture film. Compared to this technique, the limitations of even the most "realistic" stereopticon photograph became evident. The film was seen to contain the key to true objectivity, a manner of capturing the inherent aspect of the insane.

The illusion of objectivity continued unabated into the Freudian era.

PLATE 246. A group of catatonic patients from the fifth edition of Emil Kraepelin's *Psychiatrie* (Leipzig: Johann Ambrosius Barth, 1896)

PLATE 247. Cases of "Dementia Praecox" from Kraepelin

PLATE 248. A stereopticon slide of periodic mania from Robert Sommer, *Lehrbuch der psycho-pathologischen Untersuchungs-Methoden* (Berlin and Vienna: Urban & Schwarzenberg, 1899)

PLATE 249. A stereopticon slide of puerperal mania from Sommer

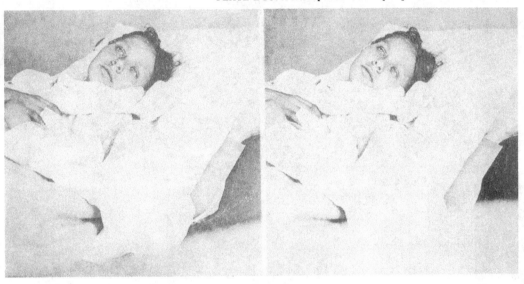

PLATES 250 and 251. Two portraits of the same case of general paresis from A. Alber, *Atlas der Geisteskrankheiten* (Berlin and Vienna: Urban & Schwarzenberg, 1902)

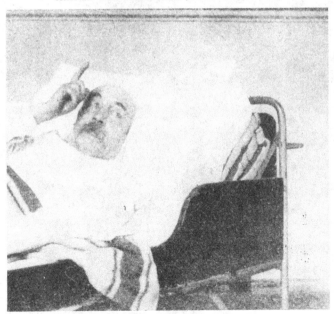

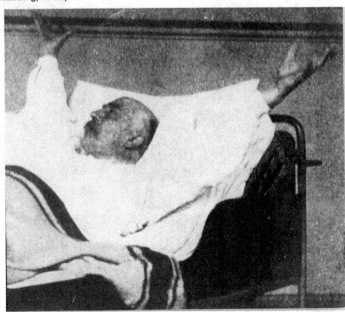

# the ONGOING ARTISTIC tradition

# seeing the insane
# at the salpêtrière

A prominent role in the interrelationship between the visualization of the insane and their treatment was played by the Salpêtrière, one of the oldest asylums in Paris, and its director during the last decades of the nineteenth century, Jean-Martin Charcot.[1] Perhaps the most influential, as well as the best known, French psychiatrist of his generation, Charcot was the first to use the human resources of the Salpêtrière to investigate a broad range of neurological and psychiatric phenomena. All of these cases were filtered through an extraordinary visual sensitivity. An excellent artist, Charcot saw the incongruities of the external manifestation of the patient and was able almost intuitively to extrapolate from them the nature of his illness.

One of his students, Henry Meige, in a long essay on Charcot as an artist, commented on the interconnection of artistic perception and diagnostic ability: "What we can conclude is that at the first glance he was able to recognize some oddity or other of the human habitude. Now, to be able to discern a comic anomaly and to project it in relief, that is the very essence of the art of the caricature. But, aside from the comic, does not the physician's art have as one of its goals the discovery of physical anomalies and making them perceptible to others? That is why it is not presumptuous to say that Charcot's talent for drawing caricatures served him well in his profession as a clinician."[2] The ability to perceive the external anomalies of his patients made Charcot a brilliant diagnostician. It also led him, during the last three decades of the nineteenth century, to make the Salpêtrière synonymous with the depiction of the insane.

Charcot did his internship at the Salpêtrière in the early 1850s. He must have found the hospital much as he described it in 1862 when he returned as the Chief of the Clinic:

> This great asylum holds a population of 5,000 persons, among whom are to be counted a large number who have been admitted for life as incurables; patients of all ages, affected by chronic diseases of all kinds, but particularly by diseases affecting the nervous system. The clinical types available for study are represented by numerous examples, which enables us to study categoric disease during its entire course, so to speak, since the vacancies that occur in any specific disease are quickly filled in the course of time. We are, in other words, in possession of a sort of museum of living pathology of which the resources are great.[3]

The concept of the "museum of living pathology" is captured in Charcot's drawings of psychiatric patients from this period [**Plates 252 and 253**]. Charcot perceived the various clinical categories, however, very much in the light of the great textbook of Esquirol which was still the standard atlas for describing the insane even as late as the 1850s. The isolated figures, stripped of any context, illustrate position (including the hidden hands of the melancholic) and expression. The sketches show not only Charcot's gifts for representation but also his debt to Esquirol and to other earlier models of depicting the insane.

In the beginning, Charcot's work was not in the area of psychiatry but of neurology. Between 1870 and 1880, he undertook major studies of neurological problems, including cerebral localization, using the resources of the Salpêtrière. He conducted painstaking post-mortems of patients with neurological disorders to pinpoint the loci of their lesions. His importance in this field can be judged by the fact that he was the first professor of neurology ever appointed at a university.

The neurological model is of importance in Charcot's perception of the insane not only for the direct relationship it postulates between physical characteristics and brain disorder but also for Charcot's choice of illustration based on this model. As Charcot himself observed, his "master of neurology" was his close friend Duchenne de

PLATE 252. "Mania" by Charcot (1854)

PLATE 253. "Melancholia" by Charcot (c. 1854)

Boulogne.[4] Duchenne's work on the application of electrical stimuli had inspired much of Charcot's work, and it was he who taught Charcot the fine points of medical photography in the 1860s. The two shared a belief in the photograph as the ultimate scientific mode of proof for neurological as well as psychiatric diagnosis, as did many psychiatrists of the period.

Duchenne entertained his dinner guests by showing lantern slides of histologic sections after the meal; Charcot incorporated similar materials into his weekly lectures on medical subjects, attended by both the medical and lay communities of Paris. The perception of psychopathologies as cross-sections, parallel to the static nature of histologic sections, provided Charcot with his model

of illustration. In his photographs, Duchenne recorded the appearance of the muscles under electrical stimulation. If one could fix the appearance of neurological and psychopathological cases one could achieve an exact description. Indeed, in the case of pathological deformities such as amyotropic lateral sclerosis, a spastic paralysis and contracture of all four extremities, first described by Charcot, he was able to undertake precisely such a task. When, however, he tried to describe cases other than neurological ones, such a model did not serve him well.

In 1870, Charcot observed the occurrence of mock-epileptic seizures among patients randomly assigned to a ward inhabited by convulsives. He isolated the symptoms, much as he had with

195

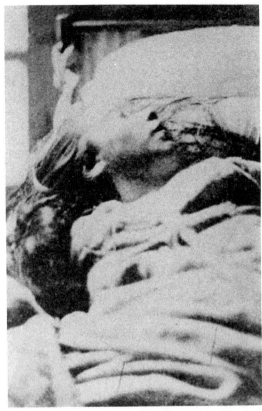

PLATE 254. The normal appearance of a hysteric, from the first volume of the *Iconographie photographique de la Salpêtrière* (1876-1877)

PLATE 255. The first phase of the hysterical episode, from the *Iconographie photographique* (1876-1877)

PLATE 256. Blanche Wittmann in a cataleptic state, from volume three of the *Iconographie* (1879-1880)

PLATE 257. Blanche Wittmann in a hypnotic trance, from volume three of the *Iconographie*

the neurological diseases, and found that a specific syndrome, the *grande hystérie*, parallel to but not identical with epilepsy, could be described in detail. Charcot and his colleague Paul Richer reported on the course of this illness. Description, however, was not considered sufficient and Charcot called upon the aid of two medical men assigned to the Salpêtrière to found the *Photographic Iconography of the Salpêtrière*, a journal devoted to the documentation of Charcot's new findings concerning the visual appearance of the hysteric [Plates 254-257]. Published from 1877 to 1880, this journal attempted to fulfill the program set out by Charcot and its editors, Desiré Magloire Bourneville and Paul Regnard:

> In submitting this first volume of the *Photographic Iconography of the Salpêtrière* for the approval of the medical public it seems necessary to say something about why and how it was conceived and executed. We have had occasion many times in the course of our studies to regret not having at our disposal the means of preserving by visual record the memory of the many cases, interesting for different reasons, that we have had the occasion to observe. This regret was felt more deeply as we saw from Mr. Charcot's example how considerable were the benefits that one could draw from such representations.
>
> Later during our collaboration at *Revue photographique* we had the idea of photographing epileptics and hysterics whom we were able to observe frequently at the time of such attacks by regularly visiting the special services of the Salpêtrière. As we were obliged to have recourse to a photographer from outside, our first attempts were not very fruitful; often by the time the photographer arrived everything was finished. To achieve our goal what we needed was someone within the Salpêtrière itself, who was knowledgeable about photography and who was devoted enough to be ready to respond to our call each time that circumstances demanded.
>
> We had the good fortune to find the devoted and talented man that we needed in our friend Mr. P. Regnard. When he came to the Salpêtrière as an intern in 1875 we explained our idea to him and he accepted it with enthusiasm. It is thanks to him that we have been able to use so effectively a portion of the manual that we assembled.
>
> First of all, Mr. Regnard and I put together an album of one hundred photographs and perhaps we would have stopped there if our excellent mentor Mr. Charcot, who had followed our clinical work and our photographic attempt with his customary care, had not encouraged us to publish the observations we

had gathered in his clinic, illustrating them with photographs taken by Mr. Regnard.[5]

Bourneville and Regnard published detailed studies of the stages of the hysterical crisis, accompanied by sequential photographs. Their interest lay in the positions assumed by the hysteric, as well as in her expression.

In 1888 the journal resumed publication under the title of the *New Iconography of the Salpêtrière*, edited by Charcot. By this date the importance of medical illustration for Charcot's argument was so apparent that he had appointed Albert Londe, a chemist, as director of photography at the asylum, the first such position in an institution. Londe was one of the great innovators in psychiatric photography.[6] As Eadweard Muybridge used sequential chronophotography[7] to document neurological cases [Plate 258], so

PLATE 258. Muybridge's study of "gait in a case of locomotor ataxia," from Francis X. Dercum, ed., *A Textbook on Nervous Diseases* (Philadelphia: Lea, 1895)

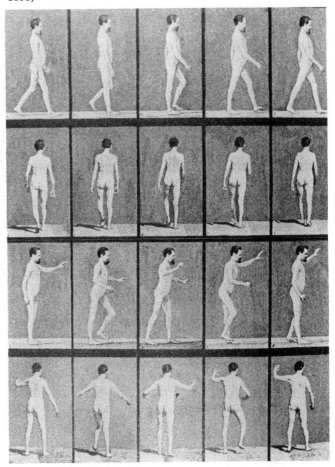

197

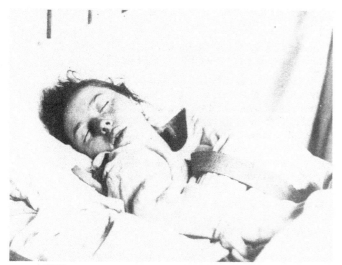

PLATE **259**. "An attack of hysterical sleep" by Albert Londe, used to illustrate Gilles de la Tourette's essay on hysterical sleep in the *Nouvelle Iconographie de la Salpêtrière* 2 (1889)

too did Londe use this technique to document cases of hysteria. Londe's work, published in the *New Iconography* until its demise in 1918 (after the publication of twenty-eight volumes), ranks with the most impressive *fin de siècle* psychiatric photography. Its focus, however, never diverges from the interests of Charcot, even after the latter's death in 1893. The illustrations continue to stress position and the sequence of position, as can be seen in Londe's illustrations accompanying the work of Charcot's students such as Gilles de la Tourette **[Plate 259]** and Pierre Janet and Fulgence Raymond **[Plate 260]**.

It soon became apparent to the students of hysteria that the photograph had the drawback of illustrating only the specific actions of single patients which, while strikingly similar, were not identical. Therefore, Paul Richer, for his massive study of the *grande hystérie*,[8] provided a series of etchings which were composite interpretations of the typical appearance of the subclassifications of the hysterical crisis **[Plates 261-264]**. Richer,

PLATE **260**. A mock dance in a case of chorea from Fulgence Raymond and Pierre Janet, *Névroses et Idées Fixes* (Paris: Félix Alcan, 1898)

PLATE 261. Paul Richer's drawing of the first stage (the epileptoid period) of the hysterical crisis, from his *Études cliniques sur la grande hystérie ou hystéro-épilepsie* (Paris: Adrien Delahaye et Émile Lecrosnier, 1881)

PLATE 262. Second stage: the clown period

PLATE 263. Third stage: the attitudes of the passions

PLATE 264. "A demonic attack" from Richer (1885)

PLATE 265. A drawing by Paul Richer (c. 1874)

like Charcot a talented artist, had sketched innumerable cases (mainly neurological ones) for the teaching collection at the Salpêtrière as early as 1874 [Plates 265-268]. The etchings were based on these drawings. The photograph had proved insufficient for this purpose.

Richer added another dimension, the historical, to his work on hysteria. He appended a long study of the "hysteric in art" to illustrate the universality of his (and Charcot's) manner of perceiving the hysteric. In 1887, Charcot and Richer published a major study, *The Possessed in Art*,[9] in which they used the illustrations to document their own visual classification. The volume concludes with a lengthy chapter, illustrated by Richer with the plates from his own study of hysteria, on "hysteria today." This chapter places all of the impressions of the hysteric from more than thirteen centuries in the status of prefigurations of the contemporary, scientific work on hysteria.

The *New Iconography*, which began in 1888, published throughout its existence many contributions from members of the staff of the Salpêt-

rière on this theme. The argument that the visual structures of hysteria paralleled all other physiologically identifiable illnesses was further pursued in the publication in 1889 of Charcot and Richer's *The Deformed and Ill in Art and Medicine*.[10] This same line of argumentation was undertaken in 1902 in the most massive of all the art history studies produced at the Salpêtrière, Paul Richer's *Art and Medicine*.[11] Here too the insane are seen as presenting parallel appearances to all other illnesses.

While the documentation of the appearance of the possessed in the studies published by Charcot and the members of his staff is important in providing a catalogue of the earlier representations of the insane (in all their forms) in art, there is a major question as to the general validity of Charcot's observations, for in dissecting hysterical episodes into specific components an expectation was created in their patients. As they selected patients for study who were extraordinarily suggestible, many of these patients were able to sense the "correct" manner of responding. This was especially evident in Charcot's prize pa-

200

PLATE **266**. A drawing by Richer (c. 1874)

PLATE 267. Drawing by Richer identified as a case of paresis (c. 1874)

tient, Blanche Wittmann, who was able to mirror Charcot's sense of the structured nature not only of the hysterical episode, but also of the stages of hypnotic treatment. While even Charcot's pupils, such as Pierre Janet, saw the oversimplifica- tion of describing the hypnotic state in a tripar- tite manner (lethargy, catalepsy, somnambulism), they did not recognize that the actions of hyster- ical patients may well have been based on fore- knowledge of their doctors' expectations.[12]

PLATE 268. A drawing by Richer (c. 1874)

Here the complicated question of the inter-action of historical models with the actions of the patients must be raised. In the case of Charcot these two aspects are so closely intertwined that they cannot be differentiated. The complex-ity of even the relatively subjective depiction of the hysteric through the camera's eye was too great to present the desired schematic nature of the appearance of the hysteric. Thus one must return to the artistic representation of the insane.

How close this tradition remained to the scientific surface at the Salpêtrière, with its famed photographic service, can be judged by the use of artistic representations of neurological cases [Plate 269] as teaching tools under Charcot. Here the strong sense of the generalized aspect of the patient as perceived by an artist-clinician overcomes any sense of the photograph as a medium reproducing single (and perhaps unique) instances. The photograph thus proves to have less value than the artist's rendering in capturing the essence of madness.

The approach at the Salpêtrière toward the investigation and treatment of hysteria had a major influence on the evolution of psychoanalysis. Freud, who spent four months with Charcot in 1885 and 1886, departed from the work done by Charcot and Janet in beginning his own work on hysteria. Freud was quite aware of the prominent role played by the perception of the insane in Charcot's nosological method. In his lengthy obituary of Charcot, Freud observed:

He was not a reflective man, not a thinker: he had the nature of an artist—he was, as he himself said, a "*visuel*," a man who sees. Here is what he himself told us about his method of working. He used to look again and again at the things he did not understand, to deepen his impression of them day by day, till suddenly an understanding of them dawned on him. In his mind's eye the apparent chaos presented by the continual repetition of the same symptoms then gave way to order: the new nosological pictures emerged, characterized by the constant combination of certain groups of symptoms. The complete and extreme cases, the "types," could be brought into prominence with the help of a certain sort of schematic planning, and, with these types as a point of departure, the eye could travel over the long series of ill-defined cases—the "*formes frustes*"—which, branching off from one or other characteristic feature of the type, melt away into indistinctness. He called this kind of intellectual work, in which he had no equal, "practising nosography," and he took pride in it. He might be heard to say that the greatest satisfaction a man could have was to see something new—that is, to recognize it as new; and he remarked again and again on the difficulty and value of this kind of "seeing." He would ask why it was that in medicine people only see what they have already learned to see. He would say that it was wonderful how one was suddenly able to see new things—new states of illness—which must probably be as old as the human race; and that he had to confess to himself that he now saw a number of things which

PLATE 269. A bust of a neurological case from the teaching collection of the Salpêtrière (c. 1880)

he had overlooked for thirty years in his hospital wards.[13]

What Freud described in 1893 was Charcot's ability to schematize the external manifestations of illness into patterns. As Freud was forced to deal more and more with the underlying causality of hysteria and abandoned first Charcot's method of treatment through hypnosis and then his visual categories, he also became wary of the illustration, Charcot's manner of empirical proof. It is noteworthy, in light of the common practice of illustrating neurological and psychiatric studies during the closing decades of the nineteenth century, that Freud's publications are barren of any such illustration. This rejection of the value of seeing the patient even extended, with an elaborate rationale, to seeing the analysand (and the patient seeing the analyst) during treatment.[14] Reacting to Charcot, Freud banished the depiction of the insane as well as the study of the external phenomena of madness from psychoanalysis.

# aRt and medicine in the nineteenth century

While the artist's role in portraying the insane may have diminished after the introduction of photography, it was by no means eliminated. The fine arts, even while reacting against the fascination of the early nineteenth century for the theme of madness, still retained the image of the insane in the gallery of portraits through the end of the century. At the same time, many aesthetic devices employed by artists were used in medical portraiture.

Perhaps the most notable effort to improve upon the lithographs which so frequently accompanied studies of the insane early in the century was undertaken by Karl Heinrich Baumgärtner in 1838. Baumgärtner's *Physiognomy of Illness* attempted to present a comprehensive study of the physical appearance of illness.[15] He saw in the outward manifestation of the disease the most accurate manner of diagnosis and thus treatment. Such a manner of diagnosis for somatic illnesses may be efficacious; however, Baumgärtner tried to apply the same criteria to psychopathologies:

It is the sum of the behavior of the insane, however, which reveals above all the deranged condition of his mind. In the majority of cases we can also recognize the illness from a single moment captured in a picture. Who would not recognize the presence of a deranged mind in the portraits of the mentally ill presented in this work. And, how easy it is, as a rule, to distinguish the warden in the midst of his charges when one goes through an asylum! As easy as it is in practice, by the way, to distinguish the derangement of the mind, it is equally difficult in individual cases as well as in general, to identify the phenomena which characterize this illness.

In portraying the insane, Baumgärtner stressed their eyes, the asymmetry of their expression, and their unique posture or gait. While emphasizing the muscular patterns which result in the specific expression of the seven case studies he presents,

he also paid careful attention to the question of skin color. This clinical observation was shared by the reader, for Baumgärtner used colored lithographs to illustrate his text [Plate 270]. The portraits by Géricault (see Plates 106-110), painted in full color, were to have been reduced to monochromatic lithographs for inclusion in Georget's textbook. Karl Sandhaas's portraits of the insane, drawn for Baumgärtner, were reproduced in intense color. While the images themselves are tra-

PLATE **270**. "Monomania" from Karl Heinrich Baumgärtner's *Kranken-Physiognomik* (Stuttgart: L. F. Rieger, 1842)

ditional, down to the melancholic (resting her head on her palm), the addition of color created a verisimilitude which even the photograph could hardly equal.

The idea of the chromolithograph as a means of capturing the essence of the insane was resurrected long after the use of the photograph had become a commonplace. In 1892, Byrom Bramwell published a series of images of the insane in his *Atlas of Clinical Medicine*.[16] While drawing in part on unpublished illustrations for Morison's atlas, Bramwell also commissioned a series of new illustrations. These chromolithographs are an excellent example of the use of an artistic technique which created the illusion of realism. Bramwell supplied a detailed commentary on the portraits, including, in a feature unique to most atlases, a specific reading of the physiognomy of the insane [**Plate 271**].

This Plate, which may be termed Melancholic Dementia, represents a woman of the bilious temperament—of short build, dusky complexion and dark hair—a type supposed to be liable to melancholia.

The expression of *melancholy* is depicted by:—

a. The drawing up of the inner portions of the eyebrows (arching of the eyebrows), by the action of the central portion of the occipito frontalis muscle.

b. The slight approximation of the inner ends of the eyebrows, owing to the action of the corrugator supercilii muscles. This is not very marked.

c. The drooping of the angles of the mouth, probably caused by the loss of tone in the cheek muscles.

d. The drooping of the eyelids, owing to loss of tone in the levator palpebrae superioris.

*Dementia* is expressed by:—

a. The permanent and deep appearance of the transverse frontal wrinkles, showing long-standing melancholy.

b. The slight corrugation of the eyebrows —strong action of the corrugator supercilii, the "muscle of thought"—expresses intelligence.

c. The coarseness of the hair—a common feature in melancholic dementia—it is often more rigid than in this case.

d. The general lack of tone or tension in the facial muscles—the presence of which expresses attention.

The expressions of melancholia are derived from two sources, viz.:—(1) The *tense* muscles of the *frightened*, fighting, struggling, or running for life; and (2) the *toneless* muscles of the captured animal suffering from *abject terror*, and perfectly *exhausted*.

PLATE **271**. "Melancholia" from Byrom Bramwell's *Atlas of Clinical Medicine* (Edinburgh: T. and A. Constable, 1892)

*Excited* melancholia illustrates (1); *passive* melancholia illustrates (2).

This is a case of passive melancholia, and the only expression of tension is in the occipitals. The reason, according to Darwin, why this muscle is contracted, is to widen the optic fissure and enable the frightened animal to see its foe or to escape better.

Melancholic dementia is not so common and seldom so profound as post-maniacal or ordinary secondary dementia.

Like Baumgärtner (and most of his contemporaries), Bramwell saw the uniqueness of the physiognomy of the insane resting in the abnormal play of muscles in their expressions. Such a view of the insane does not require reproduction of the subject's coloration, but this device served to increase the observer's impression of reality. This heightened sense of objectivity is an illusion of the artist's brush based on shared Western assumptions concerning representation. These can be and were applied to the image of the insane, continuing the older tradition of Esquirol and Morison to the end of the nineteenth century.

PLATES 272 and 273. "Chronic melancholia" and "Melancholia attonita" from Allan McLane Hamilton, *Types of Insanity* (New York: William Wood, 1883)

The use of the lithograph as a means of portraying the insane did not cease even when it became possible to reproduce photographs directly. It was not the quaintness of the lithograph in the 1880s but rather an appreciation of its special quality that appealed to the medical commentator. Allan McLane Hamilton's "illustrated guide to the physical diagnosis of mental disease,"[17] first published in 1883 and then reissued as an appendix to G. Fielding Blandford's *Insanity and Its Treatment* in 1886,[18] exemplifies such a use of lithography. Hamilton, a neurologist of wide repute, wrote a diagnostic manual based exclusively on the visualization of the insane. He emphasized expression, but also referred to color and posture:

The physiognomy of the insane consists not only in the portrayal of inharmonious types of expression, but in transitory and intensified manifestations of dominant feelings. The latter is often the case in commencing insanity, and in forms of mental disorder that have stopped short of dementia. It is well in all cases to systematically study the condition of the organs of expression themselves, and ascertain if there be functional derangements as well as general structural changes which may be the result of defective innervation. Such study should be careful and continued,

and not only the manifestation or absence of expression should be taken into account, but the possible existence of paresis of certain facial muscles, the condition of the eyes and hair, the coloring and appearance of the skin, and the general muscle tonus should be noted as well. Relaxation and rigidity of the muscles are conspicuous factors in the expression of insanity, and in states manifested by lowered emotional activity we find the former to be nearly always present.

Although Hamilton based his study on nine lithographs made from photographs [Plates 272-275], it is interesting that in his introduction he credits the lithographer, T. J. Manley, but not the photographer. The lithographs exhibit radically altered states of expression, and these are emphasized through the mode of reproduction. Yet if one compares them with the illustrations in Esquirol's atlas (see Plates 95-100) and Morison's atlases (see Plates 112-132), it is evident that the general guidelines of what is portrayed have not changed even if the manner of portrayal has. That the radical state still dominates is the more of interest in light of the neurological analogue relating radically changed appearance, gait, and posture to brain malfunction.

Blandford, in his text, is much more circumspect than Hamilton. He assumes, for the articu-

PLATE 274. "Chronic mania" from Hamilton

PLATE 275. "Dementia" from Hamilton

lation of emotional states, not a universal, generally accepted base line, a factor inherent in Hamilton's view, but a relative one:

> Much has been written concerning the physiognomy of the insane. It is supposed that insanity stamps itself in the countenance of a man, and is recognizable there. In many cases it is, but it is recognizable in some only by those persons who knew the patient in his sane state.

Indeed, he specifically warns the psychiatrist not to rely on the appearance of the insane:

> I now suppose that you are brought face to face with the alleged lunatic. If you are shown into a room where he is with other people, you may not be able to say at a glance which is the individual, and may not be at liberty to ask. It is something more than awkward to commence a conversation with the wrong person, so that I strongly advise you to make sure before you enter the room that you will have no difficulty in fixing on the right one.

> You can ask such questions concerning the number of people there, the appearance of the individual, or the distinguishing marks of his dress, so as to render any mistake impossible. This may seem a piece of trifling advice, but I have known the difficulty to occur.

Here a much more sophisticated sense of the physiognomy of the insane is introduced.

The image of the insane in the fine arts over an equivalent period from Baumgärtner's physiognomy through Bramwell's atlas also saw aesthetic traditions continued even in the light of the altered sensitivity to and understanding of insanity. Horace Vernet's *Love Madness* [Plate 276], from the first half of the century, is a conventional Romantic view of the insane female, much in the tradition of Fuseli and of Thomas Barker of Bath (see Plates 161 and 162). While stressing the pathognomy of insanity, it also reproduces the image of the deshabille and disheveled hair seen in the Ophelia-like interpretations of the Romantics.

PLATE **276**. Horace Vernet's *Love Madness*
(early nineteenth century)

By 1864, the Belgian artist Antoine Wiertz
was able to portray "hunger, madness and crime"
[Plate 277] as a comment on the social origin of
insanity. The mad mother, a figure well known
from Kaulbach's madhouse (see Plate 174), is depicted here as an infanticide driven to cannibal-
ism because society has abandoned her.[19] Her
petition for contributions lies on the floor of her
hut. She grins inappropriately while butchering
her infant. This almost surreal scene is a statement about the relationship between a meaningful role in a caring society and the neglect which
leads to death and madness. Abandonment and
madness are still represented by the opening in
the roof of the hut through which can be seen
the bare, bifurcated branch so long associated
with insanity.

PLATE **277**. Antoine Wiertz's *Faim, Folie, Crime*
(Hunger, Madness, Crime) of 1864

PLATE 278. Frontispiece of A. J. Davis, *Mental Disorders; or, Diseases of the Brain and Nerves* (New York: American News Company, 1871)

PLATE 279. Telemaco Signorini's *Disturbed Ward* (1865)

210

This carryover, along with the new consciousness of madness as a social problem, was also evident in the popular literature. In the frontispiece to A. J. Davis's *Mental Disorders; or, Diseases of the Brain and Nerves*, published in 1871, the full range of the illnesses discussed by the author is portrayed[20] **[Plate 278]**. The patients, including the melancholic with his hidden hands and the maniac brandishing his club, march from the asylum, having been freed of their literal demons by Hygeia. Thus the medieval image of madness as possession by demons (here running the gamut from mania to selfishness), along with the iconography of mental illness, remains in the popular visualization of the insane even into the late nineteenth century.

The asylum, looming large in the background of Davis's illustration, continued to play a major role in the image of the insane in this period. The 1865 painting by Telemaco Signorini of the "disturbed ward" **[Plate 279]** combines the sense of isolation present in the asylum with the conventional cast of characters found in earlier portrayals. Signorini, who is better known for his landscapes, presents the asylum as human landscape, with a series of identifiable human markers inclosed in the brilliant whiteness of the institution.[21] The blackness of Goya's asylum (see Plate 164) is altered. Here the world of the asylum is bright but not yet open. So too the image of the asylum courtyard by Daniel Urrabieta y Vierge, the Spanish illustrator, whose creative career was spent in France **[Plate 280]**. The traditional figures are placed outdoors, creating the illusion of openness, but the wall still separates them from the rest of the world. However, the brightness and openness lead to the inevitable conclusion that the asylum is not completely closed off, but rather a passage which can lead back to the world of sanity.

PLATE **280**. Daniel Urrabieta y Vierge, *Yard of an Asylum* (late nineteenth century)

PLATE **281**. A contemporary engraving of Tony Robert-Fleury's portrait of
*Pinel Freeing the Insane* (1876)

The concept of openness as a clue to the potential reintegration of the insane can be seen in what is perhaps the most famous late nineteenth-century asylum scene, the 1876 painting by Tony Robert-Fleury of Pinel freeing the insane from their chains **[Plate 281]**. In the courtyard of the Bicêtre, Pinel is surrounded by a number of female inmates who provide the familiar spectrum for the image of the insane.[22] The woman tearing her clothing in the *arc de cercle* position, the huddled figure of the melancholic, head resting on her hand, whose position is replicated by a miniscule figure seated at the rear, the tense figure of the maniac, as well as the totally passive figure chained in the foreground, are well-known inmates of the traditional asylum. The central figure, however, the woman from whom the chains are being removed, is the focus of the painting. The unnecessary use of force to restrain the insane is implied in her passive figure and her disheveled state. She is the victim, freed from her

bonds by the new humanity of Pinel. The image of the asylum as one of freedom is enhanced by the openness and light of the courtyard.

This glorification of the "freeing of the insane" is a late nineteenth-century projection of the idea of the reformed asylum, for Pinel banished chains, not restraints. The introduction of more humane restraints during the beginning of the nineteenth century and their relationship to the altered image of the insane has already been discussed. The replacement of the chain with the straitjacket was a movement in the direction of making the asylum a place of treatment, but the French reformed asylum was clearly not as far along towards that ideal as the asylums after the mid-century mark.

Robert-Fleury's massive painting hung in a very special place, in the lecture hall at the Salpêtrière. (It now hangs in the Charcot Library there.) Freud describes Charcot's lectures and the lecture hall in his obituary of Charcot:

PLATE 282. André Brouillet's portrait of *Charcot at the Salpêtrière* (1887), incorporating Richer's portrait of the hysteric (Plate 262) at the upper left

As a teacher, Charcot was positively fascinating. Each of his lectures was a little work of art in construction and composition; it was perfect in form and made such an impression that for the rest of the day one could not get the sound of what he had said out of one's ears or the thought of what he had demonstrated out of one's mind. He seldom demonstrated a single patient, but mostly a series of similar or contrasting cases which he compared with one another. In the hall in which he gave his lectures there hung a picture which showed "citizen" Pinel having the chains taken off the poor madmen in the Salpêtrière. The Salpêtrière, which had witnessed so many horrors during the Revolution, had also been the scene of this most humane of all revolutions.[23]

From this a further function of the painting may be surmised. Charcot's interest in documenting the universality of the visualization of hysteria may well account for the passive central figure as well as the figure next to her in the *arc de cercle* position. Both illustrate stages in the hysteric episode. The sense of the role of the position of the insane in determining their illness is inherent in Robert-Fleury's image.

In 1887, André Brouillet paraphrased this painting in his portrait of *Charcot at the Salpêtrière* [Plate 282], with Charcot in the place of Pinel and his colleague Joseph Babinski in the position of the servant. The patient is probably Blanche Wittmann, seen in the final stages of either a hysterical episode or hypnotic trance. But the position of the figure is strikingly like that of the young woman in the Robert-Fleury scene. The analogy to Pinel implies Charcot's position as the new liberator of the insane, in this case from the chains of hysteria. The historical value of both paintings is minimal. Their value lies in the documentation of the late nineteenth-century sense of the positive nature of treatment and the potential for reentry into society.

213

# van gogh sees the insane

As early as the 1880s, the work of Vincent Van Gogh showed a fascination with the restructuring of some of the classical images of aberrant mental and emotional states.[24] In 1881 and 1882 he drew a series of seated and weeping figures. Sketches of a weeping female, her head covered by her arms, drawn in black pencil, exist from his stay in The Hague.[25] There are at least four different views of an old man weeping from the same period. These seated, weeping figures culminate in two major works, the nude female figure in *Sorrow* [**Plate 283**], in three versions, and the seated weeping male figure in *At Eternity's Gate* in its two states [**Plates 284 and 285**]. Iconographically, all of these works stand in the tradition of the Renaissance representation of melancholy, with its strong association to mourning and grief. Van Gogh's studies reflect both his personal views of depression and the altered view of the late nineteenth century toward mental illness.

*Sorrow* exemplifies the artist's evolving view of the classic portrayal of melancholy. His earlier drawings of seated, weeping peasant women give way to the angular representation of this emaciated, pregnant figure based, like the other studies, on first-hand observation of working-class models. Van Gogh's relationship to the woman he calls "Sien," the model for *Sorrow*, is detailed in his letters to his brother Theo in 1882.[26] Perhaps even more striking is his description of the aesthetics of his model in a letter to his friend Rappard in the spring of 1882: "—I never had such a good assistant as this ugly (???), faded woman. In my eyes she is beautiful, and I find in her exactly what I want; her life has been rough, and sorrow and adversity have put their marks upon her —now I can do something with her." This effect is so successfully captured in the lithograph that the model's individuality vanishes—she becomes woman weighed down by the world.

Van Gogh has altered the initial implications of the figure of melancholy from that of the Renaissance. He has also filtered his impression of "Sien" through yet another prism. For he captions one of the drawings of *Sorrow* with a quotation from Jules Michelet's *La Femme* (which he had read as early as 1874): "How is it that on earth there can be a lonely, forsaken woman?" Jean Seznec notes that "according to Michelet, the nineteenth century was the century of woman's misery, abandonment and despair; man's mission was to liberate her, to free her from all the servitudes that oppress her."[27] Indeed, Van Gogh's *Sorrow*, even though it is rooted in the Renaissance figure of melancholy, is a substantial extension of that philosophic concept of affective disorder.

In the Renaissance, melancholy was seen as an inherent attribute of the individual, reflecting the dominance of certain internal forces under the more general influence of the cosmos. In *Sorrow* and in *At Eternity's Gate*, Van Gogh portrays individuals driven to the brink by society's inhumanity. They are isolated from society because they can no longer function in it. Both the old man, his time of constructive work behind him, and the cast-off, pregnant woman are pariahs in the ordered world of society since they offer no economic benefits. They have no way out of their dilemma and thus depression, the heightened form of grief, becomes a realistic reaction to their position in life. However, these figures of depression represent not merely a social comment, but also the potential for change, a major alteration in the nineteenth-century attitude toward mental illness, for they awaken in the observer the sense of meaninglessness pointed up in Van Gogh's quotation from Michelet: How can such waste be permitted? Van Gogh evidently felt that the portrait of *Sorrow* was sufficient to carry this message, as he did not place the Michelet quotation below the lithographed study.

PLATE **283**. Vincent Van Gogh, *Sorrow*, a lithograph from 1882

PLATE **284**  Van Gogh's *At Eternity's Gate*, a lithograph from 1882

PLATE **285**. *At Eternity's Gate*, an oil from 1890

The reworking of the classic theme of melancholy in the light of Van Gogh's strong social conscience presents a paradigm for the understanding of two late paintings. These works exist in a similar continuum of the representation of mental and emotional disorders, having their roots in the late eighteenth and early nineteenth centuries. The *Men's Ward at Arles* [Plate 286] was painted in 1889. Van Gogh describes his completion of the canvas in a letter written to his sister in October 1889 from the sanitarium at Saint-Rémy-de-Provence:

> I am now working on a ward in the hospital. In the foreground a big black stove surrounded by a number of gray and black figures of patients, behind this a very long room with a red tile floor, with two rows of white beds, the walls white, but a white which is lilac or green, and the windows with pink and green curtains, and in the background the figures of two sisters in black and white. The ceiling is violet with big beams. I had read an article about Dostoevski, who wrote a book *Souvenirs de la maison des morts*, and this induced me to resume a large study I had begun in the fever ward at Arles. But it is annoying to paint figures without models.

The painting is grounded in Van Gogh's own experiences in the hospital at Arles after his self-mutilation at the end of 1888 and again in February of the following year when he was admitted suffering from a delusion of persecution. In the spring of 1889 he voluntarily entered the private sanitarium of Saint-Paul-de-Mausole, on the outskirts of Saint-Rémy-de-Provence. During the year he remained there he painted numerous studies of the physical surroundings of the asylum, but his completion of the *Men's Ward at Arles* is unique in its presentation of a hospital scene with patients. If anything, this painting is closest in spirit to his copies from Daumier made during his hospitalization which present closed spaces, such as prisons, with figures.

Van Gogh's letter to his sister provides access to his image of the hospital. First, the picture is a composite. Begun at Arles in the "fever ward," it was completed at Saint-Rémy. His complaint about the absence of models for the figures suggests that he was reconstructing the closed world of the ward while in yet another hospital. The image of the hospital at Arles is filtered through the experience of Saint-Rémy. It becomes an abstraction of the world of the living dead, of the madmen with whom Van Gogh lived and with whom he identified. Dostoevski's work, known to him only through its title, the *Notes from the House of the Dead*, served as the motto for this

work, much as the quotation from Michelet provided a broader social context for the drawing of *Sorrow*.

Van Gogh's understanding of the suffering of the mind underwent a radical shift after his voluntary admission to Saint-Rémy. The earlier representations of mental or emotional disorders resulted from his conception of man's total suffering in this world. In Saint-Rémy he was confronted with the specific reality of mental illness as the totality of the world in which he found himself. On May 9, 1889, almost immediately after arriving at Saint-Rémy he wrote: "Though here there are some patients very seriously ill, the fear and horror of madness that I used to have has already lessened a great deal. And although here you continually hear terrible cries and howls like beasts in a menagerie, in spite of that people get to know each other very well and help each other when their attacks come on."

Just as depression came to be expressed in Van Gogh's art through his personal experiences as well as his reading, his understanding of the insane was colored by his first-hand experiences.[28] His fear of madness was present when he first arrived at the asylum: "But all joking aside, the fear of madness is leaving me to a great extent, as I see at close quarters those who are affected by it in the same way as I may very easily be in the future." He sympathized and identified with the plight of the other patients. "Formerly," he wrote, "I felt an aversion to these creatures, and it was a harrowing thought to me to reflect that so many of our profession...had ended like this. I could not even bring myself to picture them in that condition." Among the artists Van Gogh suspected were in madhouses was the illustrator Vierge, the creator of a famed asylum scene (see Plate 280).

The structure of Van Gogh's painting of the hospital ward is conventional. The clearly limited space with its inhabitants marks the universe of the asylum. The seated figure holding a cigarette is a version of the melancholic of *At Eternity's Gate*. Indeed, there exists a sketch, which Van Gogh most probably used for this figure, that is even more evidently a representation of chronic depression. But in its major aspect Van Gogh's hospital ward diverges from the traditional. The standard manic figures are absent, as they were in reality in Saint-Rémy. The difference is even more noteworthy because, rather than representing specific types or classifications of mental illness, these figures reflect the daily existence of the inmates in hospital. These are the quintessential inhabitants of the house of the dead, made dead because of forced inactivity. They smoke,

PLATE 286. Van Gogh's *Men's Ward at Arles* (1889), oil on canvas

sit, read newspapers, talk, but have no constructive roles such as Van Gogh himself had through his continuing activity as a painter. He wrote in September: "The treatment of patients in this hospital is certainly easy, one could follow it even while traveling, for they do absolutely *nothing*; they leave them to vegetate in idleness." For the nineteenth-century observer, the house of the dead was the house of idleness. Dickens, Van Gogh's favorite writer, condemned the absence of meaningful activity in the English asylums, arguing that if "the system of finding the inmates employment . . . were introduced . . . the proportion of cures would be much greater."[29] It is

this absence of work, or meaningful activity, that is expressed in the canvas begun at Arles and finished at Saint-Rémy. Van Gogh's fear of purposeless existence, of vegetating in the asylum, is triggered by the mere mention of the title of Dostoevski's novel. Van Gogh's picture is his own note from the house of the dead, the asylum.

After his release from Saint-Rémy Van Gogh was placed in the care of a doctor who was himself a patron of the arts. Paul Gachet, the friend of Gautier (see Plates 175 and 176), had earlier settled in Auvers-sur-Oise and offered to supervise Van Gogh. During his stay in Auvers, Van Gogh turned out a remarkable series of portraits and

219

PLATE **287**. Van Gogh's *Head of a Patient* (1890)

landscapes. One of the works finished in Auvers, though it may have been begun earlier at Saint-Rémy, is his *Head of a Patient* [Plate 287]. This portrait of an anonymous patient carries on yet another tradition of depicting the madman.

Van Gogh had been fascinated by Delacroix's portrait of Tasso (see Plate 168) and requested while still living at Arles that his brother send him a lithograph of it. He referred to this portrait as "representing a *real* man. Ah! portraiture, portraiture with the thoughts, the soul of the model in it, that is what I think must come."

Delacroix's image of the writer in the mad-house, however, was structured in the image of Hogarth's Bedlam, with the melancholic Tasso behind bars being gawked at by other inmates. For the prism through which he saw the inmate at Saint-Rémy, Van Gogh turned to Géricault, the artist whom he placed alongside Delacroix in his collection of prints. Van Gogh's painting of the inmate at Saint-Rémy contains a visual echo of Géricault's *Monomania, The Assassin*, painted at the Salpêtrière between 1821 and 1824 (see Plate 106). The position of the head, the coat and scarf, the lidded eyes all parallel Géricault's portrait. Van Gogh thus makes use of a classic work portraying the insane to underline the ba-nality of madness, for the abnormality of the subject is apparent only if one knows that the portrait was painted in an asylum. The line between madness and sanity in these portraits is very fine. In Van Gogh's asylum scene there is a surface appearance of normal activity, so too in his portrait of the inmate. It is primarily through his adaptation of earlier models of depicting the insane that the artist presents the abnormality of his subject.

The importance of the two paintings of the mentally ill in the total context of Van Gogh's output lies in part in their uniqueness. When one examines in particular Van Gogh's production during the final two years of his life, years spent in institutions and under the threat of imminent mental collapse, one finds few direct references to mental illness. The bulk of his work consists of landscapes, portraits, and copies, and from Delacroix he copies not the Tasso but the *Good Samaritan*. His attempt to repress his fear of insanity, a fear expressed in most of the letters following his self-mutilation, finds few direct outlets in his work and these are cast in iconographic structures based in a long tradition of classifying the insane as the inhabitants of another world, isolated from the observing eye of the artist.

# epiloGue SEEING WITH "THE THIRD EYE"

Freud rejected the idea of seeing the patient, thus centering psychoanalysis on the process of listening. Theodor Reik, one of the most orthodox of Freud's followers, stressed the need for the analyst to listen "with a third ear," to "follow his instincts":

Young analysts should be encouraged to rely on a series of most delicate communications when they collect their impressions; to extend their feelers, to seize the secret messages that go from one unconscious to another. To trust these messages, to be ready to participate in all flights and flings of one's imagination, not to be afraid of one's own sensitivities, is necessary not only in the beginnings of analysis; it remains necessary and important throughout. The task of the analyst is to observe and to record in his memory thousands of little signs and to remain aware of their delicate effects upon him. At the present stage of our science it is not so necessary, it seems to me, to caution the student against overevaluation of the little signs or to warn him not to take them as evidence. These unconscious feelers are not there to master a problem, but to search for it. They are not there to grasp, but to touch. We need not fear that this approach will lead to hasty judgments. The greater danger (and the one favored by our present way of training students) is that these seemingly insignificant signs will be missed, neglected, brushed aside. The student is often taught to observe sharply and accurately what is presented to his conscious perception, but conscious perception is much too restricted and narrow. The student often analyzes the material without considering that it is so much richer, subtler, finer than what can be caught in the net of conscious observation. The small fish that escapes through the mesh is often the most precious. Receiving, recording, and decoding these "asides," which are whispered between sentences and without sentences, is, in reality, not teachable. It is, however, to a certain degree demonstrable. It can be demonstrated that the analyst, like his patient, knows things without knowing that he knows them. The voice that speaks in him, speaks low, but he who listens with a third ear hears also what is expressed almost noiselessly, what is said *pianissimo*. There are instances in which things a person has said in psychoanalysis are consciously not even heard by the analyst, but none the less understood or interpreted. There are others about which one can say: in one ear, out the other, and in the third. The psychoanalyst who must look at all things immediately, scrutinize them, and subject them to logical examination has often lost the psychological moment for seizing the fleeting, elusive material.[1]

The pattern of interpretation here suggested by Reik is equivalent to that of the nineteenth-century psychiatrist with regard to the appearance of the patient. It is not, however, the intuitive delineation of common structures perceived in the patient that is central to Freud's shift of emphasis. For Freud and Reik, representations of the patient, whether tape recordings or transcripts, could not stand as surrogates for the patients themselves.

Freud's rejection of visual observation in psychoanalysis was not based simply on its inherent limitations. Indeed, Reik continued his argument with an example concerning his seeing a patient's abnormal reactions in passing a mirror. In rejecting the rigid representationalism of nineteenth-century theories of understanding mental processes, Freud also rejected their basis of empirical proof. Here Reik's choice of metaphor is of importance. Borrowing the image of the "third ear" from Nietzsche (where it has a totally different implication), Reik emphasizes the aural aspect of psychoanalysis to the exclusion of the visual.

The visual aspect of diagnosis has certainly not vanished from the contemporary scene. Even though modern clinical psychiatry is heavily indebted to psychoanalysis for many of its basic theoretical premises, the idea of seeing the insane has not been banned from the presentation of psychopathologies. An excellent example is the standard psychiatry handbook by Alfred Freedman, Harold Kaplan, and Benjamin Sadock.[2] In its massive multivolume form it is devoid of illustration, in line with "serious" contemporary work in psychiatry. When, however, the publishers issued a student version consisting of selections from this text, it was heralded as an "illustrated edition." Running the gamut from gynecological diagrams to brain localization studies, the illustrations include such traditional photographs as "chronic schizophrenic woman showing characteristic mannerism and facial grimacing," "chronic catatonic patient," and "hebephrenic patient." These photographs, stressing position and expression, stand directly in the line of development from the nineteenth century psychiatric atlases.

However, also included in the text is a plethora of photographic material which reveals the same influence of the atlas, but introduces an entirely new area of perception. In one instance, the reader is presented with an image of the dismembered body of a clothes mannequin lying on an open space, with two miniscule figures running in the background. The caption refers to the fact that "paranoid patients are often unable to separate the thought from the deed and fear that their angry impulses can kill others or themselves." In another, the picture of a female hugging three children while a male sits apart in the background illustrates "a patient's relationship to his parents and siblings." Such illustrations no longer represent the external aspect of man, but rather his mental life and history. Here the older model of portraying the insane is linked to the Freudian model of explanation. In teaching aids today, this combination is not only accepted but expected.

The introduction of abstraction, parallel to the introduction of psychoanalysis, removed the actual representation of the madman from the fine arts, although some artists, such as Edvard Munch, Erich Heckel, Robert Riggs, and George Bellows, carried the idea of the madman or the asylum into the twentieth century. It was only in the late 1970s that photographic documentation of the insane assumed the status of the work of art. Mary Ellen Mark's photographs from the Oregon State Hospital were judged to be a breakthrough in perceiving the insane via the artistic means of the camera.[3] In Argentina, Julio Cortázar, the famed Latin American author, provided the text accompanying a series of photographs made at the Hospicio Hecha por los Internados de Buenos Aires.[4] This sensitive reaction to the asylum and its inhabitants is introduced with a brief survey of the physiognomy of insanity by a Buenos Aires psychiatrist. Here the connection between the aesthetic and the medical modes of seeing the insane is retained.

The visualization of the insane maintains its own vocabulary of images, and these are linked to the various manifestations of mental illness in much the same way that psychiatric nomenclature relates to that same spectrum. The selection of a specific representational system is related to the entity described but is not interchangeable with that entity. It is the means by which the observer can order his perception of reality. Each age uses bits and pieces of existing systems to reorder the universe for itself. It may restructure these systems to appear as though they are new and unique, yet, since it is always relating to the reality in the world, basic common denominators of description and perception remain constant.

Thus a conclusion to the present study is impossible, as the representation and perception of the insane continues and will continue as long as society must deal with those it has designated as mentally ill. But it is to be hoped that psychiatrists as well as artists will look beyond appearance, expression, and posture to that which can only be seen by "the third eye."

# notes

## Preface

1. Oscar Wilde, "The Decay of Lying," in *The Soul of Man Under Socialism and other Essays,* ed. Philip Rieff (New York: Harper & Row, 1970), 72.

2. Gordon W. Allport, *The Nature of Prejudice* (New York: Doubleday Anchor, 1958), 127-137. See also Paul F. Secord, "Facial Features and Inference Processes in Interpersonal Perception," in Renato Tagiuri and Luigi Petrullo, eds., *Person Perception and Interpersonal Behavior* (Stanford: Stanford University, 1958), 300-315.

3. John Marshal Townsend, "Stereotypes of Mental Illness: A Comparison with Ethnic Stereotypes," *Culture, Medicine and Psychiatry* 3 (1979), 205-229.

4. Concerning the interlocking features of stereotyping in the context of visual images of the Jew see my essay "The Rediscovery of the Eastern Jew: German Jews in the East, 1890-1913," in David Bronsen, ed., *Jews and Germans from 1860 to 1933: The Problematic Symbiosis* (Heidelberg: Carl Winter, 1979), 338-365.

5. For example see the discussion of the image of the madman in Y. Mashiah, "In Search of an Insane Universe: A Study of Dār al Majānīn, The Lunatic Asylum, by Sayyid Muhammad 'Alī Jamāl-Zādeh," *Le Muséon* 86 (1973), 147-174.

6. Stephen Pepper, *World Hypotheses* (Berkeley: University of California, 1942), 91.

7. Michel Foucault, *Naissance de la clinique: Une archéologie du regard médical* (Paris: Presses universitaires de France, 1963), 107-123.

8. Nelson Goodman, "The Way the World Is," *The Review of Metaphysics* 14 (1960), 53.

9. See for example the discussion in Klaus Dörner, *Bürger und Irre: Zur Socialgeschichte und Wissenschaftssoziologie der Psychiatrie* (Cologne: Europäische Verlagsanstalt, 1969).

10. See for a recent example Joan Brockman and Carl D'Arcy, "Correlates of Attitudinal Social Distance toward the Mentally Ill: A Review and Re-survey," *Social Psychiatry* 13 (1978), 69-78.

11. Susan Sontag, *Illness as Metaphor* (New York: Farrar, Straus and Giroux, 1978), 3.

12. See F. Merke, *Geschichte und Ikonographie des endemischen Kropfes und Kretinismus* (Bern-Stuttgart-Wien: Hans Huber, 1971), 275-342.

## Part One: Icons of Madness

1. Cited from the translation of Michel Foucault's *Histoire de la Folie à l'âge classique* (1961), published in an abridged version in English under the title *Madness and Civilization*, trans. Richard Howard (New York: Vintage, 1973), 15.

2. The standard discussion of the medieval iconography of insanity is H. H. Beek, *Waanzin in de middeleewen: Beeld van de Gestoorde en Bemoeienis met de Zieke* (Haarlem: Callenbach, 1969). I have also used the Index of Christian Iconography at Princeton University to examine the appropriate biblical references.

3. The references here are to the edition edited by Ernst Schwarz (Darmstadt: Wissenschaftliche Buchgesellschaft, 1967), ll. 3309, 3345-3349. Of importance is the essay by Francis G. Gummere, "On the Symbolic Use of the Colors Black and White in Germanic Tradition," *Haverford College Studies* 1 (1889), 112-162.

4. Cited from the translation by J. W. Thomas, *Wigalois: The Knight of Fortune's Wheel* (Lincoln: University of Nebraska, 1977), 174.

5. Translated from Justus Lunzer Edler von Lindhausen, ed., *Orneit und Wolfdietrich nach der Wiener Piaristenhandschrift*, Bibliothek des litterarischen Vereins 239 (Tübingen: Litterarischer Verein, 1906), verses 1352-1354.

6. Richard Bernheimer, *Wild Men in the Middle Ages: A Study in Art, Sentiment, and Demonology* (Cambridge: Harvard, 1952), 15.

7. Reprinted in G. N. Bonwetsch and Hanns Achelis, eds., *Hippolytus: Werke I* (Leipzig: J. C. Hinrich, 1897), 359.

8. Cited from the translation by Michael P. McHugh, *St. Ambrose: Seven Exegetical Works*, The Fathers of the Church 65 (Washington: Catholic University, 1972), 19-20.

9. Cited from the translation by A Priest of Mount Lelleray, *St. Bernard's Sermons on the Canticle of Canticles* (Dublin: Browne and Nolan, 1920), 1: 21-22.

10. Penelope B. R. Doob, *Nebuchadnezzar's Children: Conventions of Madness in Middle English Literature* (New Haven: Yale, 1974), 140. See also Judith S. Neaman, "The Distracted Knight: A Study of Insanity in the Arthurian Romance" (Diss., Columbia, 1968). A popularized, shortened version appeared under the title *Suggestion of the Devil: The Origins of Madness* (Garden City, N.Y.: Anchor, 1975).

11. Stanley W. Jackson, "Galen— On Mental Disorders," *Journal of the History of the Behavioral Sciences* 5 (1969), 375.

12. Cited in the introduction to the problem of the depiction of melancholia in Western thought through the Renaissance written by Raymond Klibansky, Erwin Panofsky, and Fritz Saxl, *Saturn and Melancholy: Studies in the History of Natural Philosophy, Religion and Art* (London: Nelson, 1964), 59. Compare Lynn Thorndike, "De Complexionibus," *Isis* 49 (1958), 404. The basic introduction to the history of the classical physiognomies is Elizabeth C. Evans, *Physiognomics in the Ancient World*, Transactions of the American Philosophical Society (Phil-

adelphia: American Philosophical Society, 1969), N. S. 59, 5. See also Rudolf and Margot Wittkower, *Born under Saturn: The Character and Conduct of Artists* (London: Weidenfeld and Nicolson, 1963), especially chapter five, and Jean Starobinski, "Histoire du traitement de la mélancolie des origines à 1900," *Acta psychosomatica* (November, 1960).

13. The standard study of Galen remains Rudolph E. Siegel, *Galen's System of Physiology and Medicine: An Analysis of His Doctrines and Observations on Bloodflow, Respiration, Humors and Internal Diseases* (Basel: S. Karger, 1968), esp. 220-221, 258-321.

14. Black bile becomes the dominant feature in all later discussions of the humors and the temperaments. The seventeenth-century mystic Jacob Böhme devotes well over half of his tractate *De Quatuor Complexionibus*, written during the early 1620s, to a discussion of the origin of sinfulness in the dominance of black bile. The other humors are quickly dismissed. See the edition by Will-Erich Peuckert (Stuttgart: Frommann, 1957), 4:220-252.

15. See Rudolf E. Siegel, trans. and ed., *Galen: On the Affected Parts* (Basel: Karger, 1976). Also: F. I. Wertheimer and Florence E. Hesketh, *The Significance of the Physical Constitution in Mental Disease*, Medicine Monographs 10 (London: Baillière, Tindall and Cox, 1926), 1-9; Leo Kanner, *Judging Emotions from Facial Expressions*, Psychological Monographs (Princeton, N.J.: Psychological Review Company, 1931), 1-11; R. Kirchhoff, "Zur Geschichte und Systematik der Ausdruckstheorien," in R. Kirchhoff, ed., *Handbuch der Psychologie*, vol. 5: *Ausdruckspsychologie* (Göttingen: C. J. Hogrefe, 1965), 9-116.

16. See the discussion in Kurt Seligmann, *The History of Magic* (New York: Pantheon, 1948), 389-409.

17. Cited from W. S. Hett, trans. and ed., *Aristotle: Minor Works* (Cambridge: Harvard, 1936), 105. For a detailed presentation of the complexities of the various mind-body theories see Jerome Schaffer, "Mind-Body Problem," *The Encyclopedia of Philosophy*, ed. Paul Edwards (New York: Macmillan, 1967), 5:336-346.

18. This discussion relies on D. J. Gifford, "Iconographical Notes Towards a Definition of the Medieval Fool," *Journal of the Warburg and Courtauld Institutes* 37 (1974), 336-342, which presents numerous other examples. For the complex relationship between madness and the image of the fool see Enid Welsford, *The Fool: His Social and Literary History* (London: Faber and Faber, 1935); Barbara Swain, *Fools and Folly during the Middle Ages and the Renaissance* (New York: Columbia, 1932); and Johannes Metz, *Das Harlekinthema in der französischen Malerei des 18. Jahrhunderts und seine theatralische Aussage* (Diss., Free University Berlin, 1970) for other later parallels.

19. Numerous parallel portraits of the wild man are to be found in Bernheimer (see note 6 above) and Doob (see note 10 above). For a detailed discussion of the history of the wild man after the Middle Ages see Edward Dudley and Maximilian Novak, eds., *The Wild Man Within: An Image from the Renaissance to Romanticism* (Pittsburgh: University of Pittsburgh Press, 1972).

20. Cited in *Grimms Wörterbuch*, 14:2:315.

21. See Erhard Bahr, "Papageno: The Unenlightened Wild Man in Eighteenth-Century Germany," in Dudley and Novak (see note 19 above), 249-257.

22. It is interesting, however, that no emblems for madness are recorded in Arthur Henkel and Albrecht Schöne, eds., *Emblemata: Handbuch zur Sinnbildkunst des XVI. und XVII. Jahrhunderts* (2nd ed., Stuttgart: Metzler, 1976), the standard catalogue of seventeenth-century emblematic literature. Concerning the image of the madman in the sixteenth and seventeenth centuries see *Sapienza figurata*, Monumenta bergomensia 19 (Ber-

gamo: Edizioni 'Monumenta Bergomensia,' 1967). For the continuation of the images of madness see A. Pigler, *Barockthemen: Eine Auswahl von Verzeichnissen zur Ikonographie des 17. und 18. Jahrhunderts* I (Budapest: Ungarische Akademie der Wissenschaft, 1956): David and Saul, 132; Christ healing the possessed, 307; melancholia, 478-480; four temperaments, 500; stone-cutting, 542. See also the essay by Henry Meige, "Samuel van Hoogstraaten," *Nouvelle Iconographie de la Salpêtrière* 8, (1895), 192-204.

23. The basic discussion of the image of the possessed as witch is to be found in Gregory Zilboorg, *The Medical Man and the Witch during the Renaissance* (Baltimore: Johns Hopkins, 1935) and his (with George W. Henry) *A History of Medical Psychology* (New York: Norton, 1941). The view propounded by Zilboorg is not the one followed in this presentation. Rather, I have employed a modified manner of seeing the medieval and Renaissance stereotypes of madmen and witches as related. In analyzing this material, I have consciously avoided the medical concept of hysteria which has been used to discuss the identification of witches and the insane. See Ilza Veith, *Hysteria: The History of a Disease* (Chicago: University of Chicago, 1965) and Thomas J. Schoeneman, "The Role of Mental Illness in the European Witch Hunts of the Sixteenth and Seventeenth Centuries: An Assessment," *Journal of the History of Behavioural Sciences* 13 (1977), 337-351. This discussion of transvection relies on Rossell Hope Robbins, *The Encyclopedia of Witchcraft and Demonology* (New York: Crown, 1959), 511-514.

24. Klibansky, et al. (see note 12 above), 206-207.

25. Gifford (see note 18 above), 340-342.

26. Cited in the translation by Edwin H. Zeydel, *The Ship of Fools* (New York: Dover, 1962), 299.

27. Wolfgang Harms, *Homo Viator in Bivio: Studien zur Bildlichkeit des Weges*, Medium Aevum, 21 (Munich: Fink, 1970), with rich picture material.

28. Moshe Barasch, "Character and Physiognomy: Bocchi on Donatello's St. George, A Renaissance Text on Expression in Art," *Journal of the History of Ideas* 36 (1975), 424.

29. Translation from Leonard Forster, ed., *The Penguin Book of German Verse* (Baltimore: Penguin, 1959), 22.

30. A detailed presentation of the iconography of grief in art and literature can be found in Moshe Barasch, *Gestures of Despair in Medieval and Early Renaissance Art* (New York: New York University, 1976).

31. See Klibansky, et al. (note 12 above), 286-290. The primary work on this topic remains Hanna and Ilse Jursch, *Hände als Symbol und Gestalt* (10th ed., Berlin: Evangelische Verlagsanstalt, 1960). See also H. Ladendorf, "Zur Hand," in *Medicinae et artibus: Festschrift für Professor Dr. Phil. Dr. Med. Wilhelm Katner* (Dusseldorf: Triltsch, 1968), 61-90. The present discussion relies on the essay by Susan Koslow, "Frans Hals's *Fisherboys*: Exemplars of Idleness," *The Art Bulletin* 67 (1975), 418-432, which provides numerous parallel examples for the motif of the hidden hands.

32. Cited by Siegfried Wenzel, *The Sin of Sloth: Acedia in Medieval Thought and Literature* (Chapel Hill: University of North Carolina, 1967), 106.

33. Ibid., 108.

34. The present discussion is principally indebted to William R. Mueller, "Robert Burton's Frontispiece," *PMLA* 64 (1949), 1074-1788. See also Bergen Evans, *The Psychiatry of Robert Burton* (New York: Columbia, 1944); William R. Mueller, *The Anatomy of Robert Burton's England* (Berkeley: University of California, 1952), 13-20; Lawrence Babb, *Sanity in Bedlam: A Study of Robert Burton's Anatomy of Melancholy* (East Lansing: Michigan State University, 1959), 16-17; Bridget Gellert

Lyons, *Voices of Melancholy: Studies in Literary Treatments of Melancholy in Renaissance England* (London: Routledge and Kegan Paul, 1971), 118ff. Naomi Loeb Lipman, "Robert Burton's *Anatomy of Melancholy* and Its Relation to the Medical Book Tradition," (M. A. thesis, Columbia, 1952) does not discuss the frontispiece.

35. References to *The Anatomy of Melancholy* are to the edition of A. R. Shilleto (London: G. Bell, 1903), 1: 16-17.

36. *Love's Labour Lost*, III, i.

37. Burton (see note 35 above), 1: 39.

38. *Bedlam: A Poem* (London: Printed for the Author, 1774), 5-6.

39. The fashion of the "Melancholic portrait" is discussed by Roy Strong, *The English Icon: Elizabethean and Jacobean Portraiture* (New Haven: Yale, 1969), 35-37, 352-354.

40. This figure is discussed in Paul Richer and Henry Meige, "Documents inédits sur les Démoniaques dans l'art," *Nouvelle Iconographie de la Salpêtrière* 9 (1896), 106-107, as well as in Eugen Holländer, *Plastik und Medizin* (Stuttgart: Ferdinand Enke, 1912), 360-364.

41. John W. Basore, trans., *Seneca I: Moral Essays* (Cambridge: Harvard, 1950), 107-109.

42. See the discussion presented in Loren MacKinney, *Medical Illustrations in Medieval Manuscripts* (London: Wellcome Historical Medical Library, 1965), 43-46, 68-70; plates 36, 39, and 68.

43. In addition to Veith (see note 23 above), see also George Rosen, *Madness in Society: Chapters in the Historical Sociology of Mental Illness* (Chicago: University of Chicago, 1968), 21-138; Bennett Simon, *Mind and Madness in Ancient Greece: The Classical Roots of Modern Psychiatry* (Ithaca, N.Y.: Cornell, 1978), 238-270. The standard visual representation of the *arc de cercle* in Greek art is the so-called "Dying Baccante" in the Uffizi, a reproduction of which is to be found in Jean Rousselot, ed., *Medicine in Art: A Cultural History* (New York: McGraw-Hill, 1967), 51. See also Carl Sittl, *Die Gebärde der Griechen und Römer* (Leipzig: Teubner, 1890).

44. For the implications of the iconography of possession, see Joseph Schumacher, *Die seelischen Volkskrankheiten im deutschen Mittelalter und ihre Darstellungen in der bildenden Kunst*, Neue deutsche Forschungen, Geschichte der Medizin, 3 (Berlin: Junker und Dünnhaupt, 1937), 20-58. Surveys of the religious implications of possession are to be found in Gertrud Schiller, *Ikonographie der christlichen Kunst* (Gütersloh: Gerd Mohn, 1966), 1: 182-183, and Engelbert Kirschbaum, ed., *Lexikon der christlichen Ikonographie* (Freiburg: Herder, 1968), 1: col. 273-277. Of the older essays from the *Nouvelle Iconographie de la Salpêtrière* the following are of value for their documentary material: Jean Heitz, "Les Démoniaques et les Malades dans l'Art byzantin," 14 (1901), 84-96, 161-168; Jean Heitz, "Nouveaux Documents sur Les Possédés et les Malades dans l'Art byzantin," 17 (1904), 158-164; Henry Meige, "Les Possédés des Dieux dans l'Art antique," 7 (1904), 35-64; Henry Meige, "Documents complémentaires sur les Possédés dans l'Art," 16 (1903), 319-320 (with a discussion of the Holbein plate), 411-412. A more detailed discussion of the implications drawn by late nineteenth-century French psychiatry from this material will be found later in this volume.

45. The standard work on this subject is Herbert von Einem, *"Die Verklärung Christi" und die "Heilung des Besessenen" von Raffael*, Akademie der Wissenschaften und der Literatur in Mainz, Abhandlungen der Geistes- und Sozialwissenschaftlichen Klasse, 1966, nr. 5 (Wiesbaden: Franz Steiner, 1966). Von Einem lists a series of analogues on pp. 13-15.

46. For a discussion of the iconography of this and related works see Eugen Holländer, *Die Medizin in der klassischen Malerei* (Stuttgart: Ferdinand Enke, 1923), 248-255, and the following essays from the *Nouvelle Iconographie de la Salpêtrière*: Gilles de la Tourette, "Sur un tableau perdu de Rubens représentant la Guérison de 'Possédés'," 5 (1892), 119-120; A. Souques, "Sur une Esquisse retrouvée de Rubens représentant la Guérison de Possédés," 6 (1893), 238-240; Jean Heitz, "Un Possédé de Rubens: La 'Transfiguration' du Musée de Nancy," 14 (1901), 274-276. See also the essay by Henry Meige and L. Battaille, "Les Miracles de Saint Ignace de Loyola," *Nouvelle Iconographie de la Salpêtrière* 7 (1894), 318-323.

47. Quotes by Robbins (see note 23 above), 396.

48. *Laws*, 7, 790-791b. Cited in the translation by Edith Hamilton and Huntington Cairns, *Plato: The Collected Dialogues*, Bollingen Series, 71 (New York: Pantheon, 1961), 1363.

49. *Politics*, 1340b4. Cited in the translation by Richard McKeon, *The Basic Works of Aristotle* (New York: Random House, 1941), 1312. For further discussion of the iconography of music and dance therapy see W. Kümmel, "Melancholie und die Macht der Musik: Die Krankheit König Sauls in der historischen Diskussion," *Medizin-Historisches Journal* 4 (1969), 189-209; J. Alvin, *Music Therapy* (London: Hutchinson, 1975), 3-70; E. Schmitz-Cliever, "Zur Darstellung des Heiltanzes in der Malerei des 16. und 17. Jahrhunderts," *International Congress of the History of Medicine: Verhandlungen* (Hildesheim: Olms, 1968), 507-509; O. Rock, *Geschichte und Grundlagen der Musiktherapie* (Diss., Cologne, 1971); J. Opper, *Science and the Arts: A Study in Relationships from 1600 to 1900* (Rutherford, N.J.: Fairleigh Dickinson, 1973); H. J. Möller, *Musik und "Wahnsinn": Geschichte und Gegenwart musiktherapeutischer Vorstellungen* (Munich: Fink, 1971); and Günter Bandmann, *Melancholie und Musik: Ikonographische Studien* (Cologne-Opladen: Westdeutscher Verlag, 1960).

50. A detailed iconography of the goiter and related psychopathologies is to be found in F. Merke (see note 12, Preface, above), 275-344.

51. The literature on the stones of madness and folly is extensive. See John J. Hartman, Sarah M. White, James G. Ravin, and Gerald P. Hodge, "The Stones of Madness," *American Imago* 33 (1976), 266-295; Joan F. Menden, "Operation for Stones in the Head: An Engraving by Nicolaes Weydmans," *Journal of the History of Medicine* 24 (1969), 211; W. Braun, "Stone Cutting Scenes from the 16th and 17th Centuries," *Acta Neurochirurgica* 31 (1975), 310; and the following essays by Henry Meige from the *Nouvelle Iconographie de la Salpêtrière*: "Les Operations sur la Tête," 8 (1895), 228-264, 291-322; "Documents nouveaux sur les Operations sur la Tête," 11 (1898), 199-212, 320; "'Pierres de Tête' et 'Pierres de Ventre'," 13 (1900), 77-99. In addition he wrote a summary essay "L'Operation des Pierres de Tête," *Aesculape* 22 (1932), 50-62.

52. Henry Sigerist, ed., *Four Treatises of Theophrastus von Hohenheim called Paracelsus* (Baltimore: Johns Hopkins, 1941), 173-175. See also J. M. Grabman, "The Witch of Mallegem," *Journal of the History of Medicine* 30 (1975), 385.

53. The relevant literature on Bosch is extensive. The standard survey is Ludwig Baldass, *Hieronymous Bosch* (Vienna and Munich: Anton Schroll, 1959). Of interest is Frances Jowell, "The Paintings of Hieronymous Bosch," *Proceedings of the Royal Society of Medicine* 58 (1965), 131-136; Charles de Tolnay, *Hieronymous Bosch* (London: Methuen, 1966); A. R. Lucas, "The Imagery of Bosch," *American Journal of Psychiatry* 124 (1968), 1515-1523; Erich Fromm, "The Manifest and Latent

Content of Two Paintings by H. Bosch," *American Imago* 26 (1969), 145-166.

54. The text is available in the modernized edition by Karl Martin Schiller, *Hans Sachs: Werke* (Berlin: Aufbau, 1966), 2: 360-375.

55. Henry Meige, "Les Guérisseurs de Phantaisies," *Nouvelle Iconographie de la Salpêtrière* 18 (1916-1918), 438-452.

56. Hermann Peters, *Der Arzt und die Heilkunst in der deutschen Vergangenheit* (Leipzig: Eugen Diederichs, 1900), plate 123.

57. Clements C. Fry, "The Sixteenth-Century Cures for Lunacy," *American Journal of Psychiatry* 103 (1946), 351-354.

58. See Foucault (note 1 above), 13ff; and Dieter Jetter, *Zur Typologie des Irrenhauses in Frankreich und Deutschland (1780-1840)* (Wiesbaden: Steiner, 1971).

59. See the discussions of the image of the ship in Kathleen M. Grange, "The Ship Symbol as a Key to Former Theories of the Emotions," *Bulletin of the History of Medicine* 36 (1962), 512-523, and Horst S. and Ingrid Daemmrich, *Wiederholte Spiegelungen: Themen und Motive in der Literatur* (Bern and Munich: Francke, 1978), 39ff.

60. See Friedrich Winkler, *Dürer und die Illustrationen zum Narrenschiff*, Forschungen zur deutschen Kunstgeschichte 36 (Berlin: Deutscher Verein für Kunstwissenschaft, 1951).

61. The discussion of the inexplicability of the plate is to be found in M. Seidl and R. H. Marijnissen, *Breughel* (New York: Putnam, 1971).

62. See Helmut Vogt, *Das Bild des Kranken: Die Darstellung äusserer Veränderungen durch innere Leiden und ihrer Heilmassnahmen von der Renaissance bis in unsere Zeit* (Munich: J. F. Lehmann, 1969), 319.

### Part Two: Images of Madness

1. Alexander Pope, *Dunciad*, I, 32.

2. Three recent studies give detailed commentary on the concept of madness in the early eighteenth century: Michael V. DePorte, *Nightmares and Hobbyhorses: Swift, Sterne and Augustan Ideas of Madness* (San Marino, Calif.: The Huntington Library, 1974), especially pp. 3-53; Mervyn James Jannetta, "'The predominant Passion, and its force': Propensity, volition and motive in the Works of Swift and Pope," (Diss.: York, 1975); and Max Byrd, *Visits to Bedlam: Madness and Literature in the Eighteenth Century* (Columbia, S.C.: University of South Carolina, 1974).

3. A. C. Guthkelch and D. Nichol Smith, eds., *A Tale of a Tub* (Oxford: Clarendon, 1958), 176-179, see also xxv-xxviii.

4. See Richard Hunter and Ida Macalpine, eds., *Three Hundred Years of Psychiatry, 1535-1860* (London: Oxford University Press, 1963), 90.

5. All modern commentaries on this plate are based on Lichtenberg's analysis published in the 1790s. A full English translation is now available by Innes and Gustav Herdan, *Lichtenberg's Commentaries on Hogarth's Engravings* (London: Cresset, 1966), here 263.

6. Cited from the standard catalogue of Hogarth's works: Ronald Paulson, *Hogarth's Graphic Works* (New Haven: Yale, 1970), 1: 169. See also Paulson's magnificent study of the cultural context of the works, *Hogarth: His Life, Art and Times* (New Haven: Yale, 1971), 1: 325-328.

7. *Lichtenberg* (see note 5 above), 264.

8. Thomas Tryon, *A Treatise of dreams & visions* (London: Sowle, 1689), 261-262.

9. *Lichtenberg* (see note 5 above), 263.

10. A contemporary image of Bedlam c. 1745 influenced by Hogarth is reproduced in Daniel Hack Tuke, *Chapters in the History of the Insane in the British Isles* (London: Kegan Paul, Trench & Co., 1882), 74, from the archives at Bethlehem Hospital.

11. Ida Macalpine and Richard Hunter, *George III and the Mad-Business* (New York: Pantheon, 1969).

12. An excellent essay on the eighteenth-century image of the insane and its relationship to older images is to be found in Martin Schrenk, *Über den Umgang mit Geisteskranken*, Monographien aus dem Gesamtgebiete der Psychiatrie 10 (Heidelberg: Springer, 1973), 130-139.

13. Aldo Scapini, *Dalla 'Fisiognomica' di Giovan Battista della Porta (sec. XVII) alla morfologia costituzionalistica*, Scientia Veterum 159 (Pisa: Giardini, 1970).

14. E. Vaenius, *Tractatus physiologicus de pulchritudine. Juxta et quae de sponsa in Canticis Canticorum mystice pronunciantur* (Bruxellis: Fr. Foppens, 1662); Charles Le Brun, *La physionomie humaine comparée à la physionomie des animaux* (Paris: H. Laurens, 1927). For a detailed account and bibliography of these texts see Heinrich Laehr, *Die Literatur der Psychiatrie, Neurologie und Psychologie von 1459-1799* (Berlin: Reimer, 1900), especially 3: 213-214. From the standpoint of the history of art, the best discussion (with numerous illustrations) remains Ernst Kris, "Die Charakterköpfe des Franz Xaver Messerschmidt," *Jahrbuch der kunsthistorischen Sammlungen Wien*, N. F. 6 (1932), 169-228. See also Vogt (note 62, Icons of Madness, above), 261-272.

15. See his collected works in the French edition *Oeuvres de Pierre Camper, qui ont pour objet l'histoire naturelle, la physiologie et l'anatomie comparée* (Paris: Janson, 1803), 3 vols. and an atlas of 34 plates, and *The Works of the Late Professor Camper, in the Connexion between the Science of Anatomy and the Arts of Drawing, Painting, Statuary*, trans. T. Cogan (London: C. Dilly, 1794). For a survey of his work see the essay by G. A. Lindeboom in the *Dictionary of Scientific Biography*, ed. Charles Coulston Gillispie (New York: Scribner, 1971), 3: 37-38.

16. My discussion of the concept of the passions is indebted to an unpublished paper, M. H. Stone, "Modern Concepts of Emotion as Prefigured in Descartes' Passions of the Soul." See also Alejandro A. Jascalevich, *Three Conceptions of Mind: Their Bearing on the Denaturalization of the Mind in History* (New York: Columbia, 1926).

17. James Parsons, *Human physiognomy explain'd in the Crouian Lectures on muscular motion for the year MDCCXLVI* (London: The Royal Society, 1747), 60-62.

18. Parsons' view of the expression of the passions, especially those of fear and terror, and their relationship to concepts of insanity is prefigured in Edmund Burke's *A Philosophical Enquiry into the Origin of Our Ideas of the Sublime and Beautiful* (1757). See the edition by J. T. Boulton (Notre Dame: University of Notre Dame, 1958), 134-135.

19. Parsons (see note 17 above), 63-64.

20. From the translation by Stephen J. Gendzier, *The Encyclopedia: Selections* (New York: Harper & Row, 1967), 7. See especially Jacques Roger, *Les Sciences de la vie dans la pensée française du xviii^e siècle* (Paris: A. Colin, 1971), and Lynn Thorndike, "L'Encyclopédie and the History of Science," *Isis* 6 (1924), 361-386. An early example of illustrations of the passions is to be found in the frontispiece of J. F. Senault, *The Use of Passions*, trans. Henry Earl of Monmouth (London: John Sims, 1671).

21. See Herbert Dieckmann, *Cinq Leçons sur Diderot* (Geneva: Droz, 1959), as well as his essay "The concept of knowledge in the *Encyclopedie*," in his *Studien zur europäischen Aufklärung* (Munich: Fink, 1974), 234-257. The idea of a visual scale of the passions becomes a common-

place in handbooks and encyclopedias of the early nineteenth century. For example, there is a plate illustrating sixteen modes of expression in the *Systematische Bilder-Gallerie zur allgemeinen deutschen Real Encyclopedia* (1825-1827; Freiburg: Herder, 1977). It is apparent that the varieties of human emotion belong to the catalogue of the visible world as much as plates of buildings or ships. In this source the lithographs of the passions are no longer relegated to the rubric of "drawing" but appear as part of the study of "human physiognomy" along with anatomical plates.

22. Reinhard Kunz, *Johann Caspar Lavaters Physiognomielehre im Urteil von Haller, Zimmermann und anderen zeitgenössischen Ärzten*, Züricher Medizingeschichtliche Abhandlungen N. F. 71 (Zürich: Juris, 1970), and Christian Janentzky, *J. C. Lavaters Sturm und Drang im Zusammenhang seines religiösen Bewusstseins* (Halle: Niemeyer, 1916). The most important essay remains Hans Pollonow, "Historisch-kritische Beiträge zur Physiognomik," *Jahrbuch der Charakterologie* 5 (1928), 157-206. See also G. D. Tytler, "Character Description and Physiognomy in the European Novel (1800-1860) in Relation to J. C. Lavater's *Physiognomische Fragmente*," (Diss.: University of Illinois, 1970).

23. *Hannoverisches Magazin* 10 (1772), 148.

24. Ibid., 147.

25. From his *Von der Physiognomik* (Leipzig: Weidmann, 1772), 1:12.

26. Ibid, 1:65-66, 83-84, 91-93.

27. Albrecht von Haller, *Elementa physiologiae* (Lausannae: Grasset, 1763), 570-574.

28. *Physiognomische Fragmente zur Beförderung der Menschenkenntnis und Menschenliebe* (Leipzig und Winterthur: Weidmann, 1774-1778). The examples of psychopathologies are to be found in 1:62 (taken from Parsons); 2:35, 180, 182, 184, 189, 261, 281 (the contrast between a cretin and Plato); 4:56, 75, 128, 352.

29. Ibid., 2:34-35.

30. Ibid., 2:181.

31. See Ludwig Kaemmerer, *Chodowiecki*, Künstler-Monographien 21 (Bielefeld: Velhagen und Klasing, 1879). The image of the madman within a biographical context can also be found in Chodowiecki's portrait of the four insane brothers at St. Hiob's which accompanied Matthias Claudius' discussion of his visit to the asylum in 1782. This portrait, with its typical image of melancholic and manic patients, moves from the Hogarthian image of the asylum toward that of the illustrated biography. See Matthias Claudius, *Werke* (Gotha: Perthes, 1871), 4:86.

32. Thomas Holcroft, ed. and trans., *Essays on Physiognomy for the Promotion of the Knowledge and the Love of Mankind* (London: Whittingham, 1804), 1:64-65. The Holcroft is typical of the large number of editions of Lavater's works adapted into English and other European languages during the first half of the nineteenth century. Further editions will be discussed below.

33. Ibid., 2:280.

34. *Goethe and Lavater: Briefe und Tagebücher*, ed. Heinrich Runck, Schriften der Goethe-Gesellschaft 16 (Weimar: Goethe-Gesellschaft, 1901), 58. See also K. W. Peukert, "Die Physiognomik in Goethes Morphologie," *Deutsche Vierteljahrsschrift* 47 (1973), 400-419.

35. Immanuel Kant, *Werke*, ed. Wilhelm Weischedel (Wiesbaden: Insel, 1964), 10:643.

36. J. J. Engel, *Ideen zu einer Mimik* (Berlin: Mylius, 1785), 113-114. Engel's work, initially intended to instruct actors on the technique of imitating the scale of passions and types, reappears in numerous discussions of types of insanity, such as Gall's atlas. More recently, it assumed a central role in Karl Bühler's analysis of the development of theories of expression. See his *Ausdruckstheorie: Das System an der Geschichte aufgezeigt* (2nd ed., Stuttgart: Gustav Fischer, 1968), 36-52.

37. See Rudolf Herzog and Hans H. Walser, "Johann Konrad Fäsi-Gessner (1796-1870): Unbekannte Zeichnungen aus dem alten Züricher Spital," *Zürischer Taschenbuch auf das Jahr 1969* (Zurich: Sihl, 1968), 121-146. Fäsi-Gessner's copy of Lavater's *Fragmente* is in the possession of the Beinecke Library at Yale.

38. See A. Dorgerloh, *Verzeichnis der durch Kunstdruck vervielfältigten Arbeiten Adolf Menzels* (Leipzig: E. A. Seemann, 1905).

39. See Walther Riese, *The Legacy of Phillipe Pinel: An Inquiry into Thought on Mental Alienation* (New York: Springer [1969]).

40. George Rosen, "The Philosophy of Ideology and the Emergence of Modern Medicine in France," *Bulletin of the History of Medicine* 20 (1046), 329-339.

41. Phillipe Pinel, *Traité médico-philosophique sur l'aliénation mentale, ou la manie* (Paris: Richard, Caille et Ravier, IX [1801]). Cited from the translation by D. D. Davis, *A Treatise on Insanity* (1806; rpt. New York: Hafner, 1962), 126-127.

42. Ibid., 129-131.

43. See Edwin Clarke and Kenneth Dewhurst, *An Illustrated History of Brain Function* (Berkeley: University of California, 1974).

44. *Encyclopédie méthodique*, 172: Médecine 9 (Paris: Agasse, 1814), 136-219.

45. *L'art de connaître des hommes par Gaspard Lavater* (Paris: n.p., 1807), 8:223-233.

46. Concerning the contemporary view of the feral child as an example of a psychopathological state see Lucien Malson, *Wolf Children and the Problem of Human Nature*, trans. Edmund Fawcett, et al. (New York: Monthly Review Press [1972]).

47. Moreau de la Sarthe (see note 44 above), 233-235.

48. In the *Dictionnaire des sciences médicales* (Paris: Panckoucke, 1812-1822), Esquirol was responsible for, among others, the essays on "Démonomanie," "Folie," "Manie," and "Lypemanie."

49. J. E. D. Esquirol, *Des maladies mentales considérées sous les rapports médical, hygiénique et médico-légal* (Paris: J. B. Baillière, 1838).

50. Ibid., 2:167.

51. The translation is by E. K. Hunt, *Mental Maladies* (1845; rpt. New York: Hafner, 1965), 204-205.

52. See Jean Adhémar, "Un Dessinateur passionné pour le visage humain—Georges-François-Marie Gabriel (1775 - v. 1836)," in *Omagiu lui George Oprescu cu prilejul implinirii a 80 de ani* (Bucharest: Editura Academiei Republicii Populare Romîne, 1961), 1-4.

53. Etienne Jean Georget, *De la folie* (Paris: Crevot, 1820), 133.

54. The standard essay on this topic remains Margaret Miller, "Géricault's Paintings of the Insane," *Journal of the Warburg and Courtauld Institutes* 4 (1940-1941), 151-163. Of less interest is Hossen Cadinouche, *La médecine dans oeuvre de Géricault* (Paris: Marcel Vigne, 1929), 31-34. Recently the essay by Jerome Schneck, "Etienne Georget, Théodore Géricault, and the Portraits of the Insane," *New York State Journal of Medicine* 78 (1978), 668-671, reviewed Miller's argument.

55. Kenneth Clark, *The Romantic Rebellion: Romantic versus Classic Art* (New York: Harper & Row, 1973).

56. Charles Bell, *Essays on the Anatomy of Expression in Painting* (London: Longman, et al., 1806), 153-157. Concerning Bell see Gordon Gordon-Taylor, *Sir Charles Bell: His Life and Times* (Edinburgh and London: E. S. Livingstone, 1958), especially 17-26.

57. The German edition appeared under the title *Es-*

NOTES FOR PAGES 62 - 91

quirols allgemeine und spezielle Pathologie und Therapie der Seelenstörungen, ed. Karl Christian Hille (Leipzig: C. H. F. Hartmann, 1827), with eleven plates engraved by F. Milde from Esquirol's originals.

58. Alexander Morison, Outlines of Lectures on Mental Diseases (London: Longman, et al., 1826), 125-126.

59. Alexander Morison, The Physiognomy of Mental Disease (London: Longman Co., 1840); Physiognomik der Geisteskrankheiten (Leipzig: Ernst Schäfer, 1853). See also Vieda Skultans, ed., Madness and Morals: Ideas of Insanity in the Nineteenth Century (London: Routledge and Kegan Paul, 1975), 71-98.

60. Morison, ibid., 267.

61. Matthew Allen, Essay on the Classification of the Insane (London: John Taylor, [1837]). Allen was also the author of Cases of Insanity with Medical, Moral and Philosophical Observations (London: W. Swire, 1831).

62. Ibid., 116. A more detailed discussion of Allen's work is to be found in Hunter and Macalpine (see note 4 above), 855-856.

63. Adolph Freyherr von Knigge, Über den Umgang mit Menschen (5th ed., Hannover: Christian Ritscher, 1796), 213-220.

64. Christian Heinrich Spiess, Biographieen der Wahnsinnigen (Leipzig: Voss, 1795-1796). A modern edition by Wolfgang Promies (Neuwied: Luchterhand, 1966) presents a selection from the text as well as an appendix regarding the paucity of illustrative material depicting the insane during the eighteenth century (335-336).

65. A more detailed discussion of Alibert's contribution to the history of medical illustration is to be found in Vogt (see Icons of Madness, note 62), 48-52.

66. Jean Louis Alibert, Physiologie des Passions ou Nouvelle Doctrine des sentimens moraux (2nd ed., Paris: Bechet Jeune, 1826), 363-384.

67. Jean Baptiste Lautard, La Maison des Fous de Marseille: Essai historique et statistique (Marseille: D'Achard, 1840).

68. Karl Wilhelm Ideler, Biographieen Geisteskranker in ihrer psychologischen Entwicklung (Berlin: E. H. Schroeder, 1841), here, xvi.

69. Anatomie et physiologie du système nerveux en général et du cerveau en particulier avec des observations sur la possibilité de reconnaître plusieurs dispositions intellectuelles et morales de l'homme et des animaux par la configuration de leurs têtes (Paris: Maze, 1810-1819). Gall's discussion of mental illness appears in vol. 2: 190-212, 254-255, 261-267, 270-296, 334-343, 353-355, 417-452; vol. 3: 122-133, 157-159, 174-175, 187-190, 217-244, 269-275, 301-307, 329, 334-337; vol. 4: 49-51, 83-86, 102-103, 152, 187-188, 221, 258-263.

70. The best general introduction is David De Giustino, Conquest of Mind: Phrenology and Victorian Social Thought (London: Croom Helm, 1975).

71. P. S. Noel and Eric T. Carlson, "The Origins of the Word 'Phrenology'," American Journal of Psychiatry 127 (1970), 694-697.

72. Published by Baldwin, Cradock and Joy in London, Spurzheim's study has been reprinted with an introduction by Anthony A. Walsh (Delmar, N.Y.: Scholar's Facsimiles, 1972).

73. Ibid., pp. 141-142.

74. For Carus' discussion of the mind-body problem see lectures 11 through 13 in his Vorlesungen über Psychologie gehalten im Winter 1829-30, ed. Edgar Michaelis (Erlenbach-Zürich: Rotapfel, 1931). The atlas of skull studies appeared under the title Grundzüge einer neuen und wissenschaftlich begrundeten Cranioscopie (Stuttgart: Balz, 1841). Of importance in the general study of the interpretation of expression is Carus' Symbolik der menschlichen Gestalt (Leipzig: F. A. Brockhaus, 1858),

which does not discuss psychopathologies, and his Physis (Stuttgart: C. P. Scheitlin, 1851), which mentions this question only in passing. Concerning Carus see Gerhard Kloos, Die Konstitutionslehre von Carl Gustav Carus mit besonderer Berücksichtigung seiner Physiognomik, Biblioteca psychiatrica et neurologica 90 (Basel: Karger, 1951).

75. Richard K. Crallé, ed., The Works of John C. Calhoun (New York: D. Appleton, 1874), 5:337-338.

76. Other reactions to the census are: C. B. Hayden, "On the Distribution of Insanity in the United States," Southern Literary Messenger 10 (1844), 180; Samuel Forrey, "Vital Statistics Furnished by the Sixth Census of the United States, Bearing Upon the Question of the Unity of the Human Race," and "On the Relative Proportion of Centenarians, of Deaf and Dumb, of Blind, and of Insane, in the Races of European and African Origin, as Shown by the Censuses of the United States," New York Journal of Medicine and the Collateral Sciences 1 (1843), 151-167, and 2 (1844), 310-320.

77. The most recent and most complete discussion is in Gerald W. Grob, Edward Jarvis and the Medical World of Nineteenth Century America (Knoxville: University of Tennessee, 1978), 70-75. See also Eric T. Carlson, "Nineteenth Century Insanity and Poverty," Bulletin of the New York Academy of Medicine 48 (1972), 539-544, which presents data on earlier statistical surveys of insanity. Carlson omits the Parkman survey of the insane in Massachusetts undertaken in 1817.

78. "Startling Facts from the Census," American Journal of Insanity 8 (1851), 154, reprinted from the New York Observer. Jarvis immediately published a rejoinder, "Insanity Among the Coloured Population of the Free States," American Journal of Insanity 8 (1952), 268-282.

79. "Report on the Diseases and Physical Peculiarities of the Negro Race," [Part 1] New Orleans Medical and Surgical Journal 7 (1851), 692-713. Cartwright's views quickly became the subject of much debate. See his letter to Daniel Webster on this subject published in DeBow's Review 11 (1851), 184-187. Concerning Cartwright see James Denny Guillory, "The Pro-Slavery Arguments of Dr. Samuel A. Cartwright," Louisiana History 9 (1968), 209-227; Thomas S. Szasz, "The Sane Slave: An Historical Note on the Use of Medical Diagnosis as Justificatory Rhetoric," American Journal of Psychotherapy 25 (1971), 228-239, as well as his "Negro in Psychiatry: An Historical Note on Psychiatric Rhetoric," American Journal of Psychotherapy 25 (1971), 469-471.

80. Ibid. ("The Sane Slave"), 233-234.

81. J. F. Miller, "The Effects of Emancipation upon the Mental and Physical Qualifications of the Negro in the South," North Carolina Medical Journal 38 (1896), 287, cited by John S. Haller, Outcasts from Evolution: Scientific Attitudes of Racial Inferiority 1859-1900 (Urbana: University of Illinois, 1971), 45.

82. Quoted in Henry M. Hurd, ed., The Institutional Care of the Insane in The United States and Canada (Baltimore: Johns Hopkins, 1916), 372-373.

83. Ibid., 376.

84. Benjamin Pasamanick, "Myths Regarding Prevalence of Mental Disease in the American Negro: A Century of Misuse of Mental Hospital Data and Some New Findings," Journal of the National Medical Association 56 (1964), 17. See also William D. Postell, "Mental Health among the Slave Population on Southern Plantations," American Journal of Psychiatry 110 (1953), 52-54.

85. Pasamanick, ibid., 6.

86. M. B. Sampson, Rationale of Crime and Its Appropriate Treatment with Notes and Illustrations by E. W. Farnham (New York: D. Appleton, 1846).

87. See Madeleine B. Stern, "Matthew B. Brady and the Rationale of Crime: A Discovery in Daguerreotypes,"

The *Quarterly Journal of the Library of Congress* 31 (1974), 127-135. See especially note 8 there for a discussion of the line drawings. See also her *Heads & Headlines: The Phrenological Fowlers* (Norman: University of Oklahoma, 1971); and W. David Lewis, *From Newgate to Dannemora: The Rise of the Penitentiary in New York, 1796-1848* (Ithaca, N.Y.: Cornell, 1965), 237-256.

88. John D. Davies, *Phrenology, Fad and Science: A 19th-Century American Crusade* (New Haven: Yale, 1955), 48. Davies' chapter "Phrenology and Insanity" (89-97) is the best presentation of this question. However, he does not deal with the illustrations or visualizations of the insane, even though he presents the phrenologist's image of the scale of human existence as his frontispiece.

89. Samuel R. Wells, *New Physiognomy; or, Signs of Character* (New York: Fowler & Wells, 1883), 332-357. Wells brings illustrations from Lavater and Spurzheim, in addition to Bell and Kaulbach.

90. John Caspar Lavater, *Essays on Physiognomy*, ed. Thomas Holloway, trans. from the French by Henry Hunter (London: John Murray, 1789); Jean Gaspard Lavater, *Essai sur la physiognomie* (La Haye: Karnebeek, 1781-1803), 4 vols.

91. Lavater, *Essays*, 2: 228.

92. The discussion relies on Peter Tomory, *The Life and Art of Henry Fuseli* (London: Thames and Hudson, 1972), 84-87; see also the discussion in Gert Schiff, *Johann Heinrich Füssli 1741-1825: Text- und Oeuvrekatalog* (Zürich: Berichthaus, 1973), 515; and Frederick Anatal, *Fuseli-Studies* (London: Routledge and Kegan Paul, 1956), 121.

93. G. E. Bentley, Jr., *Blake Books* (Oxford: Clarendon, 1977), 592-595. The standard study of Blake's iconography is Kathleen Raine, *Blake and Tradition*, Bollingen Series, 35, 11 (Princeton: Princeton University, 1968), see especially 1:122-125.

94. Geoffrey Keynes, ed., *The Complete Writings of William Blake* (London: Nonesuch, 1957), 192.

95. Geoffrey Keynes, ed., *The Letters of William Blake* (Cambridge: Harvard, 1968), 106. My comments reflect the annotation given in the older edition edited by Archibald G. B. Russell, *The Letters of William Blake* (New York: Scribner's, 1906), 170. For an excellent, detailed iconography of the Blake plate see Bo Lindberg, "William Blake's Nebuchadnezzar och Mansködjuret," *Konsthistoriska stüdior* (Helsinki) 1 (1974), 10-18.

96. See Raine (note 93 above), 1: 6; also Anthony Blunt, "Blake's Pictorial Imagination," *Journal of the Warburg and Courtauld Institutes* 6 (1943), 203-204, and Jean H. Hagsrum, *William Blake: Poet and Painter* (Chicago: University of Chicago, 1964), 38.

97. As late as the beginning of the nineteenth century publishers vied to keep Le Brun's physiognomy before the public, for example *Bowles's Passions of the Soul, represented in several heads from the designs of the late celebrated M. Le Brun* (London: Bowles and Carver, 1800).

98. John Varley, *A Treatise on Zodiacal Physiognomy; illustrated by Engravings of Heads and Features* (London: By the Author, 1828). The Blake-Varley notebook has been reproduced in an edition by Martin Butlin, *The Blake-Varley Sketchbook of 1819* (London: Heinemann, 1969). The present plate is closely related to page 12, "8 profiles plus two beginnings."

99. Murdoch's work was published in Dublin for J. Rea, 1783.

100. This discussion is grounded on Ronald Paulson, *Rowlandson: A New Interpretation* (New York: Oxford, 1972), especially 33-35. See also M. Dorothy George, *Hogarth to Cruikshank: Social Changes in Graphic Satire* (London: Allan Lane, 1967).

101. V. S. Pritchett, *The Living Novel* (New York: Vintage, 1967), 21.

102. H. S. Milford, *Cowper: Poetical Works* (London: Oxford, 1967), 140-141. For discussion of related works see Tomory (note 92 above), 172-174.

103. A most useful review of the criticism on Goya is available in Nigel Glendinning, *Goya and His Critics* (New Haven: Yale, 1977).

104. The standard study of Goya's debt to the iconography of insanity is Folke Nordström, *Goya, Saturn and Melancholy: Studies in the Art of Goya* Figura, NS 3 (Stockholm: Almqvist & Wiksell, 1962).

105. Ibid., 59-75.

106. Cited by Valerian von Loga, *Francisco de Goya* (Berlin: G. Grote, 1921), 163-164.

107. See Nordström (note 104 above), 72-73, and Nicolas Powell, *Fuseli: The Nightmare* (New York: Viking, 1973).

108. See J. L. Foy, "The Deafness and Madness of Goya," in I. Jakab, ed., *Conscious and Unconscious Expressive Art*, Psychiatry and Art, 3 (Basel: Karger, 1971), 2-24.

109. The drawings are reproduced in Pierre Gassier and Juliet Wilson, *The Life and Complete Works of Francisco Goya* (New York: Regnal, 1971), drawings 1725, 1737-1742, 1744-1750; see also p. 339.

110. See the discussion of Lavater in José Lopez-Rey, *Goya's Caprichos: Beauty, Reason and Caricature* (Westport, Conn.: Greenwood, 1970).

111. Jean Stewart, ed. and trans., *Eugène Delacroix: Selected Letters 1813-1863* (London: Eyre and Spottiswoode, 1971), 56.

112. Ernest H. Coleridge, ed., *The Works of Lord Byron* (London: John Murray, 1901), 4, 145-146.

113. See especially Uve Fischer, *Das literarische Bild im Werk Eugène Delacroix* (Diss., Bonn 1963), 343-344; and Colomba Calcagni, "La validita' dell'arte pittorica nella patologia ed in particolare nelle malattie mentali," *Congresso nazionale de storia della Medicina* Florence 1966 (Rome: Società italiana di storia della medicina, 1967), 590-610.

## Part Three: The Reform of Madness

1. W. Scott Peterson, "The Author Run Mad," *Journal of the History of Medicine* 27 (1972), 325.

2. Concerning the development of the image of the insane see Werner Leibbrand and Annemarie Wettley, *Der Wahnsinn: Geschichte der abendländischen Psychopathologie* (Freiburg: Karl Alber, 1961). Comparative studies of interest are W. Weygandt, "Die Darstellung abnormer Seelenzustände in der japanischen Kunst," *Zeitschrift für Neurologie und Psychiatrie* 150 (1934), 500-506; and L. S. Copelman and Liliane Copelman-Fromant, "Les portraits psychiatriques dans le miroir des beaux-arts," in I. Jakab, ed., *Conscious and Unconscious Expressive Art*, Psychiatry and Art, 3 (Basel: Karger, 1971), 25-29.

3. See Patricia Allderidge, *The Late Richard Dadd 1817-1866* (London: The Tate Gallery, 1974), 95-96.

4. Concerning Kaulbach see Fritz von Ostini, *Wilhelm von Kaulbach* (Bielefeld: Velhagen und Klasing, 1906). See also Carl Zigrosser, ed., *Medicine and the Artist* (New York: Dover, 1970), 113-120.

5. Guido Görres, *Das Narrenhaus von Wilhelm Kaulbach gestochen von H. März nebst Ideen über Kunst und Wahnsinn* (n.p.: Besonders abgedruckt aus dem Morgenblatt, 1836), here 29.

6. Ibid, 40.

7. Karl Rosenkranz, *Aesthetik des Hässlichen* (Königsberg: Bornträger, 1853), 308-309.

8. Johann August Schilling, *Psychiatrische Briefe oder die Irren, das Irresein und das Irrenhaus* (Augsburg: J. A. Schlosser, 1863), 387-473.

9. Concerning the introduction of the figure of the unmarried mother see Oscar H. Werner, *The Unmarried Mother in German Literature* (1917; rpt. New York: Ams Press, 1966).

10. See Jean Vinchon, "En marge des dessins de folies du Docteur Paul Gachet," and Paul Gachet, "Médecine et Art," *Histoire de la médecine*, numéro spécial 8 (1958), 9-22, 23-27. Of more general interest is G. J. Reimann-Hunziker, "Dr. med. Paul-Ferdnand Gachet (Paul van Ryssel) als Radierer und sein Einfluss auf die Impressionisten," *International Congress for the History of Medicine*, Basel 1964 (Basel: S. Karger, 1966), 637-643. Also see L. Garrison, "History of Illustrations in Psychiatry," *British Journal of Photography* 117 (1970), 880-883.

11. Johanthon Mayne, ed., *Art in Paris 1845-1862: Salons and Other Exhibitions Reviewed by Charles Baudelaire* (London: Phaidon, 1965), 165.

12. All references to this essay are to the edition of Harry Stone, ed., *Charles Dickens' Uncollected Writings from Household Words 1850-1859* (Bloomington: Indiana University, 1968), II: 381-391. Stone describes the state of the preserved manuscript of the essay and provides editorial commentary on it. Other literature on the essay, as well as on the question of Dickens' knowledge of nineteenth-century psychiatric theories and practice, is not great. The major studies are: Richard A. Hunter and Ida Macalpine, "A Note on Dickens' Psychiatric Reading," *The Dickensian* 53 (1957), 49-51; and Leonard Manheim, "Dickens' Fools and Madmen," *Dickens Studies Annual* 2 (1971), 69-97, 357-359. Also of interest are: H. P. Sucksmith, "The Identity and Significance of the Mad Huntsman in *The Pickwick Papers*," *The Dickensian*, 68 (1972), 109-114; A. and P. Plichet, "Charles Dickens et ses observations neuro-psychiatriques," *Presse médicale* 64 (1956), 2230-2233; L. Schotte, "La médecine et les médecins dans la vie et l'oeuvre de Charles Dickens (1812-1870)," *Chronique médicale* 19 (1912), 97-105; Isaak Oehlbaum, *Das pathologische Element bei Dickens* (Diss., Zürich, 1944); *Dickens and Medicine*, Exhibition Catalogue No. 5, The Wellcome Institute of the History of Medicine (1970), 9-10; and Fred Kaplan, *Dickens and Mesmerism: The Hidden Springs of Fiction* (Princeton: Princeton University, 1975).

13. Hunter and Macalpine (see Images of Madness, note 4), 998-999.

14. See the note on Katharine Drake by P. D. Gibbons, *Journal of the History of Medicine* 21 (1966), 184.

15. *Frank Leslie's Illustrated Newspaper*, December 9, 1865, 188.

16. Cited by Skultans (see Images of Madness, note 59), 172.

17. *Ceremonies et coutumes religieuses de tous les peuples du monde* (Amsterdam: J. F. Bernard, 1728-1743). For a discussion of Picart, see Vogt (Icons of Madness, note 62), 309-310. A more general introduction to this problem is offered by Margarite Putscher, "Changes in medical illustration in the first half of the seventeenth century," *Proceedings of the Twenty-Third International Congress of the History of Medicine* (London: Wellcome Institute, 1974), 2:911-913.

18. Cited by Hunter and Macalpine (see Images of Madness, note 4), 478.

19. *Della pazzia in genere e in specie tratto medico analitico con una centuria de osservazioni* (Firenze: Carlieri, 1793-1794).

20. Cited by George Mora, "Vincenzo Chiarugi (1759-1820): His Contribution to Psychiatry," *Bulletin of the Isaac Ray Medical Library* 2 (1954), 58.

21. Cited by Hunter and Macalpine (see Images of Madness, note 4), 699-700.

22. The standard study of masturbatory insanity is E. H. Hare, "Masturbatory Insanity: The History of an Idea," *The Journal of Mental Science* 108 (1962), 1-25. Also of interest are Karl-Felix Jacobs, *Die Entstehung der Onanie-Literatur im 17. und 18. Jahrhundert* (Diss., Munich 1963); and R. P. Neuman, "Masturbation, Madness, and the Modern Concepts of Childhood and Adolescence," *Journal of Social History* 8 (1975), 1-26. None of these studies treats the eighteenth-century literature on masturbation printed in German.

23. See especially Gudrun Burggraf, *Christian Gotthilf Salzmann im Verfeld der französischen Revolution* (Germering: Stahlmann, [1966]).

24. Benjamin Rush, *Medical Inquiries and Observations upon The Diseases of the Mind* (1812), facsimile edition (New York: Hafner, 1962), 349-350.

25. G. W. Becker, *Verhütung und Heilung der Onanie mit allen ihren Folgen bey beyden Geschlechten* (Leipzig: Karl Tauchnitz, 1803), 250-251.

26. D. M. Rozier, *Des Habitudes secrètes ou des maladies produites par l'onanisme chez les femmes* (3rd ed., Paris: Audin, 1830). This is one of the very rare illustrated studies of masturbatory insanity.

27. *Philadelphia Medical Museum* N.S.1 (1811), 169-173.

28. A presentation of illustrations of treatment without any discussion of their implications is to be found in A. A. Roback and Thomas Kiernan, *Pictorial History of Psychology and Psychiatry* (New York: Philosophical Library, 1969), 197-208. See also Otto L. Bettmann, *Pictorial History of Medicine* (Springfield, Ill.: C C Thomas, 1956), 48-49, 228-229.

29. Ernst Horn, *Öffentliche Rechenschaft über meine zwölfjährige Dienstführung als zweiter Arzt des königlichen Charité-Krankenhauses zu Berlin* (Berlin: Realschulbuchhandlung, 1818).

30. Peter Joseph Schneider, *Entwurf zu einer Heilmittellehre gegen psychische Krankheiten* (Tübingen: Heinrich Laupp, 1824).

31. Joseph Guislain, *Traité sur l'Aliénation mentale et sur les hospices des aliénés* (Amsterdam: van der Hey, 1826).

## Part Four: Photography and Madness

1. Concerning this question see H. S. Dommasch, "The Development of Medical Photography," *Journal of the Biological Photographic Association* 33 (1965), 169-170; Alison Gernsheim, "Medical Photography in the Nineteenth Century," *Medical and Biological Illustration* 11 (1961), 85-92; "Victorian Clinical Photography," *Medical and Biological Illustration* 9 (1959), 70-77; Robert Ollerenshaw, "Medical Illustration: The Impact of Photography on Its History," *Journal of the Biological Photographic Association* 36 (1968), 3-13; Daniel M. Fox and James Terry, "Photography and the Self Image of American Physicians, 1880-1920," *Bulletin of the History of Medicine* 52 (1978), 435-457.

2. Arthur Schopenhauer, *Parerga and Paralipomena*, trans. E. F. J. Payne (Oxford: Clarendon Press, 1974), 2: 634.

3. The detailed background on Diamond is provided in my earlier book, *The Face of Madness: Hugh W. Diamond and the Origin of Psychiatric Photography* (New York: Brunner/Mazel, 1976). The text of Diamond's unpublished paper is also reproduced there for the first time. In addition to that paper see Diamond's report printed in the *Eighth Report of the Commissioners in Lunacy* (29 June 1854), 140-142, concerning his introduction of reforms into the Surrey Asylum.

4. See Roger Lancelyn Green, ed., *The Diaries of Lewis Carroll* (London: Cassell, 1953), 1:74. For a fuller description of Diamond's role in Victorian intellectual life see W. C. Hazlitt, *Four Generations of a Literary Family* (London: G. Redway, 1897), 2: 29-34.

5. *The Photographic Journal* 3 (1857), 289.

6. John Conolly, "Religious Mania" (see following note).

7. Conolly's papers "On the Physiognomy of Insanity" ran as follows in *The Medical Times and Gazette*: N. S. 16 (1858) No. 1, "Religious Melancholy," 2-4; No. 2, "Suicidal Melancholy," 56-58; No. 3, "General Melancholy," 134-136; No. 4, "Melancholia passing on to Mania," 238-241; No. 5, "Mania and Convalescence," 314-316; No. 6, "Chronic Mania and Melancholy," 397-398; No. 7, "Senile Dementia," 498-500; No. 8, "Puerperal Mania," 623-624; N. S. 17 (1858) No. 9, "Religious Mania," 81-83; No. 10, "Religious Mania-Convalescence," 210-212; No. 11, "Religious Melancholia," 367-369; No. 12, "Insanity Supervening on Habits of Intemperance," 651-653; N. S. 18 (1859), No. 13, "Illustrations of the Old Methods of Treatment," 183-186.

8. H. G. Wright, "On Medical Uses of Photography," *The Photographic Journal* 9 (1867), 204.

9. J. Thompson Dickson, *The Science and Practice of Medicine in Relation to Mind* (London: H. K. Lewis, 1874).

10. Ernst Lacan, *Esquisses photographiques à propos de l'exposition universelle et la guerre d'orient* (Paris: A. Gaudin, 1856), 40-41.

11. B. A. Morel, *Traité des degénérescences physiques, intellectuelles et morales de l'espèce humaine et des causes que produisent ces variétés maladies: Atlas de XII Planches* (Paris: J. B. Baillière, 1857).

12. [Isaac Newton Kerlin], *The Mind Unveiled; or, A Brief History of 22 Imbecile Children* (Philadelphia: U. Hunt and Son, 1858).

13. Dietrich Georg Kieser, *Elemente der Psychiatrik* (Breslau and Bonn: Kaiserliche L.-C. Akademie, 1855). See also Walter Brednow, *Dietrich Georg Kieser: Sein Leben und Werk* (Wiesbaden: Franz Steiner, 1970), 86-98.

14. Max Leidesdorf, *Lehrbuch der psychischen Krankheiten* (2nd ed., Erlangen: Ferdinand Enke, 1865).

15. Cited from the facsimile introduced by Francis J. Braceland (New York: Hafner, 1968), 282-289. Some references to the problem of the physiognomy of insanity can be found in Wilhelm Griesinger's classic *Pathologie und Therapie der psychischen Krankheiten* (Stuttgart: Krabbe, 1845), without, however, any illustrative material. Griesinger was instrumental in founding the *Archiv für Psychiatrie und Nervenkrankheiten* in 1868 which included in its very first volume visual representations of psychopathological cases.

16. Henri Dagonet, *Traité des maladies mentales* (Paris: J. B. Baillière, 1894), 265-266; the first edition was entitled *Nouveau traité élémentaire et pratique des maladies mentales* (Paris: J. B. Baillière, 1876).

17. "The first principle of physiognomy," *Cornhill Magazine* 4 (1861), 570.

18. To place Darwin's study in the overall scope of his work see Sir Gavin de Beer, *Charles Darwin: Evolution by Natural Selection* (Garden City, N.Y.: Doubleday, 1967), 220-225. Perhaps the most influential work of nineteenth-century physiognomy influenced by Darwin was that of Paolo Mantegazza, *Fisionomia e Mimica* (Milano: Fratelli Dumolard, 1881), which was dedicated to Darwin. Mantegazza does not discuss the physiognomy of mental illness.

19. All references are to the first edition published in London by John Murray in 1872. Here, 13-14.

20. I am indebted to Mr. P. J. Gautrey of the Cambridge University Library for making this material available to me. Browne's letters to Darwin are preserved in their original holograph form; Darwin's to Browne, however, are preserved only in Francis Darwin's transcription. None of the correspondence was included in published collections of Darwin's letters. Francis Darwin mentions Browne in passing in his *Life and Letters of Charles Darwin* (New York: D. Appleton, 1896), 2: 314. For the context of the Browne-Darwin exchange see pages 310-324 of that volume as well as Francis Darwin and A. C. Seward, eds., *More Letters of Charles Darwin* (New York: D. Appleton, 1903), 98-111.

21. Biographical information on Sir James Crichton Browne can be found in the *Dictionary of National Biography* supplement for 1931-1940 (London: Oxford University Press, 1949), 106-107. See also Richard Hunter and Ida Macalpine (Images of Madness, note 4), 882.

22. See Edwin Clarke and Kenneth Dewhurst (Images of Madness, note 43), especially 101-113.

23. Guillaume Benjamin Duchenne [de Boulogne], *De l'électrisation localisée et de son application à la pathologie et à la thérapeutique* (Paris: J. B. Baillière, 1861), as well as his *Mécanisme de la physionomie humaine* (Paris: Nenouard, 1862). See also Emanuel B. Kaplan, "Duchenne of Boulogne and the *Physiologie des Mouvements,*" in Solomon R. Kagan, ed., *Victor Robinson Memorial Volume* (New York: Froben, 1948), 177-192.

24. In this regard see Peter Pollack, *The Picture History of Photography* (New York: Harry Abrams, 1958), 175; also Cecil Beaton and Gail Buckland, *The Magic Image: The Genius of Photography from 1839 to the Present Day* (Boston: Little, Brown, 1975), 51-53.

25. For the history of the mind-body problem, especially in the light of nineteenth-century neurological and psychological views, see the discussion in Jerome Schaffer (Icons of Madness, note 17), 5: 336-346; and Barbara von Eckardt Klein, "Conceptions of Sensory Experience and Mind-Body Identity" (Diss., Case Western Reserve, 1975). See, in addition, the reflection of this problem in the following German discussions of the physiognomy of illness: Hans Killian, *Facies dolorosa: Das schmerzenreiche Antlitz* (Leipzig: G. Thieme, 1934); Michel Hertl, *Das Gesicht des kranken Kindes: Physiognomisch-mimische Studie und Differentialdiagnose unter Bevorzugung des seelischen Ausdruckes* (Munich and Berlin: Urban & Schwarzenberg, 1962); Georg Volk, *Neural-personale Diagnostik: Anleitung zur patho-physiognomischen Betrachtung des Menschen* (Ulm: K. F. Haug, 1955); and Hans Kirchhof, *Das menschliche Antlitz im Spiegel organisch-nervöser Prozesse* (Göttingen: Verlag für Psychologie, 1960).

26. Pierre Gratiolet, *De la physionomie et des mouvements d'expression* (Paris: J. Hetzel, 1865); Theodor Piderit, *Grundsätze der Mimik und Physiognomik* (Braunschweig: F. Vieweg, 1858).

27. Piderit (2nd ed., Detmold: Meyer, 1886), 189. He also cites his correspondence with Darwin in the introduction to this edition.

28. Hermann Oppenheim, "Beiträge zum Studium des Gesichtsausdrucks der Geisteskranken," *Allgemeine Zeitschrift für Psychiatrie* 40 (1884), 840-863.

29. Luigi Mongeri, "Étude de la physionomie chez les Aliénés," *Internationale Medizinisch-photographische Monatsschrift* 1 (1894), 353-360. This journal, in its early numbers, devoted extensive space to the question of representing the insane. Quickly, however, it became an organ of the newest wave of medical photography, the x-ray. See there also Ludwig Jankau, "Physiognomische Betrachtungen," 1 (1894), 74-81.

30. Augusto Tebaldi, *Fisionomia ed Espressione Studiate nelle Loro Deviazioni* (Padua: Drucker e Tedeschi, 1884), with a detailed atlas of photographs of the insane supplemented with images from Morison and Leidesdorf.

31. See John Turner, "Asymmetrical Conditions met with in the Faces of the Insane; with Some Remarks on the Dissolution of Expression," *Journal of Mental Science* 38 (1892), 18-29, 199-211. See also his essay "Some Further Remarks on Expression in the Insane," *Journal of Mental Science* 39 (1893), 177-185.

32. For a detailed discussion see Theodor Kirchhof, *Der Gesichtsausdruck und seine Bahnen beim Gesunden und Kranken besonders beim Geisteskranken* (Berlin: Julius Springer, 1922), 135-140. A complete bibliography to this question is appended to a modern atlas of the insane: Gerhard Mall, *Das Gesicht des seelisch Kranken* (Konstanz: Schnetztor, 1967), 281-288.

33. See Theodor Ziehen, "Der Gesichtsausdruck des Zorns und des Unmuts bei Geisteskranken," *Internationale Medizinisch-photographische Monatsschrift* 2 (1895), 225-232; *Psychiatrie für Ärzte und Studierende bearbeitet* (Berlin: Friedrich Wreden, 1894).

34. Richard Krafft-Ebing, *Textbook of Insanity*, trans. Charles Gilbert Chaddock (Philadelphia: F. A. Davis, 1905), 124.

35. A discussion of Galton's use of composite photography is to be found in Karl Pearson, *The Life, Letters and Labours of Francis Galton* (Cambridge: Cambridge University, 1914-1933), 2:290.

36. William Noyes, "Composite Portraiture of the Insane," *Science* 9 (1888), 252-253; "Composite Portraits of General Paresis and of Melancholia," *Journal of Nervous and Mental Diseases* NS 13 (1888), 1-2.

37. James Shaw, "Facial Expression as one of the Means of Diagnosis and Prognosis in Mental Disease," *The Medical Annual* 12 (1894), 344-374; 15 (1897), 305-323; 21 (1903), 407-415. These essays were republished as *The Physiognomy of Mental Disease and Degeneracy* (Bristol: John Wright, 1903).

38. See Sommer's *Lehrbuch der psychopathologischen Untersuchungs-Methoden* (Berlin: Urban & Schwarzenberg, 1899), 5-10.

39. Emil Kraepelin, *Psychiatrie: Ein Lehrbuch für Studierende und Aerzte* (Leipzig: Johann Ambrosius Barth, 1896), vi.

40. A. Alber, *Atlas der Geisteskrankheiten im Anschluss an Sommer's Diagnostik der Geisteskranken* (Berlin and Vienna: Urban & Schwarzenberg, 1902). At the turn of the century see also Wilhelm Weygandt, *Atlas und Grundriss der Psychiatrie* (Munich: F. Lehmann, 1902), and Gilbert Ballet, ed., *Traité de Pathologie Mentale* (Paris: Octove Doin, 1903).

## Part Five: The Ongoing Artistic Tradition

1. Relevant books are: Georges Guillain, *J.-M. Charcot 1825-1893: His Life—His Work*, trans. Pearce Bailey (New York: Paul B. Hoeber, 1959); A. R. G. Owen, *Hysteria, Hypnosis and Healing: The Work of J.-M. Charcot* (London: Dennis Dobson, 1971); Henri F. Ellenberger, *The Discovery of the Unconscious: The History and Evolution of Dynamic Psychiatry* (New York: Basic Books, 1970), 89-101. Ilza Veith (see Icons of Madness, note 23) makes passing mention of Charcot's interest in the visual arts but does not relate this interest to his schematic representation of hysteria.

2. Henry Meige, "Charcot artiste," *Nouvelle Iconographie de la Salpêtrière* 9 (1898).

3. Cited by Guillain (see note 1 above), 9.

4. See Paul Guilly, *Duchenne de Boulogne* (Paris: J. B. Baillière, 1936).

5. This preface, signed by Bourneville, is published at the beginning of the first volume of the *Iconographie photographique de la Salpêtrière* 1 (1876-1877). Compare the photographs in J. Luys, *Les émotions chez sujets en état d'hypnotisme* (Paris: J. B. Baillière, 1887).

6. Londe's central role in the development of medical photography is outlined in Nicolas M. Graver, "Photographie Médicale: Albert Londe's 1893 book, first in the field," *Journal of the Biological Photographic Association* 43 (1975), 95-102. Interestingly, none of Londe's

published studies deals with photographing psychiatric patients. See his *La photographie médicale: application aux sciences médicales et physiologiques* (Paris: Gauthier-Villars et fils, 1893) where he discusses, in the third chapter, the problems of photographing patients in an informal setting. Here Londe reproduces a photograph of an hysteric patient which had already appeared in the *Nouvelle Iconographie*, without, however, any specific explanation.

7. Muybridge's importance in the study of human and animal movement through chronophotography has always been known; his contribution to the study of pathological movement has been ignored. See Anita Ventura Mozley, ed., *Muybridge's Complete Human and Animal Locomotion* (New York: Dover, 1979). For the documentation to his studies of pathology see Francis X. Dercum, ed., *A Textbook on Nervous Diseases by American Authors* (Philadelphia: Lea Brothers, 1895), plate 206.

8. See Paul Richer, *Études cliniques sur la grande hystérie ou l'hystéro-épilepsie* (Paris: Adrien Delahaye et Emile Lecrosnier, 1881).

9. *Les Démoniaques dans l'art* (Paris: Adrien Delahaye et Émile Lecrosnier, 1887), v-viii.

10. *Les Difformes et les malades dans l'art* (Paris: Lecrosnier et Babé, 1889), v-vi.

11. *L'art et la médecine* (Paris: Gaultier, Magnier et Cie, 1902), 10-11. A detailed list of the discussions of the representations of the mentally ill in art (to 1903) which were published in the *Nouvelle Iconographie de la Salpêtrière* appeared in the sixteenth volume of that journal (1903), 425-429.

12. See Pierre Janet, "J.-M. Charcot, son oeuvre psychologique," *Revue Philosophique* 39 (1895), 569-604.

13. "Charcot," in *The Standard Edition of the Complete Psychological Works of Sigmund Freud* (London: Hogarth Press, 1953-1974), 3:12-13.

14. "On Beginning the Treatment," ibid., 12:133-134, 139.

15. *Kranken-Physiognomik* (2nd ed., Stuttgart: L. F. Rieger, 1842), 17-18, 226.

16. Byrom Bramwell, *Atlas of Clinical Medicine* (Edinburgh: T. and A. Constable, 1892), 1801.

17. *Types of Insanity: An Illustrated Guide in the Physical Diagnosis of Mental Disease* (New York: William Wood, 1883).

18. G. Fielding Blandford, *Insanity and Its Treatment*, Wood's Library of Standard Medical Authors (New York: William Wood, 1886), 315-316.

19. See *Antoine Wiertz, 1806-1865* (Paris-Bruxelles: Jacques Damase 1974).

20. A. J. Davis, *Mental Disorder; or, Disease of the Brain and Nerves, Developing the Origin and Philosophy of Mania, Insanity, and Crime with Full Directions for Their Treatment and Cure* (New York: American News Company, 1871).

21. Enrico Somaré, *Signorini* (Milano: "L'Esome," 1926).

22. The painting of scenes of historical madness in the late nineteenth century also mirrored many of the late nineteenth-century presuppositions concerning the appearance of the insane. Emile Wauters' painting of the madness of the medieval monk Hugo van der Goes (1872) stressed the use of music therapy, a factor in his treatment, yet portrayed him in the light of late nineteenth-century theories of physiognomy. A painting by Karl Müller, identical in theme to that of Robert-Fleury, is reproduced in A. A. Roback and Thomas Kiernan (see The Reform of Madness, note 28), 184.

23. Freud (see note 13 above), 3:17-18. Freud was wrong about the location of Pinel's act.

24. For the present study the following works were

of value: Karl Jaspers, *Strindberg und Van Gogh* (Berlin: Springer, 1926); Charles Mauron, "Vincent et Theo," *L'arc* 2 (1959), 3-12; Jan Hulsker, "Van Gogh's Threatened Life in Saint-Rémy and Auvers," *Vincent* 2 (1972), 21-39.

25. All references to Van Gogh's works are based on the J. B. De La Faille, *L'Oeuvre de Vincent Van Gogh: Catalogue raisonée* (Paris et Bruxelles: Van Oest, 1928), 5 volumes. Specifically, the sketches of a weeping female, F 1060, 1069; view of an old man weeping, F 863, 864, 997, 998; three versions of *Sorrow*, F 929, 929 bis, 1655; two states of *At Eternity's Gate*, F 702, 1662; *Men's Ward at Arles*, F 646; *Head of a Patient*, F 703.

26. All references to the letters are to *The Complete Letters of Vincent Van Gogh* (Greenwich, Conn.: New York Graphic Society, n.d.). Specifically, to Theo 1882, 3, 323; to Rappard 1882, 125; to his sister 1880, 461; to Theo, 204; from Saint-Rémy 1889, 170, 174, 213; on Delacroix, 25.

27. Jean Seznec, "Literary inspiration in Van Gogh," in Bogomila Welsh-Ovcharov, ed., *Van Gogh in Perspective* (Englewood Cliffs, N.J.: Prentice-Hall, 1971), 132.

28. There is one landscape of Van Gogh's from March of 1884 (F 1130) which presents an evocative scene under the title of "Melancholy."

29. Dickens (see The Reform of Madness, note 12), II:387.

### Epilogue: Seeing with "the Third Eye"

1. Theodor Reik, *Listening with the Third Ear* (New York: Farrar, Straus and Company, 1949), 144-145.

2. Alfred Freedman, Harold Kaplan, and Benjamin Sadock, *Comprehensive Textbook of Psychiatry* (Baltimore: Williams and Wilkins, 1967); student ed., *Modern Synopsis of Comprehensive Textbook of Psychiatry II* (Baltimore: Williams and Wilkins, 1976). This is not merely an American anachronism, see for example Dietfried Müller-Hegemann, *Neurologie und Psychiatrie: Lehrbuch für Studierende und Ärzte* (Berlin: Volk und Gesundheit, 1966), the textbook used in the general psychiatry classes in the German Democratic Republic; and Yakov Pavlovich Frumkin and Georgy Leonidovich, *Uchebnny atlas psikhiatrii* [Teaching Atlas of Psychiatry] (Kiev: Gos. Med. Izd. USSR, 1962).

3. Douglas Davis, "A Glimpse of Madness," *Newsweek* (January 23, 1978), 82; and Robert Hughes, "Pictures at an Institution," *Time* (January 23, 1978), 91.

4. Sara Facio, Alicia D'Amico, Julio Cortázar, *Humanario* (Buenos Aires: La Azotea, 1976).

# supplemental BIBLIOGRAPHY

[In addition to the works cited in the Notes, the following have also been consulted.]

Adam, Hermann August. *Über Geisteskrankheit in alter und neuer Zeit: Ein Stück Kulturgeschichte im Wort und Bild.* Regensburg: L. Rath, 1928.

Anonymous. "Medical Books Illustrated By Their Authors." *Crookes Digest* 15 (1949), 178-181.

Arroya, Jose Maria. *La medicina en el Museo del Prado.* Madrid: J. Morata, 1933.

*Art et Médecine.* Paris, 1930.

*Arte y medicina.* Habana, 1952.

Bland, David. *A History of Book Illustration: The Illuminated Manuscript and the Printed Book.* Berkeley: University of California, 1969.

Boettiger, C. A. *Les furies d'après les poètes et les artistes ancien.* Paris: Delalain, 1862.

Burns, Stanley B. "Early Medical Photography in America (1839-1883): V. The Beginnings of Psychiatric Photography." *New York State Journal of Medicine* 80 (1980), 270-282.

Burrows, Adrienne, and Schumacher, Iwan. *Doktor Diamonds Bildnisse von Geisteskranken.* Frankfurt: Syndikat, 1979.

Cahier, Charles. *Charactéristiques des saints dans l'art populaire.* Paris: Poussielque frères, 1867.

Choulant, Ludwig. *Geschichte und Bibliographie der anatomischen Abbildung nach ihrer Beziehung auf anatomische Wissenschaft und bildende Kunst.* Leipzig: Weigel, 1852.

————. *History and Bibliography of Anatomic Illustration in its Relation to Anatomical Science and the Graphic Arts.* Ed. and trans. Mortimer Frank. Chicago: University of Chicago, 1920.

Clark, Leon Pierce. "Mental and Nervous Diseases in Classic and Pictorial Art." *Medical Pickwick* 2 (1916), 1-15.

De La Fuente, Juan-Ramon, and Alarcón-Segovia, Donato. "Depression as Expressed in Pre-Columbian Mexican Art." *American Journal of Psychiatry* 137 (1980), 1095-1098.

Dumesnil, René. *Histoire illustrée de la médecine.* Paris: Plon, 1935.

Fülöp-Miller, René. *Kampf gegen Schmerz und Tod: Kulturgeschichte der Heilkunde.* Berlin: Süd-Ost, 1938.

Gilman, Sander L. "Zur Physiognomie des Geisteskranken in Geschichte und Praxis, 1800-1900," *Sudhoffs Archiv* 62 (1978), 201-234.

————. "Die psychiatrische Abbildung," in *Psychologie des XX. Jahrhunderts*, Bd. X: *Psychiatrie*, ed. U. H. Peters (Zurich: Kindler, 1980), 1071-1078.

Graham, John. *Lavater's Essays on Physiognomy: A Study in the History of Ideas.* Bern: Lang, 1980.

Hahn, André, and Dumaitre, Paul. *Histoire de la médecine et du livre médical.* Paris: Olivier Perrin, 1922.

Heintel, H. "Grundzüge einer Ikonographie des Epileptikers." In Heinz Goerke und Heinz Müller-Dietz, eds., *Verhandlungen des XX. Internationalen Kongresses für Geschichte der Medizin.* Hildesheim: George Olms, 1968.

Henschen, Folke. *The History of Diseases.* Trans. Joan Tate. London: Longmans, 1966.

————. *The Human Skull: A Cultural History.* Trans. Stanley Thomas. London: Thames and Hudson, 1966.

Holländer, Eugen. *Die Karikatur und Satire in der Medizin.* Stuttgart: Ferdinand Enke, 1905.

————, ed. *Katalog zur Ausstellung der Geschichte der Medizin in Kunst und Kunsthandwerk zur Eröffnung des Kaiserin Friedrich-Hauses 1. März 1906.* Stuttgart: Ferdinand Enke, 1906.

Jones, T. S. "The Evolution of Medical Illustration." In *The Illinois University College of Medicine Essays in Honor of David J. Davis.* Chicago: Davis Lecture Committee, 1965. Pp. 158-167.

Kiell, Norman, ed. *Psychiatry and Psychology in the Visual Arts and Aesthetics.* Madison: University of Wisconsin, 1965.

————. "Medicine and Art, 1934-1964: A Bibliography." *Journal of the History of Medicine* 21 (1966), 147-172.

Knipping, H. W., and Keuter, H. *Heilkunst und Kunstwerk: Probleme zwischen Kunst und Medizin aus ärztlicher Sicht.* Stuttgart: Friedrich-Karl Schattauer, 1961.

Laignel-Lavastine, M., and Vinchon, Jean. *Les malades de l'esprit et leurs médicins du XVIe au XXe siècle: Les étapes des connaissances psychiatriques de la Renaissance à Pinel.* Paris: Éditions médicales, 1930.

————. "La psychose périodique dans l'histoire, la littérature et l'art." *La Semaine des hôpitaux de Paris* 12 (1936), 314-325.

Lemke, Rudolf. *Psychiatrische Themen in Malerei und Graphik.* Jena: Gustav Fischer, 1958.

*L'illustrazion medica italiana.* Genoa, 1919-1932.

MacKinney, Loren. "Medical Illustration: Ancient and Medieval." *Ciba symposia* 10 (1949), 1062-1071.

————. "Medical Illustrations in Medieval Manuscripts of the Vatican Library." *Manuscripta* 3 (1959), 3-18, 76-88.

Margoth, R. *An Illustrated History of Medicine.* Ed. Paul Lewis. Feltham: Hamlyn, 1968.

Marti-Ibanez, Félix. *The Patient's Progress.* New York: MD Publications, 1967.

Melicow, Meyer M. "Interrelationships of medicine and art." *Bulletin of the New York Academy of Medicine* 33 (1957), 347-356.

Meyer-Steinig, Theodor, and Sudhoff, Karl. *Illustrierte Geschichte der Medizin.* 5th ed. Stuttgart: Gustav Fischer, 1965.

Netter, Frank H. "Medical Illustration: Its History, Significance and Practice." *Bulletin of the New York Academy of Medicine* 33 (1957), 357-368.

Paulson, Ronald. *Emblem and Expression: Meaning in English Art of the Eighteenth Century.* Cambridge: Harvard, 1975.

Peugniey, Paul. *L'histoire et la médecine dans l'art religieux: L'église St. Géry de Cambria.* Amiens: Yvert et Tellier, 1903.

Praz, Mario. *Studies in Seventeenth Century Imagery.* London: The Warburg Institute, 1939-1947.

Portigliotti, Giuseppe. *I Pazzi anell'arte.* Turin: Streglio, 1907.

Rosenthal, O. *Wunderheilungen und ärztliche Schutzpatrone in der bildenden Kunst.* Leipzig: F. C. W. Vogel, 1925.

Rothkopf, A. " 'Das Narrenhaus' von W. Kaulbach und die Deutung des Bildes durch J. A. Schilling 1863," *Confinia psychiatrica* 23 (1980), 51-64.

Rumann, Arthur. *Das illustrierte Buch des XIX. Jahrhunderts in England, Frankreich und Deutschland, 1790-1860.* Leipzig: Insel, 1930.

Schadewaldt, H. "Kunst und Medizin." In *Medicinae et artibus: Festschrift für Prof. Dr. med. Wilhelm Katner.* Düsseldorf: M. Triltch, 1968. Pp. 146-160.

Schipperges, Heinrich. "Melancolia als ein mittelalterlicher Sammelbegriff für Wahnvorstellungen." *Studium generale* 20 (1967), 723-736.

Schramm, Albert, ed. *Der Bilderschmuck der Frühdrucke.* Leipzig: W. Hiersemann, 1922 ff.

Sheon, Aaron. "Caricature and the Physiognomy of the Insane," *Gazette des Beaux-Arts,* October, 1976, 145-150.

————. "Courbet, French Realism, and the Discovery of the Unconscious," *Arts Magazine* 55 (1981), 114-128.

Sigerist, Henry E. "The Historical Aspect of Art and Medicine." *Bulletin of the Institute of the History of Medicine* 4 (1936), 271-296.

————. *Civilization and Disease.* Ithaca, N.Y.: Cornell, 1943.

Sudhoff, Karl. "Medizin und Kunst" and "Malerei und die Geschichte der Medizin." In Eugen Holländer, ed. *Katalog zur Ausstellung,* op. cit., 21-26, 27-33.

Temkin, Owsei. *The Falling Sickness: A History of Epilepsy from the Greeks to the Beginnings of Modern Neurology.* Baltimore: Johns Hopkins, 1945.

Townsend, John Marshal. "Stereotypes of Mental Illness: A Comparison with Ethnic Stereotypes." *Culture, Medicine and Psychiatry* 3 (1979), 205-229.

Vinchon, Jean. *L'art et la folie.* Paris: Stock, 1950.

"Wahnsinnigendarstellungen." *Lexikon der Kunst.* Leipzig: E. A. Seemann, 1978.

236

# name index for TEXT and [PLATES]

# tıtle ındex for PLATES

# sources of the plates

| | | | | | |
|---|---|---|---|---|---|
| ii [27] | 34 [28] | 69- 77 [30] | 137-140 [10] | 175-192 [12] | 250-251 [10] |
| 1- 7 [30] | 35 [16] | 78- 82 [11] | 141-143 [30] | 193 [40] | 252-253 [ 4] |
| 8- 9 [ 6] | 36 [10] | 83 [30] | 144-146 [29] | 194 [30] | 254-264 [10] |
| 10 [ 7] | 37-38 [30] | 84- 88 [12] | 147-153 [30] | 195 [27] | 265-269 [ 4] |
| 11 [ 2] | 39 [ 7] | 89- 90 [30] | 154 [12] | 196 [10] | 270 [10] |
| 12 [42] | 40 [41] | 91- 94 [10] | 155 [44] | 197-198 [12] | 271 [27] |
| 13 [30] | 41 [ 1] | 95-101 [11] | 156 [26] | 199-200 [10] | 272-275 [10] |
| 14 [ 2] | 42-43 [30] | 102-105 [ 5] | 157-158 [12] | 201 [27] | 276 [12] |
| 15-17 [30] | 44-45 [27] | 106 [25] | 159 [50] | 202-209 [10] | 277 [22] |
| 18 [15] | 46 [ 1] | 107 [34] | 160-161 [30] | 210-214 [49] | 278 [10] |
| 19 [20] | 47-48 [32] | 108 [24] | 162-163 [12] | 215 [10] | 279 [23] |
| 20 [16] | 49-54 [12] | 109 [17] | 164 [18] | 216 [49] | 280-281 [12] |
| 21-22 [11] | 55-56 [27] | 110 [19] | 165 [33] | 217 [30] | 282 [27] |
| 23-24 [48] | 57 [17] | 111 [11] | 166 [28] | 218-226 [10] | 283-284 [43] |
| 25-27 [36] | 58 [21] | 112 [30] | 167 [45] | 227 [11] | 285 [37] |
| 28 [46] | 59 [13] | 113-121 [10] | 168 [34] | 228-230 [10] | 286 [34] |
| 29 [14] | 60 [35] | 122-124 [39] | 169-170 [12] | 231-239 [ 8] | 287 [38] |
| 30 [12] | 61 [30] | 125-128 [10] | 171 [27] | 240 [11] | |
| 31 [ 7] | 62 [27] | 129-132 [39] | 172 [12] | 241 [ 8] | |
| 32 [ 9] | 63-64 [12] | 133-135 [10] | 173 [ 3] | 242-247 [10] | |
| 33 [47] | 65-68 [10] | 136 [30] | 174 [31] | 248-249 [11] | |

[1] Albertina, Vienna
[2] Beinecke Library, Yale
[3] Bethlem Royal Hospital Archives
[4] Bibliothèque Charcot, Paris
[5] Bibliothèque nationale, Paris
[6] Bodleian Library Oxford
[7] The British Library, London
[8] Cambridge University Library
[9] The Denver Art Museum, Kress Collection
[10] Oskar Diethelm Historical Library, Cornell
[11] Ex Libris/Mazel, Larchmont, New York
[12] Clements Fry Collection, Yale
[13] Germanisches Nationalmuseum, Nurenberg
[14] Hessisches Landesmuseum, Darmstadt
[15] Herbert F. Johnson Museum of Art, Cornell
[16] Kunsthistorisches Museum, Vienna
[17] Louvre, Paris
[18] Meadows Museum, Southern Methodist University, Dallas, Texas
[19] Musée des Beaux Arts, Lyon
[20] Musée Magnin, Dijon
[21] Musée Mayer van den Bergh, Brussels
[22] Musées royaux des Beaux-Arts, Brussels
[23] Museo d'Arte Moderne, Venice
[24] Museum of Fine Arts, Springfield, Massachusetts
[25] Museum voor schone Kunsten, Ghent

[26] National Galleries of Scotland, Edinburgh
[27] National Library of Medicine, Bethesda, Maryland
[28] National Museum, Stockholm
[29] New York State Historical Association, Cooperstown
[30] Olin Library, Cornell
[31] Pennsylvania Academy of Fine Arts, Philadelphia
[32] Museo del Prado, Madrid
[33] Real Academia de Bellas Artes de San Fernando, Madrid
[34] Oskar Reinhart Collection, Winterthur
[35] Rijksdienst voor de Monumentenzorg, Amsterdam
[36] Rijksmuseum, Amsterdam
[37] Rijksmuseum Kröller-Müller, Otterlo
[38] Rijksmuseum Vincent Van Gogh, Amsterdam
[39] Royal College of Physicians, Edinburgh
[40] The Royal College of Psychiatrists, London
[41] Stadtbibliothek, Nurenberg
[42] Statens Museum for Kunst, Copenhagen
[43] Stedelijk Museum, Amsterdam
[44] The Tate Gallery, London
[45] Collection of Mr. and Mrs. Eugene V. Thaw, New York
[46] Universitätsbibliothek, Erfurt
[47] Vatican: Pinacoteca
[48] Victoria and Albert Museum, London
[49] Wellcome Historical Library, London
[50] Yale Center for British Art, Paul Mellon Collection

CPSIA information can be obtained
at www.ICGtesting.com
Printed in the USA
LVHW061049220821
695852LV00003B/28

9 781626 548763